WordPerfect 6

SELF-TEACHING GUIDE

Wiley SELF-TEACHING GUIDES (STG's) are designed for first time users of computer applications and programming languages. They feature concept-reinforcing drills, exercises, and illustrations that enable you to measure your progress, and learn at your own pace. Other Wiley Self-Teaching Guides:

DOS 5 STG, Ruth Ashley and Judi N. Fernandez
INTRODUCTION TO PERSONAL COMPUTERS STG, Peter Stephenson
OBJECTVISION 2 STG, Arnold and Edith Shulman, and Robert Marion
QUATTRO PRO 3 STG, Jennifer Meyer
LOTUS 1-2-3 FOR WINDOWS STG, Douglas J. Wolf
PARADOX 3.5 STG, Gloria Wheeler
Q&A 4 STG, Corey Sandler and Tom Badgett
FOXPRO 2 STG, Ellen Sander
ALDUS PERSUASION FOR IBM PC'S AND COMPATIBLES STG, Karen Brown and Diane Stielstra
PERFORM STG, Peter Stephenson
NOVELL NETWARE 2.2 STG, Peter Stephenson and Glenn Hartwig
MICROSOFT WORD 5.5 FOR THE PC STG, Ruth Ashley and Judi Fernandez
MICROSOFT WORD FOR WINDOWS 2 STG, Pamela S. Beason and Stephen Guild
WORDPERFECT 5.0/5.1 STG, Neil Salkind
WORDPERFECT FOR WINDOWS STG, Neil Salkind
SIGNATURE STG, Christine Rivera
MICROSOFT WINDOWS 3.0 STG, Keith Weiskamp and Saul Aguiar
WINDOWS 3.1 STG, Keith Weiskamp
PC DOS 4 STG, Ruth Ashley and Judi Fernandez
PC DOS 3.3 STG, Ruth Ashley and Judi Fernandez
MASTERING MICROSOFT WORKS STG, David Sachs, Babette Kronstadt, Judith Van Wormer, and Barbara Farrell
QUICKPASCAL STG, Keith Weiskamp and Saul Aguiar
GW BASIC STG, Ruth Ashley and Judi Fernandez
TURBO C++ STG, Bryan Flamig
SQL STG, Peter Stephenson and Glenn Hartwig
QUICKEN STG, Peter Aitken
COREL DRAW 2 STG, Robert Bixby
HARVARD GRAPHICS 3 STG, David Harrison and John W. Yu
HARVARD GRAPHICS FOR WINDOWS STG, David Harrison and John W. Yu
AMI PRO 2 FOR WINDOWS STG, Pamela S. Beason and Stephen Guild
EXCEL 4 STG, Ruth K. Witkin

To order our STG's, you can call Wiley directly at (201)469-4400, or check your local bookstores.
"Mastering computers was never this easy, rewarding, and fun!"

WordPerfect 6

SELF-TEACHING GUIDE

Neil Salkind

John Wiley & Sons, Inc.
New York ▲ Chichester ▲ Brisbane ▲ Toronto ▲ Singapore

Associate Publisher: Katherine Schowalter
Editor: Tim Ryan
Managing Editor: Frank Grazioli
Editorial Production: Mary Ray Worley/Impressions, a Division of
    Edwards Brothers, Inc.

This text is printed on acid-free paper.

This publication is designed to provide accurate and authoritative information in regard to the subject matter covered. It is sold with the understanding that the publisher is not engaged in rendering professional services. If legal, accounting, medical, psychological or any other expert
assistance is required, the services of a competent professional person
should be sought. FROM A DECLARATION OF PRINCIPLES JOINTLY
ADOPTED BY A COMMITTEE OF THE AMERICAN BAR ASSOCIA-
TION AND A COMMITTEE OF PUBLISHERS.

Library of Congress Cataloging-in-Publication Data:

Salkind, Neil J.
    WordPerfect 6: self-teaching guide / by Neil Salkind.
        p. cm.
    Includes index.
    ISBN 0–471–58422–3 (paper: alk. paper)
    1. WordPerfect (Computer file) 2. Word processing. I. Title.
Z52.5.W65S245   1993
652.5'536--dc20   93-5306
                                                                            CIP

Printed in the United States of America
10 9 8 7 6 5 4 3 2 1

For Micah
on the occasion of his ninth birthday
and for his unending curiosity
about how the world, and his parents, work

Contents Overview

Contents

Introducing WordPerfect

You're lucky. Out of all the word processing programs that are available, you chose WordPerfect. Besides being the number one selling word processing program available today, it is also one of the best business, writing, and document creation tools you can own.

If you want to learn how to use WordPerfect, you've come to the right place. As you work through each lesson in *WordPerfect 6.0: A Self-Teaching Guide*, you'll learn how to enter and edit text, prepare tables, and use great graphics to make your documents shine. When you finish this book, you'll have mastered an excellent set of skills that will allow you to do almost anything that WordPerfect is capable of. In this lesson you'll learn:

▲ **What's in *WordPerfect 6.0: A Self-Teaching Guide***

▲ **What you need to use WordPerfect programs**

▲ **How to use the keyboard and mouse**

▲ **How to use this book**

Important Keys
Alt
Ctr
Del
Enter
Esc
Ins
Shift
Tab

Important Terms
function keys
pull-down menus
template

The Difference Between WordPerfect 5.0/5.1 and 6.0

When software developers release a new version of a program, they assign a number to differentiate that version from others. When the changes are minor, a version increment goes by a decimal such as from 5.0 to 5.1 and so on. When the changes are major, the version increment is a whole number such as 5.1 to 6.0. And that's where we are with WordPerfect 6.0.

Version 6.0 of WordPerfect is quite different from previous versions. The difference is not so much in how you use the program, but in what features the program offers. For example, with WordPerfect 6.0 you can create and send a fax; view your documents in text, page, or graphic format; save time and effort with button bars to select a button that allows you to print, save, or change fonts with a click of the mouse; open up to nine (count 'em) screens at a time; and use a new and very powerful File Manager to help keep your documents well organized and easy to access.

Although all of the features from earlier versions of WordPerfect are still here, this new version does take on somewhat of a different appearance. For those of you who have used WordPerfect in the past, the key combinations will be the same, but the screens these combinations bring up when used will appear a bit different and take a bit of time (but not much) to get used to.

Who Should Use This Book

*Who Should
Use This Book*

This book is intended for anyone who is interested in learning how to use WordPerfect. We assume that you have some experience using computers and are somewhat familiar with the operating system (such as MS-DOS or DR DOS) that your computer uses. Though you don't need experience with another word processor to learn how to use WordPerfect, you will find many elements from other word processors (especially terminology) to be similar.

What's in This Book

This *Self-Teaching Guide* has 20 chapters. Each chapter consists of a set of lessons that lead you through the steps you need to master a particular WordPerfect skill. The lessons are brief and to the point so that you can finish one in a relatively short amount of time, apply what you have learned, and then move on to learning about the next skill.

Chapter 1, "Getting Started," does just that. It covers what you need to know to get WordPerfect up and running, including starting the program, understanding the opening screen, and getting help when you need it.

The most basic and important task of any word processing system is to make the creation of documents easy. That's just what reading and working through Chapter 2, "Creating Your First Document," will do for you. You'll learn how to enter, save, and print text, and then sign off when you want to finish a session.

As much as we would like to think it is the case, none of us is perfect. Chapter 3, "Editing Documents," reveals the tips and tricks needed to fix everything from correcting typos to rearranging pages of text work with WordPerfect blocks, and even restore text that you might have inadvertently deleted!

One of the things that all word processor users want is to be able to see their document exactly as it would appear when printed. WordPerfect has taken care of that in earlier versions, but version 6 introduces different views of WordPerfect, which we'll discuss in

Chapter 4. Text, Graphics, and Page views all provide different amounts of information and each has its advantages.

One of WordPerfect's new and most exciting features is the creation of button bars, featured in Chapter 5. These allow you to use and create icons that represent different WordPerfect tasks. All you do is click on an icon and the task is done!

Good housekeeping on your computer is just as important as good housekeeping in your home or apartment, and Chapter 6, "Managing Files," shows you how to work with WordPerfect files to keep things in order.

Another part of the editing process is locating what you need to correct. WordPerfect's powerful search and change tools are the focus of Chapter 7, "Searching Through Documents."

Good words are good, but good-looking words and documents are wonderful! Chapters 8, 9, and 10—"Dressing Up Text," "Dressing Up Lines," and "Dressing Up Pages"—cover the tools that WordPerfect has available to change the way a document looks. These tools include different fonts, the appearance of text, styles and sizes, margin settings, line spacing, tabs, numbering pages, headers and footers, and even comments that you can see on the WordPerfect screen but don't print on your document.

How did you do on those spelling tests in elementary school? Good for you. But if you're not a whiz at spelling or if your vocabulary goes on vacation at the most important times, turn to the spell checker or thesaurus that WordPerfect provides. Chapter 11, "Spell Checker and Thesaurus," will introduce you to each of these fast and useful tools that are bound to improve your writing and the quality of your presentation.

Tables make your word processing life easier in many ways and WordPerfect offers so many options that tables will become an everyday WordPerfect activity for you. From the simplest table to a detailed and complex business form, Chapter 12, "Creating and Using Tables," will cover these and more.

Did you know that WordPerfect can double as a spreadsheet? That it can add column totals, work in tables, and even be used with formulas? "WordPerfect Math" can do all that, and we'll show you how in Chapter 13.

Next on the list of what you'll learn is Chapter 14, "Word-Perfect Columns." Interested in newspaper columns that snake from the bottom of one column to the top of another? You'll be amazed at how often text needs to be formatted in columns and how practical it is. Here's where you find out how to use WordPerfect to accomplish this.

Lists, lists, and more lists and nothing in order? Use Word-Perfect's sorting tools (Chapter 15, "Sorting with WordPerfect") to sort words, lines, and paragraphs and to sort first or last names or both!

Letters, letters, letters. You either send out or get hundreds, or both! WordPerfect uses the Merge feature to allow you to prepare personalized form letters so that you can customize your mailing lists, catalogs, or any printed document. See Chapter 16 for a step-by-step guide to writing and using the Merge feature.

By this time in this *Self-Teaching Guide*, you'll already have printed a document, but WordPerfect holds much more in store with its powerful printing features. Controlling your printer's many different options and printing such things as labels and envelopes are only part of the content contained in Chapter 17, "Printing with WordPerfect."

You may find that you have a very long document and you want to simultaneously view more than one part of it, or even see two documents on your screen at the same time and switch back and forth between them as you work. In Chapter 18, "Multiple Documents," you'll learn such things as switching screens and sharing text between two documents.

WordPerfect has come quite far since version 1.0 was introduced almost ten years ago. One of the most useful of the new features is the program's ability to incorporate and work with graphics. And while you might want to forget all the math you've ever learned, should you need to construct an equation, you can do so easily and with a great degree of control. Chapter 19, "Great Graphics," takes you through step-by-step instructions on how to create and modify graphics, including equations.

What's in This Book

This *Self-Teaching Guide's* short lessons will surprise you, since you'll see results immediately. At the end of each lesson, we'll check on your progress with some hands-on checkpoints that will allow you to determine if you've mastered the material in that lesson. At the end of each chapter, you'll find exercises that will review the basic skills you learned in the lessons contained in that chapter.

The book can also be used as a reference source to which you can return time and again to refresh your memory on a particular feature.

To help you remember some of the more important points in lessons, you'll find *TIP*s throughout the book to remind you about particularly important shortcuts or things that can make Word-Perfect work for you.

What You Need to Use WordPerfect 6.0

WordPerfect is designed to run with most computers that are IBM or IBM compatible, but you still have to be sure that your system has certain features. Here's a brief description of what they are.

The Computer

WordPerfect will work with the most basic IBM PC, XT, or AT computer that has at least 520K of internal memory or RAM and at least a 80286 (called a 286) model central processing unit. It should also work with any IBM compatible or clone. It is designed to work with extended memory.

The Disk Drives

Unlike earlier versions of WordPerfect, you can only use version 6.0 with a hard drive. And if you're thinking of adding one to your machine (or adding another), follow this advice. Buy the biggest one you can afford. Only 10 years ago people thought that a 20-megabyte drive was all they would ever need. Now they find that WordPerfect and some other big applications just about fit on a drive that size!

The Printer

WordPerfect is designed to work with more than 1,500 different types of printers and will probably work with yours. You'll learn more about printing documents in Chapter 17.

The Monitor

Whether you have a monochrome (such as black and white or amber) or a color monitor (which will show a minimum of 16 different colors), WordPerfect will work just fine, and you have nothing to be concerned about.

However, monitors do differ from one another. The display card contained in your computer provides directions about how information is displayed on the monitor. While some display cards allow very high resolution (and very detailed images), others might not be able to display WordPerfect graphics that include images, equations, and the view screen feature. If you find that your monitor does not support WordPerfect graphics and you want to use them, contact your dealer or the company who manufactured the monitor to see if you need a different display card or a new monitor.

Using the Keyboard

Just like a typewriter, your keyboard consists of rows of keys that correspond to numbers and other characters such as @, #, and &.

The difference between the keyboard and a standard typewriter is that the keyboard contains some keys that do special WordPerfect things.

For example, the Backspace key [←] is used to delete characters that you no longer want in a document. Here's a list of what some of those special WordPerfect keys are.

Key	Function
Tab	Indents the space where text begins. You can set the amount of the space that is indented.
Enter	When this key is pressed, you tell WordPerfect that you have finished a paragraph. This is also called the Return key. In this book, Enter means you need to press the Enter or return key.
Esc	Cancels the current WordPerfect window.
Ins	Allows you to insert text wherever the cursor is located.
←↑→↓	Moves the location of the cursor left, right, up, or down.
Del	Deletes a selected amount of text or a special code (called a reveal code) that WordPerfect inserts into a document.

Besides these keys, there are special keys that are the heart of the interface between you and WordPerfect. These are the **Ctrl,** the **Shift,** and the **Alt** keys used in conjunction with function keys (**F1, F2, F3** and so on, up to **F10** or **F12** depending on the type of keyboard and computer you have). These combinations of keys perform every function WordPerfect has available except the entry of original text. You'll learn more about using these key combinations throughout the rest of the book.

Keyboard Conventions

Keyboard
Conventions

Since we want you to use this book in a hands-on fashion, we'll be using certain conventions regarding how you should enter keystrokes.

First, WordPerfect uses many key combinations such as **Shift+F7** to begin the printing process, or **Ctrl+F4** to select a sentence, paragraph or page of text. When you see any two keys separated by a plus sign (**+**), it means that you press and hold down the first key while you press the second.

For example, to begin the printing process, you would hold down the **Shift** key and press the **F7** function key. In this *Self-Teaching Guide*, this keyboard operation would look like this: **Shift+F7**. When you use one of these two key combinations, you often have to make additional selections. For example, to print the current page of a document, the sequence of keys is **Shift+F7,2 Enter**. These keystrokes are executed as follows: While holding down the **Shift** key, press the **F7** function key, release both keys, then press only the number **2** key. Finally, press the **Enter** key. Keys that are separated by commas are entered in sequence.

You might have noticed that along with your WordPerfect package of disks and documentation, a **template** was included. This fits over or next to the function keys that are located on the left-hand side of your keyboard or across the top of the keyboard, depending on the type of keyboard you have.

As you become more proficient in using WordPerfect, you will see how different key combinations do different things. For example, one of the most basic is the **Ctrl+F2** key combination to begin the spell check process. Here, you hold down the **Ctrl** key and press the **F2** key. Or, if you want to begin using WordPerfect's powerful graphics tools, you use the **Alt+F9** key combination. Try this combination now.

TIP

You can always exit from any WordPerfect screen by pressing the Esc **key.**

Worried about remembering what keys do what? Don't. First, the key combinations and what they control will soon become second nature. Without even thinking about it, you'll be able to select the combination that does just what you want. It just takes practice. When in doubt you can always refer to the template. You should place yours over your function keys if you have not done so already, and leave it there until you are comfortable with the various keystrokes.

Last, and most certainly not least, you can see an on-screen representation of the template when you are in WordPerfect by selecting the **Template** option in the **Help** screen (press **F1** and then use the arrow keys to move down to Template and press **Enter**). As you see in Figure I.1, this template indicates which combination of keys accomplishes what task.

For example, the on-screen template shows you that if you want to open a file that is being stored, you would use the **Shift+F10** key combination and then provide the name of the file you want to retrieve.

▼ *Figure I.1.   The WordPerfect Template*

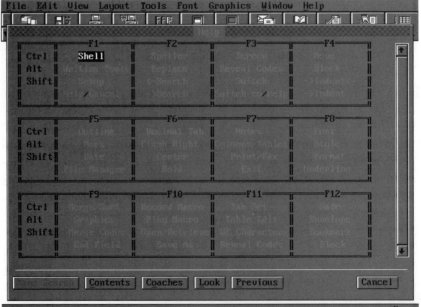

Mouse or Keyboard?

As you probably know, you can access all of WordPerfect's commands from a mouse or from the keyboard. It's no surprise to find that some people prefer the mouse while others prefer using just the keyboard. There are advantages to each.

A mouse allows you to move quickly to any part of the screen to make a menu selection or to work with text. Nothing is faster for getting from one point on the screen to another. If you have used a mouse with other applications (such as drawing or engineering tools) or other computers (such as the Macintosh), you might already be used to the feel and control.

The big advantage of using the keyboard is that your fingers never leave the keys, so that basic entry of text is not interrupted. Some people find it irritating to have to leave the keyboard and then return again and prefer the various key combinations to the use of the mouse. Fortunately with WordPerfect, you can use **pull-down menus** with the keyboard as effectively as you can with the mouse for almost all WordPerfect features. It's just a matter of choice. In Lesson 3, you'll learn how to use the mouse and pull-down menus.

Throughout this book, all of the mouse equivalents for a WordPerfect feature will be shown following the keystrokes. For example, here is how the mouse moves for opening a file would appear:

[Mouse Moves: **F**ile, **O**pen]

The boldface letter is the one you press to invoke the command if you are using pull-down menus from the keyboard.

TIP

To start using main menus, you have to use the Alt **key along with the letter, such as** Alt+F **to access the File menu.**

About Selecting

Throughout this *Self-Teaching Guide* you will often have to **select** a WordPerfect option such as opening a file, numbering pages, or changing fonts. You can make selections in WordPerfect in a variety of ways.

First, you can simply place the mouse pointer on the selection and click or double-click the left mouse button (depending on what you want to do with the option).

Second, you can use the arrow keys (↑, ↓, →, ←) to move through a list of options and then press the **Enter** key to select the highlighted option.

Finally, you can use the **Tab** key to move throughout a Word-Perfect menu or set of options and then press the **Enter** key to select the highlighted option.

For example, when you see an instruction such as, Select **S**ize from the **F**ont dialog box, you can use one or all of these three techniques to make the selection you want.

Helping You Work

As you work through the various exercises in this book, keep the following things in mind.

When you see a bolded letter, you know that it can substitute for whatever WordPerfect option is available on the screen. For example, when it comes time to work with Fonts (see Chapter 8), the first window you see contains a variety of options as you can see in Figure I.2.

You can select the number **3** or press the bolded letter **A** to change the appearance of text. A press of the **Esc** function key returns you to the document.

▼ *Figure I.2.   A Sample WordPerfect Window Showing Bold Letters That Make It Easy to Select What You Want*

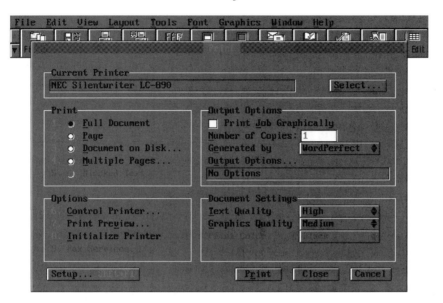

How to Use This Book

We hope that we have created a book that you will find easy to use, helpful, and informative. No matter how simply the material is presented, however, there are always steps you can take to make the learning process even more successful. Here are a few tips you can follow to help you get the most out of this *Self-Teaching Guide*.

We are assuming that you are somewhat familiar with the basics of the operating system that your computer uses. If you are completely new to computers and WordPerfect, you would be well served to read one of the many fine, introductory books available.

▲ Don't try to do too much at a time. The book was organized into brief lessons so that you can master a small part of a larger skill before moving on. For example, there's no reason to try and work through every section of creating and using tables. Take one lesson at a time. Work in small chunks, perhaps a few lessons, but no more than 45 minutes at a time.

▲ Work through the examples, the self-checks at the end of each lesson, and the exercises at the end of each chapter. They're all included to help you take a hands-on approach to learning the ins and outs of WordPerfect. They've all been tested for usefulness. If you find that when you follow the step-by-step directions you don't get the results you want, start at the beginning and try again. If things really get rough, take a break.

▲ Don't rush or have unreasonable expectations for yourself. If you're new to WordPerfect (or computers), as many of you probably are, take your time. If you find yourself getting frustrated, stop for a walk around the block or a cookie break. Being frustrated leads to more errors, and more errors lead to more frustration and then nothing gets done.

▲ If you are new to WordPerfect, you're about to learn all about word processing. If you are already using another word processor and are switching to WordPerfect, from now on use only WordPerfect and not the other word processor. You can use the WordPerfect convert utility to convert documents created with many other word processors. Don't switch back and forth between different word processors no matter how much you love your old standby. If you loved it so much, you wouldn't be switching. Go cold turkey. It's too easy to get confused otherwise. The more you stick with one word processor, the faster you will learn how to use it and the better you will become at using it as well. This version of WordPerfect can work with documents created using other versions.

Finally, personal computers and wonderful programs such as WordPerfect were designed to help you work more efficiently and enjoy yourself while you're doing it. By all means, take advantage of these tools and let them do the tedious work so you can have some fun!

Great. You've been formally introduced to WordPerfect and some of the techniques you will need to master to become a pro. Now, it's time to move on to the next step: how to start WordPerfect and use menus and Help.

Getting Started

Almost ready to go. Before we begin learning about how to start WordPerfect and see WordPerfect's opening screen, you need to make sure that three things have been done. First, you should have already made a backup copy of your original WordPerfect application disks and, second, stored the originals in a safe place. This insurance never hurt anyone! Next, WordPerfect should have been installed on your hard disk. In this chapter you'll learn how to:

- ▲ **Start WordPerfect**
- ▲ **Exit WordPerfect**
- ▲ **Understand the WordPerfect opening screen**
- ▲ **Use pull-down menus with WordPerfect**
- ▲ **Use WordPerfect Help**
- ▲ **Use the WordPerfect template**

Important Keys	Important Terms
Alt+=	Coaches
wp	cursor
	Help
	Main menu
	Name Search
	pull-down menu
	status line

Lesson 1: Starting WordPerfect

Before WordPerfect can do its work, the program itself has to be loaded into the memory of your computer.

To start WordPerfect:

1. Switch to the directory where WordPerfect is stored. Do this by entering the following command at the C> prompt:

   `cd\wp60`

   WP60 is the name of the directory where WordPerfect is stored. If you followed the instructions on installing WordPerfect in the original manual then the directory will be named WP60.

2. Type **wp** and then press **Enter**. You will soon see WordPerfect's opening message to you and then the opening screen you see in Figure 1.1.

TIP

The command you need to start WordPerfect is wp.

Exiting WordPerfect

To exit WordPerfect at any time, press the **F7** function key and then follow WordPerfect's prompts. WordPerfect will ask you if you

▼ *Figure 1.1. The WordPerfect 6.0 Opening Screen*

Lesson 1:
Starting
WordPerfect

want to save the document you are working on. If you do, provide a name and then WordPerfect will exit. If you do not want to save the current document, press the **N** key (for No) and WordPerfect will exit.

CHECK YOURSELF

1. What exact keystrokes start WordPerfect?
2. Look at your WordPerfect template (see Figure I.1) and indicate which keystrokes you would use to access the following features.
    Help
    Footnote
    Font
    Bold

ANSWERS

1. Type **WP** and then press **Enter**.
2. For Help, press **F1**. For Footnotes, press **Ctrl+F7**. For Fonts, press **Ctrl+F8**. For Bold, press **F6**.

Lesson 2: The WordPerfect Opening Screen

We'll assume that you have followed the instructions in Lesson 1 and now have in front of you WordPerfect's "clean screen" (shown in Figure 1.1). You'll see the following information in the lower right-hand corner of the screen on the **status line**:

```
Doc 1 Pg 1 Ln 1" Pos 1"
```

The status line consists of four indicators on the right that provide you with the following information.

Status Line Indicator	*What It Means*
Doc	Shows the number of the document that you are currently working on, which can be document 1 through document 9.
Pg	Shows the page number of the current document.
Ln	Shows the line number from the top of the page where the cursor is located.
Pos	Shows the position of the blinking cursor relative to the left-hand margin. If the setting for the left margin is one inch and the cursor is placed at the left-most point, you'll see a Pos indicator of 1".

In the lower left-hand corner, WordPerfect shows you the default font it is using. You'll learn all about fonts and how to select them in Chapter 8.

One of the reasons people like to work with WordPerfect is because there is no clutter on the screen. If you want, the only things you will ever see on the screen when you are entering text are the **cursor,** the text, and the status line. After you have saved a document for the first time, you will then also see the name of the document in the lower left-hand corner of the screen. The cursor is the blinking square that indicates where text will be entered.

TIP

You can always look to the status line to learn your position within any WordPerfect document.

Given the indicators in the status bar, you can tell the document number, page number, line number, and the position of the cursor.

TIP

WordPerfect allows you to work with up to nine (!) windows at a time, so it's a good idea to keep your eye on the status line so you can track the use of multiple windows. More about that in Chapter 18.

If you were working on a document, such as one named *chap1*, then the status line would look like this:

```
C:\CHAP1                 Doc 1 Pg 1 Ln 1" Pos 1"
```

As you can see, the name of the current directory and file becomes part of the status line.

CHECK YOURSELF

1. What would the status line look like if you were at the beginning of the third line on the fourth page of the first document?
2. What would the status line look like if you were at the beginning of the third line on the fifth page of the eighth document?

ANSWERS

1. Doc 1 Pg 4 Ln 3" Pos 1"
2. Doc 8 Pg 5 Ln 3" Pos 1"

Lesson 3: Using Pull-Down Menus

You already know that you can use various combinations of keys to access any of WordPerfect's different features. For example, the **Ctrl+F8** key combination provides you access to the set of WordPerfect Font options.

There's another way to interact with WordPerfect, and that's through the use of **pull-down menus**. A pull-down menu is a listing of WordPerfect features that appears across the top of the screen from which various options can be selected. You actually pull down all the alternatives listed on the menu using the keyboard or the mouse.

Displaying the Main Menu Bar

The appearance of the **Main menu bar** on the WordPerfect opening screen is the default setup. You saw the menu bar in Figure 1.1 (File, Edit, View, Layout, etc.). Each time you start up WordPerfect, you will see the same set of menus across the top of the screen.

Selecting a Pull-Down Menu

To select an individual pull-down menu using a mouse, just place the mouse pointer on the menu you want to select (such as **F**ile or **Fo**nt) and click the left button once.

To select an individual pull-down menu using the keyboard, use the **Alt** key, plus the highlighted menu character combination. For example, if you wanted to select the Tools menu, you would use the **Alt+T** key combination. The highlighted characters are usually bold in appearance and are often the first letters (F for **F**ile, E for **E**dit, V for **V**iew, etc.). The only exception to this is that you use the **Alt+O** key combination to select the Font menu.

TIP

If you are using a mouse to work with pull-down menus, be sure that you are working on a flat surface and using a mouse pad so the mouse ball doesn't slip when you try to move the cursor.

Selecting Options from Pull-Down Menus

Once the options on a menu are visible you can select the option you want from any pull-down menu in one of three ways:

1. Use the arrow keys to move to the selection you want on a particular menu. Then press the **Enter** key to make the selection.
2. Enter the boldface letter of the option you want.
3. Place the mouse pointer on the option and click the left button. For example, Figure 1.2, shows the sequence of menu commands for editing a button bar. The mouse or the following sequence of keystrokes could have been used:

   Alt+V, S, E

   V for **V**iew, **S** for Button Bar **S**etup, and **E** for **E**dit.

   The keys **V**, **S** and **E** are pressed in sequence, one after another.

TIP

In this *Self-Teaching Guide*, when we use the word *Select*, we mean using the mouse or keystrokes and menus.

Don't Like Menus?

If you don't like menus appearing on your screen, you can tell WordPerfect to start up without the Main menu appearing. To do this, follow these steps.

▼ *Figure 1.2. Selecting an Option from a Menu*

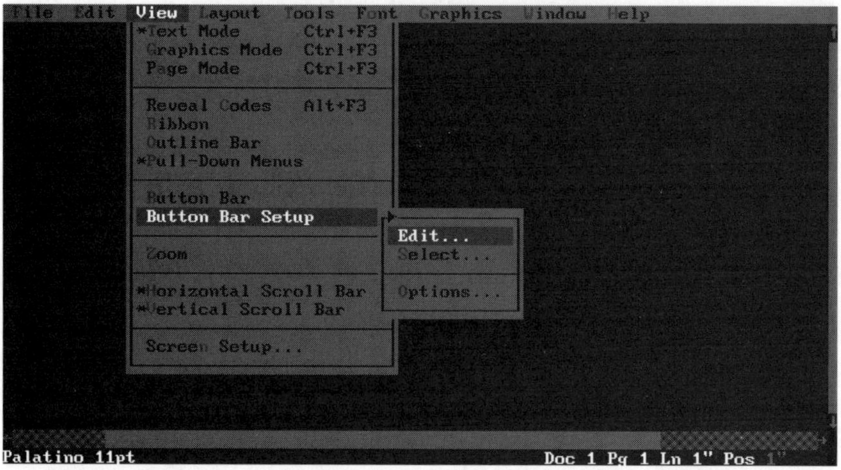

1. Select **P**ull-Down Menus from the **V**iew menu. Since the default is to have pull-down menus appear, this option will have an asterisk (*) next to it.
2. Select **P**ull-Down Menus. Once you select this option (and in effect turn it off), the menu bar, and access to pull-down menus) will disappear from the screen.

Oops! You want them back? Since you can't see the menus, it's tough to get back to the View menu and turn on the Pull-Down Menus option.

To see the WordPerfect menu bar again, simply use the **Alt+=** key combination. That will turn on the menu bar (temporarily) so you can use it as needed. You can then use the arrow keys to navigate from menu to menu and make the selection you want.

TIP

Once you turn off the Pull-Down Menus option from the View menu, WordPerfect will not show you the menu bar when it first starts. You'll have to use the Alt+= key combination and then turn menus on using the View menu.

If you're a mouse user and the Main menu is not visible, clicking on the right-hand button will reveal the menu bar. You can then select the option you want.

TIP

You may want to work with a clean screen. Why not turn off the menus and then just use the Alt+= **key combination or mouse to use what you need when you need it?**

Using Dialog Boxes

Besides the pull-down menus that are available in WordPerfect 6.0, you will also use dialog boxes that are standard WordPerfect fare. For example, in Figure 1.3, you can see the dialog box that is used to control the printing options accessed through the **Shift+F7** key combination or the **File, Print** mouse move.

A dialog box provides you with a series of options from which you can select. It's also WordPerfect's way of asking for additional information. For example, in Figure 1.3, you can see how you can print a full document (option 1), preview what you want to print (option 7), or print more than one copy (Number of Copies:). A dialog box will always follow a menu option that has three dots (called an ellipsis). For example, in Figure 1.2, the Edit option produces a dialog box that requires you to provide information about editing a button bar.

You can make a selection in a dialog box in one of three ways.

▲ Click on the selection using the mouse.
▲ Use the **Tab** or arrow keys until the area that you want selected is highlighted and then press the **Enter** key.
▲ Enter the highlighted or bolded letter of the option you want such as **F** for printing a **F**ull Document.

▼ *Figure 1.3. The Print Dialog Box Where WordPerfect Asks You for Additional Information*

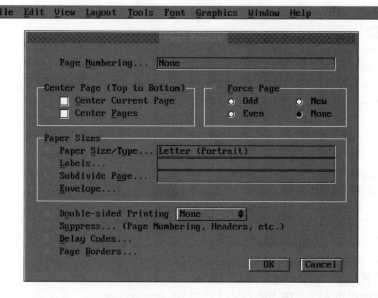

CHECK YOURSELF

1. What pull-down menu is highlighted if you use the Alt+= key combination?
2. What are the exact keystrokes you need to underline text using pull-down menus (if the means are not visible)?

ANSWERS

1. The File menu.
2. The keystrokes are **Alt+=,o,u**. The **F8** function key also underlines as you will learn in Lesson 24.

Lesson 4: Using WordPerfect Help

*Lesson 4:
Using
WordPerfect
Help*

Everyone needs help sometime, and with WordPerfect, it is only as far away as a few keystrokes. This quick and easy help is especially useful if you are in the middle of working with a document and need a certain feature but forget what keystroke or menu combination you need to access it.

You can use **Help** with WordPerfect in a variety of ways.

The WordPerfect Help Template

As you saw in Figure I.1 in the Introduction, the WordPerfect template illustrates the various keystrokes and the corresponding WordPerfect features. This template is an exact on-screen duplicate of the plastic one that you should place by your function keys on your keyboard (if you haven't done so already). The template will either go on the left-hand side of your keyboard or across the top, depending on the location of the function keys.

TIP

WordPerfect Help is always available within any WordPerfect document.

Using WordPerfect Context-Sensitive Help

Perhaps WordPerfect's best Help feature is that it can produce help for the feature in which you are currently working. For example, let's say that you are trying to check the spelling in a document and pressed the **Ctrl+F2** key combination but don't know where to go from there. By pressing the **F1** key, WordPerfect will provide detailed instructions regarding the next step [Mouse Moves: **Help**].

For example, in Figure 1.4, you can see **context-sensitive help** for creating a new file. Any option that is selected will produce a screen full of help on that option.

You can use the **Esc** key to exit the Help menu.

The WordPerfect Help Index

You can also locate help on a particular WordPerfect feature by using a Help index.

To use the Help index:

1. Press the **F1** key once [Mouse Moves: **H**elp]. You'll see the Help screen as shown in Figure 1.5.
2. Press **Enter** to use the index and you'll see a listing of WordPerfect topics.
3. Press the letter **N** for Name Search.

▼ *Figure 1.4. Help Using WordPerfect's Context-Sensitive Help Feature*

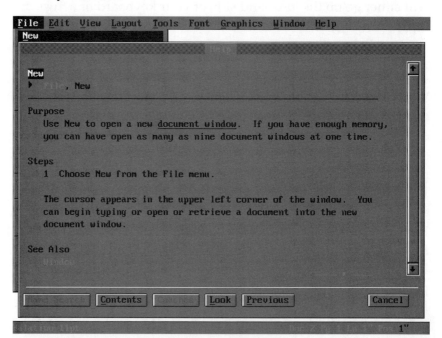

▼ *Figure 1.5. The WordPerfect Help Index*

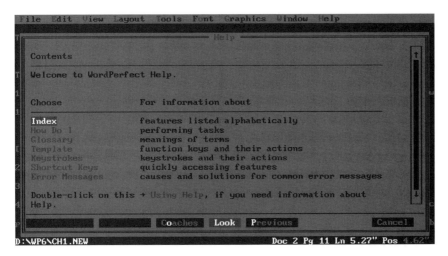

4. Now press the first letter of the feature you want help with (such as **C** for copy, **P** for print, or **S** for save) and WordPerfect will deliver you to the first topic that begins with that letter. The more characters you enter, the more precisely WordPerfect can find the help you need.

5. When you find the index topic you want help in, just press **Enter** and it will be there.

Using a Coach

On the Help screen that you see in Figure 1.5, you can see the **Coaches** option. If you select this with the mouse or using the keyboard, WordPerfect will provide you with a set of step-by-step directions for performing a task. For example, let's say you want to know not just about using an outline, but the actual steps it takes to do it.

To use the Coaches option:

1. Select **H**elp.
2. Press **Enter** to begin the index.
3. Press **N** for Name Search.
4. Enter the words **save document**.
5. Press **Enter.** Select Coaches.
6. Select the coach you want to use.

CHECK YOURSELF

1. How would you get context-sensitive help for opening a new file? (New or the File menu?)
2. What are the first two entries in the Help Index?

ANSWERS

1. Select **N**ew from the **F**ile menu (using the mouse or keyboard) and then press **F1**.
2. About Help, Absolute Position, Advance

Knowing how to start WordPerfect is the first step toward becoming a confident and competent user. And with your knowledge of how to find help on almost any feature, you'll find that learning about new features will be even easier than you thought. With that clean screen still in your mind, let's get to the real job at which WordPerfect shines; the creation of your first WordPerfect document.

PRACTICE WHAT YOU'VE LEARNED

1. What directory must you be in when you start WordPerfect?
2. What does the status line tell you?
3. What is one situation when you would want to use pull-down menus instead of the keyboard to access WordPerfect commands?
4. Name two ways that you can get help when saving a WordPerfect document.

ANSWERS

1. The directory where the WP.EXE files are stored, which is probably WP60.
2. The document number you are working in and the location of the cursor as far as page, line, and position on the line and the default font.
3. When you are using a mouse.
4. Using the Help index or the F1 key for context-sensitive help.

Creating Your
First Document

Your patience will now pay off. It's time to actually use WordPerfect for what it was designed for: the creation of text documents. Some of the most basic yet most important WordPerfect techniques will be discussed in this chapter. When you're finished with the text, self-checks, and exercises, you'll know how to create and save anything from a one-page memo to an encyclopedic treatise! In this chapter you'll learn how to:

- ▲ **Enter text**
- ▲ **Save a file for the first time**
- ▲ **Work with the save feature to save files to new locations**
- ▲ **Print a document**
- ▲ **Exit from a WordPerfect session**

Important Keys	*Important Terms*
F7	exit
F10	Backspace
	path
	save
	word wrap

Lesson 5: Entering Text with WordPerfect

Entering text using WordPerfect is just like using a typewriter, with two big differences. The first, of course, is that what you type appears on a monitor screen and not on a piece of paper. The second is the amazing **word wrap** feature that almost all word processing programs offer. Word wrap means that as you enter text and you come to the right-hand margin, the text automatically continues on the next line. No concerns about margin releases, bells, or carriage returns.

For example, in Figure 2.1, you can see a sentence that was entered without having to worry about where the right-hand margin stops. Be sure that you have a clear WordPerfect screen and enter that sentence now. Don't be concerned if when you enter this sentence, the lines "break" at different words. Where WordPerfect stops on one line and continues on the next depends on the type of printer you have.

TIP

Entering text using WordPerfect is just like using a typewriter, except you don't have to be concerned about where lines end.

After you've finished entering that first sentence, press the **Enter** key twice and continue by entering the text that follows in Figure 2.2. If you make a mistake, just use the **Backspace** key to erase the error and retype the correct text.

Besides word wrap, WordPerfect offers many other useful features. It can check your spelling, underline words, and more. Best

▼ *Figure 2.1. An Example of How Word Wrap Works*

Lesson 5:
Entering
Text with
WordPerfect

of all, you'll be amazed at how it can save you time and a great deal of work.

Congratulations! You finished your first document, which should look the same on your screen as the illustration shown in Figure 2.2. If yours doesn't match the figure exactly, don't worry. Just use the **Backspace** key to make corrections and the **Enter** key to insert line spaces until they match up.

CHECK YOURSELF

▲ Enter the following text to experiment how the word wrap feature works. Be sure to note where WordPerfect breaks at the end of one line and starts another. What happens?

WordPerfect is the leading word processor that is available for IBM compatible machines. It has been in existence for over ten years and has gone through many different modifications. Almost everyone who uses it finds it easy to learn and simple to use.

ANSWER

▲ Word wrap automatically forwards you to the next line of text without having to press the Enter or Return keys.

▼ *Figure 2.2. Adding More Text for Practice and Watching How Word Wrap Works*

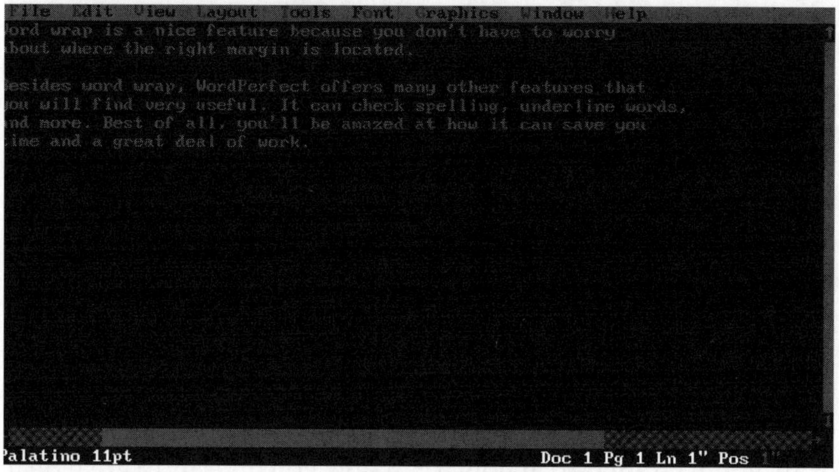

Lesson 6: Saving a File

What good would any word processor be if we could not save our work? Not much. We either save it or it's lost when the computer is turned off.

You need to remember three things about saving WordPerfect documents:

1. *Save your work as you work.* You can use WordPerfect's automatic save feature to save every certain number of minutes. For example, if you save every ten minutes, you will never be out more than ten minutes of work should you accidentally lose your work (the electricity goes off, the dog kicks the plug out, or you accidently delete the file).

2. When you save a document for the first time, you assign a name to that file. *Use names that are descriptive* and give you some indication of the file's contents. Names such as *letter1* or *letter2* tell you nothing. Instead, *springer.ltr* or *intro.ltr* are much more useful.

3. Make at least *two backups* of each file, one to a hard disk for safe keeping and one to a floppy disk for additional insurance. You

don't want the only copy to be on your hard disk, since they have been known to fail.

TIP

When you save a file, be sure to use names that convey the content of the file.

Saving a File for the First Time

Now that you have entered some text, you need to save it.

To save new text that you have entered in WordPerfect:

1. Press the **F10** function key [Mouse Moves: **F**ile, **S**ave] and WordPerfect will show you the Save Document 1 dialog box shown in Figure 2.3.
2. You now need to enter a name for the document you want to save in the Filename box. Enter the name you want to use, including the complete path. (You can use up to eight characters for a DOS name, with three more characters following a period. These three characters are called an extension.)

▼ *Figure 2.3. The Save Document Dialog Box*

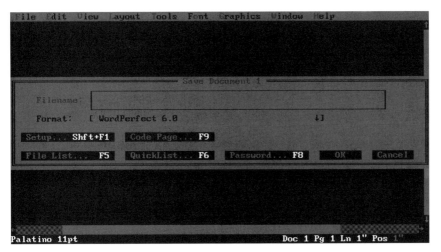

TIP

Remember, a WordPerfect file name is like any other DOS name. It can only be eight characters long and have a three-character extension.

The **path** is the order of directories and subdirectories where files are located. For example, the file named *psych* would be saved in the document directory named *manu* using the following command:

`C:\manu\psych`

If you want to save a file to a directory that does not exist, you must first create the directory. You can do this using the DOS command, or through the WordPerfect File Manager, which you'll learn about in Chapter 6.

3. Once you enter the name of the file, press **Enter** and Word-Perfect will save the file under the name that you assigned and the location you specified. You'll now see the name of the file in the lower left-hand corner of your screen.

Assigning a Password

While most of us are not in the business that James Bond was, we may need to use a password to protect access to a particular file. As you can see in Figure 2.3, there is an option for assigning a password to a file when you save it for the first time.

To assign a password:

1. Press the **F10** function key [Mouse Moves: **F**ile, **S**ave] and WordPerfect will show you the Save Document 1 dialog box.
2. Enter the name of the file you want to use.
3. Press the **F8** function key.
4. Enter the password. It must be less than eight characters long.
5. Press **Enter**. After you enter the password for the first time, WordPerfect will ask you to enter the password again to confirm it was entered as you intended.
6. Enter the password again.
7. Press **Enter**.

The password is now in effect. Should you want to open this file again at a future time, you will have to provide this password. Otherwise, WordPerfect will not provide access to the file and you will not be able to work with it.

TIP

Don't mess around with passwords unless you really need to use them. If you forget the password, there's no way that you can open the file and even the fabulous, best-in-the-world WordPerfect technical support won't be able to help you either.

Removing a Password

It's just as easy to remove a password as it is to assign one. Be sure that the document for which you want to remove the password is active.

To remove a password:

1. Press the **F10** function key [Mouse Moves: File, **S**ave] and WordPerfect will show you the Save Document 1 dialog box.
2. Press the **F8** function key. When you do this, you will see the Password box.
3. Press the **F6** function key and the password will no longer be in effect. You can tell this because the **Remove (F6)** button is dimmed and not available.

Saving a File After It Has Been Saved Once

Once you assign a name and save a file for the first time, WordPerfect remembers the name that you used.

To save a file after it has been saved once (using the same file-name):

1. Press the **F10** function key [Mouse Moves: File, **S**ave] and WordPerfect will show you the name that is currently used to save the file.

2. Press **Enter**.
3. WordPerfect will prompt you to determine if you want to re-place the already saved file with the content that is currently on your monitor screen (or in WordPerfect's memory). This is WordPerfect's way of checking that you are sure you want to replace the old file with the changes that have been made.
4. Press **Y** and WordPerfect will save the changes that were made using the original filename.

Saving a File to Another Disk

There are occasions when you want to save a file to a floppy disk, such as when you want to back up a file.

To save the file to a disk other than a hard disk:

1. Place a *formatted* disk into the floppy drive to which you want to save the file.
2. Press the **F10** function key [Mouse Moves: **F**ile, **S**ave] and you'll see the Save Document dialog box.
3. Enter the letter that represents the disk drive, a colon, and the name of the file. For example, the following will save the file named *psych* to the disk inserted in disk drive A.

   ```
   a:psych
   ```

4. Press **Enter**.

   WordPerfect will remember that it stored the file there and the next time you press the **F10** function key to save the file, WordPerfect will want to save the file to the A drive. If you want to switch back to the original file storage location, you will have to enter the path command that will take you to the original directory.

   These instructions also hold true if you want to save a file to another location, such as another directory on a hard disk.

Saving a File Under a New Name

You may need to save an existing file under a different filename. For example, you might want to use the same document over again, but instead of naming it *springer.ltr*, you want to name it *jackson.ltr*. Everything is almost the same, except for a different filename.

To save an existing file under a different name:

1. Press the **F10** key [Mouse Moves: **File, Save As**]. Enter the new name you want to use, such as *jackson.ltr*. When you start entering the new name for the file, it will automatically replace the old name. Be sure to specify the complete path.
2. Press **Enter**. Since it is a new name that has not been used before, WordPerfect will not ask you if you want to replace the existing file with a new one. WordPerfect will just go ahead and make the save.

Saving and Clearing the WordPerfect Screen

To save your file and then start a new document (and clear or exit your screen):

1. Press the **F7** function key [Mouse Moves: **File, Exit WP**]. WordPerfect will then ask you if you want to save the document under its current name.
2. Press the **Y** key for Yes to be sure that you save whatever changes might have been made.
3. WordPerfect will then ask you, Exit WordPerfect? Since you only want to clear the screen and not exit the program, press **N**. You don't want to exit at this point, but continue with the creation of a new document.

Saving and Exiting the WordPerfect Screen

To save your file and then exit WordPerfect:

1. Press the **F7** function key [Mouse Moves: **File, Exit WP**]. WordPerfect will then ask you if you want to save the document under its current name.
2. Press **Enter** for Yes.

3. WordPerfect will then ask you, Exit WordPerfect? Press **Y**. You will then be returned to the system level where you will see the C> prompt.

Here's a summary of commands for saving files and exiting WordPerfect files.

Keystrokes	Function
F10,[filename],<Enter>	Save a file for the first time.
F10,<Enter>,Y	Save a file that has already been saved once.
F10,[enter new filename], <Enter>	Save a file under a new name.
F10,[enter new drive and filename],<Enter>	Save a file to another disk.
F7,Y, N	Save a file and clear the screen.
F7,Y, Y	Save a file and exit.

TIP

The F7 **key is used to begin the exit process from WordPerfect. The** F10 **key is used to save WordPerfect files.**

CHECK YOURSELF

1. Enter your name, address, city, state, and zip code and save it under a file named *address*.
2. Place a formatted disk in a floppy drive and save the address file that you created above to that floppy disk under the new filename *address.new*.

ANSWERS

1. Remember to use names that reflect the content of the file you are saving. Otherwise, when you have a large number of files from which to choose, you will have difficulty selecting the correct one.

2. Until a file is saved, none of the changes that you made will be recorded.

Lesson 7: Printing Your Document

If you still have text entered from Lesson 5, you're in great shape. If not, go back and write your best friend a short two-paragraph letter. It's time to print. First be sure that the document is active and on your screen.

To print a WordPerfect document:

1. Use the **Shift**+**F7** key combination [Mouse Moves: **F**ile, **P**rint] and you will see the Print dialog box as shown in Figure 2.4.

    As you can see in Figure 2.4, many different print options are available to you. For example, you can print a single page of a document (option 2) or print multiple pages from the same document (option 4).
2. Select option 1, for **Full Document**.
3. Press **Enter** and you'll see the text that you entered being printed. We'll explore all of the options you see in Figure 2.4 later on in Chapter 17.

CHECK YOURSELF

▲ Enter the following list of five items.
    hat
    shoe
    shirt
    sweater
    glove
    a. Save them as a file named *list*.
    b. Print the file named *list*.

▼ *Figure 2.4. The Print Dialog Box*

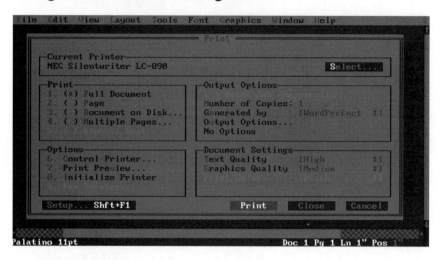

ANSWER

▲ Using the **Shift+F7** key combination provides you with a ton of printing options!

TIP

If you don't clear your WordPerfect screen before you recall a document, the new document will be inserted wherever the cursor is located in the previous document.

Lesson 8: Ending a WordPerfect Session

When you are ready to stop working, you never just turn your computer off. This could lead to a disaster. First, what you have been working on is not saved. Second, WordPerfect needs some warning to do some housekeeping and get its files in order so that the next time you begin to work everything runs smoothly.

TIP

WordPerfect will ask you to save your document one last time before you exit.

To end a WordPerfect session:

1. Press the **F7** function key [Mouse Moves: **F**ile, E**x**it]. WordPerfect will ask if you want to save the current document.
2. Press **Y** and respond to the prompts that WordPerfect provides.
3. WordPerfect will then ask you if you want to exit the program. Indicate Yes and you will be returned to the DOS prompt (C>).

TIP

Press the F7 function key to begin the exiting process. Now press the F1 function key and describe what happens—you get help!

Creating a document is the first step of many along the way in becoming familiar with WordPerfect's many features. In this chapter, you learned how to enter text and the variety of different ways and locations that text can be saved. Finally, you saw how easy it is to print a document and then exit from a WordPerfect session. Now that you're familiar with the basics of entering and saving text, we'll move in Chapter 3 to the process of editing a document once the text is entered and saved.

PRACTICE WHAT YOU'VE LEARNED

1. Provide an example of when you would want to save a file under another name.
2. Write the keystrokes you use to print a full document.
3. What keystroke combination would you use to save a WordPerfect document and then clear the screen in preparation for a new document?
4. How often should you save a file?
5. Write the exact sequence of keys you would press to save a newly created document.

ANSWERS

1. When you want to use some of the contents of that file again as a new document.
2. Shift+F7,1
3. F7,Y,N
4. About 10 minutes between saves is a good start, since this means that you will never lose more than that amount of work.
5. F10, [filename], Enter

Editing
Documents

It's rare that your first draft is your last one. That's why WordPerfect has so many built-in editing tools that are easy to use. Learning how to edit is an essential part of learning WordPerfect. You may want to correct a simple mistake, delete an entire section of a paper, or move three paragraphs from one place in a document to another or even to an entirely different document! WordPerfect lets you do it all. Whatever your editing task, WordPerfect and you can handle it. In this chapter you'll learn how to:

▲ **Retrieve a document**

▲ **Use reveal codes**

▲ **Move around a document**

▲ **Use blocks in WordPerfect**

▲ **Insert and delete text**

▲ **Copy and move text**

▲ **Undo and Undelete**

Important Keys	***Important Terms***
Alt+F3	Backspace key
Ctrl+Backspace	block
Ctrl+F4	buffer
Ctrl+Home	copy
Ctrl+End	cut
Ctrl+Right and Left Arrows	drag insert
	open
	move
	restore
	retrieve
	typeover
	undelete

Lesson 9: Opening a Document

When you create a document for the first time, you'll probably work with it a little bit, make the corrections you want, and then end your WordPerfect session.

The more usual circumstance, however, is to create a document, save it, end your work session, and come back at a later time to work with (and edit) the document. That's because few documents (except maybe for memos or short letters) can be written start to finish in one sitting.

The first step in this process is to open a document, since it is only when a document is loaded (or in the memory of your computer) that it can be modified.

Before we begin talking about opening a document, just one short note. In WordPerfect, you can use the File menu to create a **N**ew document (you already did this), **O**pen an already saved document, or **R**etrieve one that's been saved as well. What's the difference between the Open and Retrieve options? Open creates a new window or screen within which the file you want to work with will appear. Retrieve will take the file you want to work with and retrieve it at the location of the cursor, even if there is something else in the current window. You'll read more about this distinction later, but for now let's continue with the basics of opening a document so that you can work with it.

Opening a Document

The first thing you need to do to edit a document that is stored on a hard or floppy disk is to open that document.

To open a document:

1. Use the **Shift+F10** key combination [Mouse Moves: **F**ile, **O**pen] to see the Open Document dialog box shown in Figure 3.1.
2. Enter the name of the document you want to open in the Filename box. Be sure to include the complete path. In Figure 3.1, you can see the path (c:\taxes\qtr.1) indicates that the file has been stored using the name *qtr.1* in the *taxes* directory.

Once you press the Enter key, you're in business. WordPerfect will then load the file from the directory that you indicated. If you entered the wrong filename, then WordPerfect will beep and tell you that it can't find the file and ask you for another filename (it assumes you know the name but just entered it incorrectly). The problem may be that you are either using the wrong filename or you are asking WordPerfect to look for a file in the wrong location.

▼ *Figure 3.1.   The Open Document Dialog Box*

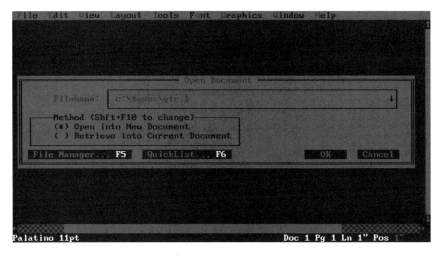

TIP

If you entered the wrong filename and want to escape the Shift+F10 **file retrieve command, use the** Esc **key to cancel the command.**

Retrieving a Document Using the File Manager

There's an alternative way to retrieve a document that is especially helpful if you don't remember the name of the document (but do remember where it's stored). It's through the use of Word-Perfect's **File Manager,** which you'll learn all about in Chapter 6.

To retrieve a file using the File Manager:

1. Press the **F5** function key [Mouse Moves: File, File Manager].
2. When you see the Specify File Manager List dialog box, enter the location (and the name if you know it) of the file.
3. Press **Enter**. When you do this, you will see the File Manager dialog box as you see in Figure 3.2.
4. Use the arrow keys to move up and down the list of files until you have highlighted the one you want to open.
5. Select **Open into New Document** (option 1) and the file you highlighted will appear in a new window all by itself.

TIP

If you cannot find the file, you can use the F5 **key to get back to the Specify File Manager List dialog box and try another location.**

The File Manager shows you a list of all the files in the current directory in alphabetical order with all kinds of valuable information on the screen. For example, all the files that are in the current directory (named *WP6* in this example) are listed and include their names, how big they are (in kilobytes or thousands of pieces of information), and the date they were created.

▼ *Figure 3.2.*   *The File Manager Dialog Box*

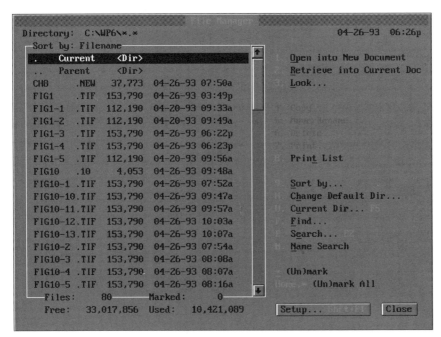

```
Directory:  C:\WP6\*.*                                    04-26-93  06:26p
 Sort by: Filename
    .     Current      <Dir>                        Open into New Document
    ..    Parent       <Dir>                         Retrieve into Current Doc
  CH8     .NEW     37,773  04-26-93 07:50a          Look...
  FIG1    .TIF    153,790  04-26-93 03:49p
  FIG1-1  .TIF    112,190  04-20-93 09:33a
  FIG1-2  .TIF    112,190  04-20-93 09:49a
  FIG1-3  .TIF    153,790  04-26-93 06:22p
  FIG1-4  .TIF    153,790  04-26-93 06:23p
  FIG1-5  .TIF    112,190  04-20-93 09:56a          Print List
  FIG10   .10       4,053  04-26-93 09:48a
  FIG10-1 .TIF    153,790  04-26-93 07:52a          Sort by...
  FIG10-10.TIF    153,790  04-26-93 09:47a          Change Default Dir...
  FIG10-11.TIF    153,790  04-26-93 09:57a          Current Dir...
  FIG10-12.TIF    153,790  04-26-93 10:03a          Find...
  FIG10-13.TIF    153,790  04-26-93 10:07a          Search...
  FIG10-2 .TIF    153,790  04-26-93 07:54a          Name Search
  FIG10-3 .TIF    153,790  04-26-93 08:08a
  FIG10-4 .TIF    153,790  04-26-93 08:07a          (Un)mark
  FIG10-5 .TIF    153,790  04-26-93 08:16a             (Un)mark All
 Files:      80      Marked:        0
  Free:  33,017,856  Used:  10,421,089        Setup...            Close
```

To practice using the File Manager to open a file (be sure you have a clear WordPerfect screen):

1. As an exercise, enter the following text: **The List Files screen has many handy tools**.
2. Save the file (**F10**) under the name **tools**.
3. Clear the WordPerfect screen (**F7,N,N**).
4. Press the **List Files** function key (**F5**).
5. Press **Enter** (since you are already in the correct directory).
6. Use the up and down arrow keys to highlight the file you want to retrieve.
7. Select **Open** (option 1) to make this file an active WordPerfect window.

TIP

You can use the List Files feature to open a file located in another directory by pressing F5, **then selecting** Change Default Dir **(option H),** then supplying the new directory and filename.

Combining Files

Here's where the Retrieve option in the File menu (and in the File Manager) comes in handy. You may have just finished a four-part report and you want to combine each of the parts into a totally new file. The easiest way to combine files so they appear active in the same screen is to use the Retrieve option in the File menu. All you need to be sure of is that the cursor is located where you want the new information placed, *before you retrieve the document.* Word-Perfect will always insert a retrieved file at the cursor location.

Second, you can use the **Retrieve into Current Doc** (option 2) to retrieve subsequent documents as well. You still have to make sure, however, that your cursor is placed at the appropriate location when you retrieve another file. What you retrieve will be inserted into your document at the location of the cursor.

TIP

If you want to combine files into one large one, keep in mind that the name of the file (unless you change it) will be the same as the name of the first file that you retrieved.

CHECK YOURSELF

1. Clear your WordPerfect screen and open two other files. Create them if you have not saved two previously.
2. Create three separate documents that each consist of one sentence and save them under the names of *first.doc, second.doc,* and *third.doc.* Now retrieve them (in numerical order) using the **Retrieve** option in the File Manager. What is the current name of the document?

ANSWERS

1. Notice that WordPerfect opens a new window for each file.
2. first.doc

Lesson 10: Using Reveal Codes

Lesson 10:
Using Reveal
Codes

The people who designed WordPerfect thought it was essential to keep the window you see and use for entering and working with text unencumbered by anything.

For example, when you press the **Enter** key, the cursor moves to the next line on the screen, but you don't see an on-screen entry in the document such as [Enter key pressed]. Or when you underline a word, WordPerfect does not show you [underline word] or some other message. That would make the screen very messy and difficult to work with.

But WordPerfect is hard at work recording all of your keystrokes, even if they are not immediately apparent by just looking at the screen. To see these keystrokes and key combinations, use the **Alt+F3** [Mouse Moves: **V**iew, Reveal **C**odes] key combination, which shows WordPerfect's embedded codes, called **reveal codes**. If you are using a mouse, select the Reveal **C**odes option from the **V**iew menu.

TIP

WordPerfect will by default place the reveal code [Open Style: Initial Codes] at the beginning of each document. This style code contains the default settings for each WordPerfect session.

For example, look at the first few paragraphs of the following letter. Enter it now for practice.

```
April 12, 1990

Mr. Jack Jordan
1827 Altoona
Pittsburgh, PA 12345
```

Dear Jack:

It was great to hear from you yesterday. I was pleased to find that you are happy with your new job and that your family is fine.

Now if you press the **Alt+F3** key combination, you'll see the codes associated with the letter as shown in Figure 3.3. What you see in Figure 3.3 is the letters and the codes screen for the letter. Some interesting things appear in this figure.

First, you see a portion of the actual document itself in the top portion of the window along with the status line indicator (that appears in any window).

TIP

You can undo what a code does by deleting the code itself. Just place the cursor to the right of the code (be sure you can see it using the Alt+F3 **key combination) and use the** Backspace **key to delete it.**

Next, there's a line of triangles separating the document from the codes. This line contains brackets (**{** and **}**) that represent the document's left and right margins and triangles that represent tab settings. We'll learn more about tabs in Chapter 9.

▼ *Figure 3.3.   Examining Reveal Codes*

```
 File  Edit  View  Layout  Tools  Font  Graphics  Window  Help
April 27, 1993

Mr. Jack Jordan
1827 Altoona
Pittsburgh, PA 12345

Dear Jack:

It was great to hear from you yesterday. I was pleased to find
that you are happy with your new job and that your family is
fine.
      ▲                   ▲               ▲          }  ▲       ▲       {
[Open Style:InitialCodes][Rgt Mar]April 27, 1993[HRt]
[HRt]
Mr. Jack Jordan[HRt]
1827 Altoona[HRt]
Pittsburgh, PA 12345[HRt]
[HRt]
Dear Jack:[HRt]
[HRt]
It was great to hear from you yesterday. I was pleased to find[SRt]
that you are happy with your new job and that your family is[SRt]

Palatino 11pt                                    Doc 1 Pg 1 Ln 1" Pos 1
```

TIP

The mouse will not work in the reveal codes section of the screen.

Finally, the bottom of the screen shows the text of the letter and the famous reveal codes that we have been discussing. Though there are hundreds of codes, the only ones you see here are a [Rgt Mar] for a right margin settting, [HRt] for hard return, indicating a hard return or a pressing of the Enter key, and [SRt] for soft return, indicating that the end of a line was reached and WordPerfect automatically ended the line there (remember word wrap?) and started a new one.

As you learn more about WordPerfect, you will see how useful codes can be. In Figure 3.4, you can see the codes for a stationary heading. They're a bit more complex, but they give valuable information as to types of commands that are inserted in the document that you could not otherwise see.

Here's what some of the codes do:

[Paper Sz/Typ: 8.5i x 11i,Standard-bin2] Goes to paper bin #2 and selects a particular size of paper.

[Font: Helvetica Narrow] [Size: 18.9pt] Changes the font or type style to 18.9 point Helvetica Narrow.

[Cntr on Mar] moves the text that follows so it is centered.

▼ *Figure 3.4.* **An Example of Some Other Reveal Codes**

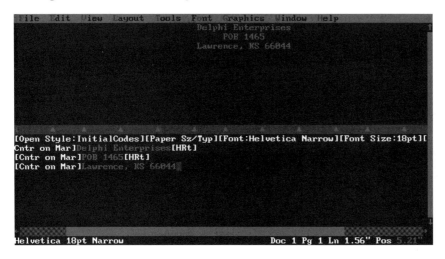

Why worry about codes? For one simple reason. They provide information about the way a document will appear when printed, as well as other features that you don't want to appear on the screen. They allow you to have precise control over the appearance of a document, since placement of codes affects how documents look.

You'll see and learn how to work with different codes throughout this *Self-Teaching Guide*. They're your key to seeing and understanding the fine features that separate WordPerfect from the rest.

TIP

Don't even try to memorize reveal codes. As you work with WordPerfect you'll find the most common ones easy to remember.

When it's time to return to a full screen so that the codes are no longer visible, just use the **Alt+F3** key combination once again or select Reveal Codes from the View menu to turn reveal codes off.

CHECK YOURSELF

1. Create a new file or retrieve one that you have already used. Now, use the **Alt+F3** key combination to reveal the codes. How do you delete a code?
2. What happens on your WordPerfect screen if you press the **Alt+F3** key twice?

ANSWERS

1. By placing the cursor to the right of the code and pressing the **Backspace** key or placing the cursor right on the code and pressing the **Del** key.
2. You return to the WordPerfect screen without any reveal codes.

Lesson 11: Moving Around Your Document

The editing process consists of moving the cursor to the position where you want the edit to take place and then either deleting text, inserting text, or doing both. You also need to locate the cursor in the proper position to take advantage of using WordPerfect's blocking feature, which we'll talk about later in this chapter.

Here's a summary of how the cursor is moved from one place in a document to another.

TIP

The first step in editing is moving the cursor to the appropriate location.

To move the cursor	Press
to the left one character	left arrow key
to the right one character	right arrow key
to the beginning of the word to the left	Ctrl+left arrow key
to the beginning of the word to the right	Ctrl+right arrow key
to the beginning of a line	Home+left arrow key
to the end of line	Home+right arrow key
up one line	up arrow key
down one line	down arrow key
to the top of the window	Home+up arrow key
to the bottom of the window	Home+Down arrrow key
to the beginning of the next page	PgDn key
to the top of the previous page	PgUp key
to the beginning of the document	Home, Home, up arrow key
to the end of the document	Home, Home, down arrow key

For example, if you want to move to the end of the text, no matter how long the document, press the **Home, Home, down arrow** key combination (that's the three keys in sequence) and the cursor will be moved to the end of the last character in the document.

CHECK YOURSELF

1. Create a small WordPerfect document and practice moving the cursor from one word to the next, from one line to the next, and from the left margin to the right.

2. Move to the end of document by pressing the down arrow key. What's the fastest way to get to the top of the document? Do it.

ANSWERS

1. The most important "moving" keys are the up, down, right, and left arrow keys found on the numeric keypad.
2. Use the **Home, Home**, up arrow key combination to move to the top of the document.

Scrolling and Scroll Bars

If you are going to be using WordPerfect with a mouse, using scroll bars and scrolling is another way to move vertically and horizontally through a document.

Scrolling allows to you to move through a window or a document when the entire document cannot fit in one screen. Scroll bars are tools that are located on the right-hand edge of a window (vertical scroll bar) or on the lower edge (horizontal scroll bar) and, as you can see in Figure 3.5, consist of two different parts, the scroll box and the scroll arrow.

▼ *Figure 3.5.   A Vertical and Horizontal Scroll Bar*

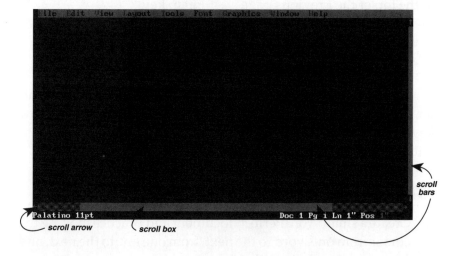

Here's how you can use them to move around, using the mouse.

To . . .	Click (with the mouse)...
scroll one line at a time	the scroll arrow in the direction you want to move
scroll one screen at a time	above or below the scroll box
scroll through an entire document	place the mouse pointer on the scroll box and drag it in the direction you want to move then release it

When you drag the scroll box from one part of the scroll bar to another and then release the mouse button, the distance that the screen scrolls is proportionate to how far you drag the scroll box. For example, if you are at the beginning of a document and drag the scroll box halfway down the scroll bar and then release the mouse button, you will be approximately at the halfway point in the document.

Scroll bars are very handy tools, but where in the world are they? Nowhere, until you tell WordPerfect to show them for you.

To show the scroll bars:

1. Use the **Alt+V,H** key combiantion [Mouse Moves: **V**iew, **H**orizontal Scroll Bar].
2. Use the **Alt+V,V** key combination [Mouse Moves: **V**iew, **V**ertical Scroll Bar].

You can select either the horizontal or vertical scroll bars or both. In Figure 3.5, both were selected for illustrative purposes.

Lesson 12: Working with Blocks

As you learn to edit, you will often want to work with more than one character or more than one word. To do this, WordPerfect allows you to create blocks of text. A **block** is a selection of text from a document. It might be a sentence or a paragraph, or even the text included from the middle of one sentence to the middle of another.

In Figure 3.6, you can see how a portion of text is blocked. Once it is blocked (or selected) we can then perform a variety of different operations, such as moving the block to another part of the document, checking the spelling of the blocked text, and more. For example, if you want to save a specific part of a document, you can block that part and then use the **F10** key to save that block of text. Very handy, indeed.

Blocking Text from the Keyboard

To create a block of text using keyboard commands:

1. Place the cursor at the location in the text that will mark the beginning of the block.
2. Turn on the WordPerfect block feature by pressing the **Alt+F4** key combination [Mouse Moves: **E**dit, **B**lock]. When you do this, you will see a **Block On** message in the lower left-hand corner of the WordPerfect window. If you are having trouble turning the blocking feature on, be sure you are using the **Alt+F4** key combination and not the Ctrl+F4 key combination.
3. Move the cursor to the location in the text where you want the block to end. You'll notice that as you move the cursor, the blocked or selected text is highlighted. You're done! If you

▼ **Figure 3.6.   Blocked Text**

make a mistake and block text that you don't want to, you can turn off the block feature and start again (just use the **Alt+F4** key combination to toggle between on and off).

TIP

Blocks of text are like little documents that you can print, save, move, and even check the spelling of.

Blocking Using a Mouse

Once you've tried blocking text with a mouse, you may believe that the mouse was invented just to make blocking text easier.

To create text blocks with a mouse:

1. Using the mouse, place the cursor at the location in the text that will mark the beginning of the block.
2. Press down the left mouse button and drag the mouse cursor to the location in the text where you want the block to end. As you drag, the text is highlighted.
3. Release the left mouse button and you have your block. If you have any problems, just click on the left mouse button again and the text will no longer be highlighted.

Using Blocks

Once you have created a block, you can do many useful things with that chunk of material. In fact, when you create a block, in many ways it's like creating an entirely new document. As you learn new WordPerfect skills, such as checking spelling and sorting, you'll find that you can perform these same operations on a smaller amount of text, by first creating a block and then invoking the command to spell or sort.

Printing Blocks

Once you have created a block and text is highlighted on your screen, you can print only the contents of that block by using the

Shift+F7 key combination. You will see the Print dialog box (which you saw earlier in Chapter 2) only this time Blocked Text (option 5) will be preselected to go.

Saving Blocks

Let's say that you've worked hard at creating a list or a table or an equation, all of which are part of a larger document but you want to save only that small part. Simple.

To save a block:

1. Create a block of what you want to save.
2. Press the **F10** function key [Mouse Moves: **F**ile, Save **A**s]. As you can see in Figure 3.7, the Save Block dialog box will appear.
3. Provide a name for the block of text you want to save in the Filename box.
4. Press **Enter**.

WordPerfect will save the blocked text as a file using the name you provided.

CHECK YOURSELF

1. Enter two sentences in a new WordPerfect document. Now block the first sentence and save it as a separate file.

▼ *Figure 3.7.   The Save Block Dialog Box*

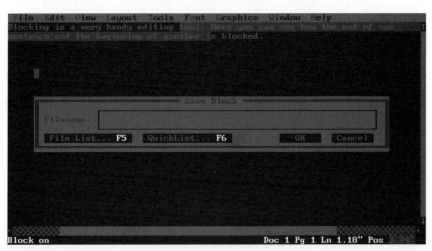

2. Enter a third sentence into the same WordPerfect document. Block the second sentence and print it out.

Lesson 12: Working with Blocks

ANSWERS

1. You can always save a block just by pressing the **F10** key.
2. You can easily print a block of text, using the **Shift+F7, Enter** key combination.

Lesson 13: Inserting and Deleting Text

Here's where we get to the meat of editing: actually changing the text that you've already created. Although you can modify text at any time, it's usually a good idea to save your documents as you work, and always a good idea to save your document before you do any major changes. More about that in a moment.

Inserting Text

The easiest way to insert text is to place the cursor at the location where you want the text to be inserted (either using the arrow keys or the mouse) and then just enter the new text from the keyboard. WordPerfect's **default** is to insert text at the location of the cursor. For example, to change the sentence:

```
This is a good example of how WordPerfect in-
serts text.
```

to

```
This is a very good example of how WordPerfect
inserts text.
```

you would follow these steps:

1. Place the cursor after the word *a.*
2. Type a space and the word *very.*
3. Type another space.

As you enter the word *very*, all the characters to the right of the cursor move to make room for the insertion. That's all there is to it!

You may not, however, want to insert text, but instead, type over text that is already there. This is the **Typeover** mode, which is entered by pressing the **Ins** key in the lower right-hand area of your keyboard. When you press **Ins**, the word **Typeover** will appear on the status line in the lower left-hand corner of your screen. This indicates that whatever you enter from the keyboard will be entered at the cursor location and not be inserted between existing characters. For example, to change the sentence:

```
This is the best that we can do.
```

to

```
This is the only option available for us.
```

you would follow these steps:

1. Place the cursor before the letter *b* in the word best.
2. Press the **Ins** key and the word **Typeover** will appear on the status line.
3. Enter the text *only option available for us*.
4. Press the **Ins** key to return to the Insert mode.

TIP

If you ever find that your keyboard entries are writing over text already entered, you are probably in the Typeover mode. Press the Ins **key to get back to the Insert mode.**

Deleting Text

The easiest way to delete characters is to place the cursor after the characters or words that you want to delete and press the **Backspace** key the number of times necessary to delete the text. For example, to edit the sentence:

```
This is the worstt thing that ever happened.
```

to

```
This is the worst thing that ever happened.
```

you would follow these steps:

1. Place the cursor to the right of either letter *t* in the word *worstt*.
2. Press the **Backspace** key once. You're done!

You can delete multiple characters the same way. Just place the cursor after the character and backspace once or as many times as necessary.

Deleting Words

Deleting words is even easier than deleting characters because it only takes one key combination, the **Ctrl+Backspace** [Mouse Moves: **Edit, Delete**].

To delete any word in a WordPerfect document:

1. Place the cursor any where on the word you want to delete.
2. Use the **Ctrl+Backspace** key combination and the word will be deleted.

You can delete a series of words by continuing to use the **Ctrl+Backspace** key combination. Words will be deleted to the right of the location of the cursor.

Deleting Lines

To delete more than one word of text at the same time all on the same line (*not sentence!*), use the **Ctrl+End** key combination, which deletes everything from the right of the cursor to the end of the screen line. For example, to change the line:

```
wants to be the first one to climb the mountain
using the new technique.
```

to

```
wants to be the first one to climb the mountain
```

follow these steps:

1. Place the cursor in the line of text where you want to delete everything from that point to the right. In this example, it is on the first letter of the word *using*.
2. Use the **Ctrl+End** key combination to delete the text to the end of the line.

Deleting Sentences, Paragraphs, and Pages

When it comes time to delete larger amounts of text than characters or words (such as a sentence or paragraph) that is fixed, use the **Ctrl+F4** key combination to first create a block out of what it is you want to delete.

To delete a sentence, paragraph, or page:

1. Use the **Ctrl+F4** key combination [Mouse Moves: **E**dit, **S**elect] to see the Move dialog box as shown in Figure 3.8.
2. Press **1**, **2**, or **3**, depending on what it is you want to select and delete. As you can see, there are other options as well (such as Cut and Paste), which we will deal with later. Even though it is a Move dialog box, don't be concerned. WordPerfect considers moving text to mean blocks as well.

▼ *Figure 3.8.* *The Move Dialog Box*

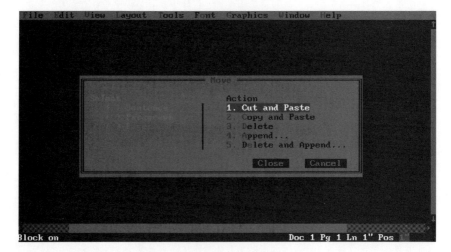

When your selection (Sentence, Paragraph or Page) is made, it will be highlighted. If the cursor is located in the middle of a word when you select a sentence, then the sentence containing the word will be highlighted. Or the paragraph. Or the page.

You can also use the mouse to select a sentence, paragraph, or page by selecting the appropriate menu item from the Select options on the Edit menu as you see in Figure 3.9. The menu option you choose will determine what is selected.

How does WordPerfect know that a set of words is a sentence? Easy. It just goes from one period to another.

TIP

If you have a sentence containing a number with a decimal point, watch out. WordPerfect will view that decimal point (which is the same as a period) as part of a sentence and only block that.

It knows paragraphs because each paragraph must end with a hard carriage return. If you look at Figure 3.3, you can see the **[HRt]** code that indicates a carriage return and the end of a paragraph.

WordPerfect knows pages, since it automatically gets to the end of a page depending on how the length has been set up. As

▼ **Figure 3.9.** **Options from Which You Can Make a Selection to Work with Text**

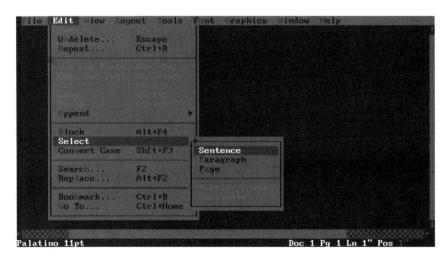

with paragraphs and looking for the **[HRt]** code, when it comes to pages, WordPerfect looks for the **[SPg]** reveal code, indicating a soft page.

3. Once you have decided what you want to delete (by indicating **1**, **2**, or **3**), then WordPerfect wants to know which of the five action options (shown in Figure 3.8) you will want to perform.

   In this example, the option is Delete (option 3).

Deleting a Block of Text

You just saw how WordPerfect will create blocks for you, but the blocks are sentences, paragraphs, or pages. What about when you need to delete a block of text that is not one of these?

To delete a block of text that is not a sentence, paragraph, or page:

1. Select the block of text you want to delete as we previously described, using either the **Alt+F4** key combination or the mouse.
2. Press the **Del** or the **Backspace** key.

   WordPerfect will delete the selected block of text.

CHECK YOURSELF

1. Enter two sentences into a WordPerfect document. Place the cursor at the end of the first sentence and enter another sentence.
2. Repeat check 1, but this time press the **Ins** key before you enter the third sentence. What is the difference between the two?
3. What are the exact keyboard steps you would take to delete a page of text?

ANSWERS

1. Be sure to place the cursor where you want to begin the insertion.
2. In the Typeover mode, charcters you enter replace those that are already there.
3. **Ctrl+F4,3,3**.

Lesson 14: Cutting and Copying Text

Lesson 14: Cutting and Copying Text

In the last lesson you saw how text can be selected either as an irregular block or as a predefined amount of text such as a sentence, paragraph, or page. You also saw that when you select text, you can then have WordPerfect delete it. Now we'll do more with the Move dialog box you first saw in Figure 3.8.

Cutting and Pasting Text

The Cut and Paste command, one of the action options you see in the Move dialog box shown in Figure 3.8, is produced by the **Ctrl+Del** [Mouse Moves: **Edit**, **Cut and Paste**] key combination (plus the text you want to select); it removes text from the location in which it appears and places it in a buffer. A **buffer** is a temporary storage place that can hold only one chunk of information. If you select a block of text and place it in the buffer and then select another, the contents of the first block will disappear.

When you select the **Cut and Paste** option and press the **Enter** key, the selected text, be it a sentence, paragraph or page, will disappear from the WordPerfect window. Where there is text that has been cut and is waiting to be placed somewhere, the following message appears in the status line:

```
Move Cursor; Press Enter to retrieve.
```

TIP

When you perform a Move operation on a block of selected text, WordPerfect already knows it is a block and you need not worry about identifying it as a sentence, paragraph or page.

You can now place the cursor anywhere in the document (or in another document) and, once you press the **Enter** key, whatever text was selected will then appear!

For example, Figure 3.10 shows a list of ten items, with the last five blocked.

To move the last five to the beginning of the list:

1. Use the **Alt+F4** key combination or use the mouse and highlight the five items you want to move.
2. Use the **Ctrl+F4** key combination [Mouse Moves: **Edit**, **Cut and Paste**] and you will see the Move Block dialog box.
3. Select **Cut and Paste** (option 1).
4. Move the cursor to the top of the document.
5. Press **Enter**.

The results are shown in Figure 3.11. The move was easy and successful. You can move text to any location, but remember these important things.

▲ WordPerfect only lets you place one block (be it a sentence, word, page, character, anything) at a time in that temporary storage place. The last block selected always replaces the earlier one.

TIP

To cancel the move operation, press the Esc **key.**

▼ *Figure 3.10.* *Moving Items in a List*

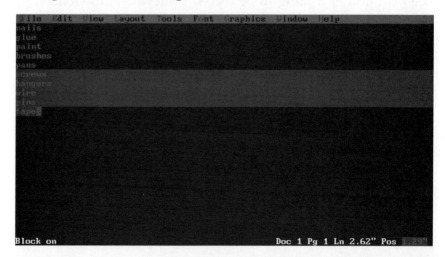

▼ *Figure 3.11.* **After the Big Move!**

▲ Once you select text to cut, it disappears from its original location and the only way you can get it back is by pressing the **Enter** key. If you mistakenly press the **Enter** key, whatever is in the buffer will pop up at the cursor location.

TIP

When you exit WordPerfect or turn off your computer, anything in the buffer disappears. That's why it's called temporary.

TIP

Here's a good one. You can retrieve whatever is in the buffer by using the Skip+F10 Enter **key combination as many times as you want. Whatever was last cut, will appear again.**

Copying Text

When you cut text, you are removing it from its original place and moving it to a new location. When you copy text, you are making an exact copy of whatever the highlighted text consists of.

Both operations are done in exactly the same way, except that when you copy text, you select Copy and Paste (option 2) in the Move Block dialog box rather than Cut and Paste (option **1**).

For example, let's say that you have a particularly interesting equation that you don't want to retype but would rather just copy.

To copy text:

1. Select the equation you want to copy by highlighting it using the **Alt+F4** key combination or the mouse. Remember, you simply want to duplicate the text without removing it from its original location.
2. Press the **Ctrl+F4** key combination.
3. Select **Copy and Paste** (option 2).
4. Move the cursor to the location where you want to copy the selection. It could be in a new window or in another part of the same document.
5. Press the **Enter** key and the selection will appear.

TIP

When you highlight text to cut or copy, WordPerfect provides you with the prompt for moving a block. When you don't have any text selected, WordPerfect provides you with a prompt for moving a sentence, paragraph, or page.

CHECK YOURSELF

1. Enter two sentences on a clean WordPerfect screen. Now select (use the **Cut and Paste** command) the first sentence as if you were ready to move it. What happens when it is selected?
2. Enter a list of ten things you need to do. Now use the Move feature to prioritize them with the most important item on the list coming first.

ANSWERS

1. It disappears from your screen and goes into the temporary buffer.

2. Be sure to remember that when you move or copy text, WordPerfect can only hold one set of information in the buffer at a time.

Lesson 15:
The Fabulous
Undelete
and Undo

Lesson 15: The Fabulous Undelete and Undo

Imagine this. It's 2 A.M. The report is almost finished. Just a little more cleaning up and . . . Zap! Tired and confused, you just deleted the last three pages of the document. You can:

Pull your hair out

Retype the missing material (if you have it to begin with)

Use WordPerfect's Fabulous Undelete Feature

Pulling your hair out might provide some temporary relief, but it certainly won't do anything for the report. Retyping is an option, but after all your work, you can barely face that music.

On to two of WordPerfect 6.0's best features, **Undelete** and **Undo**. These features virtually allow you to reverse the deletion process. If you don't lose your mind altogether when you inadvertently delete text and don't go vertical trying to recover it (which means leave everything alone), there's an excellent chance you can get everything (that's right, everything) back.

Now, we are not talking about resurrecting a file. That's an entirely different story. We are talking about restoring text that has been deleted. And WordPerfect does it in much the same way as moving a block of text. WordPerfect turns what you delete into a block and stores it. But, just as with a block of selected text in the buffer, once you exit WordPerfect or turn off your computer, you can forget about being able to undelete anything! And, if you do accidently delete text, don't do anything to try and get it back but the following. Anything!

To undelete text:

1. Immediately after the deletion, press the **Esc** key. The last text deleted will be displayed along with the Undelete dialog box you see in Figure 3.12.
2. Press option **1** (Restore) to restore the text you see.

If you are using the mouse, just select the **U**ndelete option from the **E**dit menu. Text is always restored at the location of the cursor, so don't expect it to return to its rightful place unless the cursor is there to act as a marker for where the text should go.

You can even undelete text that has inadvertenly been deleted before the last deletion. If you select option **2** (Previous Deletion) in the Undelete dialog box, you'll see the next to last deletion and you can then restore that.

CHECK YOURSELF

1. Delete one word from a sentence, then another, then another. Practice undeleting the words one at a time using the arrow keys.
2. Create a three sentence document.
   a. Delete sentence 1.
   b. Delete sentence 2.
   c. Delete sentence 3.

▼ *Figure 3.12.   The Undelete Dialog Box*

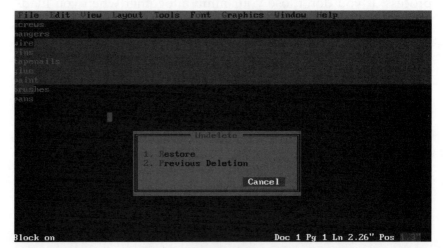

ANSWERS

1. WordPerfect can delete only up to the last three things that you have entered.
2. Restore the sentences in the order that they were deleted.

The As Fabulous Undo

There's another *Un* option that, like Undelete, can work wonders and save your day (or night!). The Undo option works much like the Undelete option, but goes one better. Instead of worrying about what it is that you have deleted, **Undo** will undo whatever it is that you have just done (to a point that is).

For example, let's say that you changed the font of an entire document and realize that you made a terrible mistake. You could just delete the font reveal code. Or, you could select **U**ndo from the **E**dit menu or use the **Ctrl+Z** key combination. Ctrl+Z will undo the last WordPerfect operation that was performed.

So if you created a table and don't want it, underlined everything and don't want it, changed the margins and don't like them, or sorted a list of names and addresses by last name and don't want the sort to stay, feel free to **Ctrl+Z** and undo what you have done.

TIP

The WordPerfect people have worked hard to help you with Undelete and Undo, but these commands cannot work major miracles. So if you delete a file, or continue far beyond a deletion you need to restore, you probably won't find much help here.

Wow! That's a lot of WordPerfect skills to master in one chapter, but the importance of being able to move around a document, insert and delete text, and cut and copy text when and where you want are basic to good WordPerfect usage. Practice these skills. You'll find them invaluable as you learn in the next chapter how to search for and find the text you want to edit, move, or copy.

PRACTICE WHAT YOU'VE LEARNED

1. Enter a simple sentence, save it as a file under the name *sent1*, and do the following:
   a. Clear the WordPerfect screen.
   b. Retrieve the file using the **Shift+F10** key combination.
   c. Repeat step a.
   d. Retrieve the file using the **F5** List Files option.
2. Correct the error in the following paragraph:
   There were too hundred people who came to the concert last week. That is a nice showing, but we have to work harder to increase attendance.
3. Under what conditions would you want to retrieve a document using the File Manager versus just using the **Shift+F10** key combination and the document's name?
4. How do you use the **Backspace** key to delete a word? How do you use the **Ctrl** key along with the Backspace key to delete a word?
5. What is the difference between the Typeover and Insert modes and when would you use each?
6. What happens if you copy text and you're ready to move it, and you accidentally press the Enter key?
7. Why can't the Restore feature restore a file that has been accidentally deleted?

ANSWERS

2. There were two hundred people who came to the concert last week. That is a nice showing, but we have to work harder to increase attendance.
3. When you cannot remember the exact name of the file.
4. Place the cursor on the character or space to the right of those you want to delete and press the **Backspace** key once for each character you want to delete. Place the cursor on a word and use the **Ctrl+Backspace** key combination to delete the entire word.

5. Typeover places text on top of already existing text, while Insert places text at the location of the cursor and thus places it within already existing text. Typeover is used when text is substantively changed whereas Insert is used mostly for editing.
6. The blocked text reappears.
7. Because Restore only restores text within a file and not files themselves.

Different Views of WordPerfect

One of the neatest things about this new version of WordPerfect is that you have a choice of modes in which to work, including the Text mode, the Graphics mode, or the Page mode. These different views allow a great deal of flexibility in creating exactly the document you want. In this chapter you'll learn:

▲ **What each of the different WordPerfect modes looks like**

▲ **The advantages of each mode**

▲ **How to switch from one mode to another**

Important Keys
Ctrl+F3

Important Terms
Text mode
Graphics mode
Page mode
Screen dialog box

Lesson 16: The Different WordPerfect Modes

You can view a WordPerfect document in three different ways. Each way you view WordPerfect is also a different way to work with a document.

The first is through the **Text mode**, which you may be used to, if you are a user of an earlier version of WordPerfect, since that's all that was available. In the Text mode, all you see are text and other special WordPerfect codes, such as those used for graphics. For example, in Figure 4.1, you can see an example of how a document that includes a graphic looks in the Text mode. Notice that you cannot tell anything about the size of characters or how they will appear as printed.

The second mode or WordPerfect view is the **Graphics mode,** shown in Figure 4.2. To say that there's a difference in the visual appeal of what you see in Figure 4.1 (the Text mode) and the Graphics mode you see in Figure 4.2 is quite an understatement. The Graphics mode provides you with a view of how your WordPerfect document will look when it is printed, including the exact placement of graphics, the appearance of text, and any other special formatting features that you might include, such as full justification of the lines.

TIP

The Text mode is the fastest for entering and editing of text.

One of the complaints that WordPerfect users had about earlier versions of the program is that although in the Print Preview option (see Lesson 24 for more about this), you could see what you

▼ **Figure 4.1.** **A WordPerfect Document in the Text Mode**

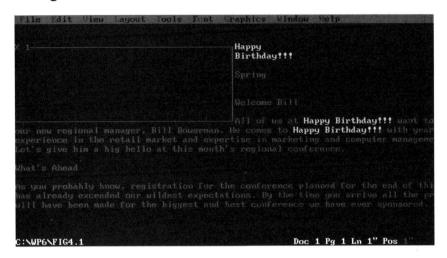

▼ **Figure 4.2.** **A WordPerfect Document in the Graphics Mode**

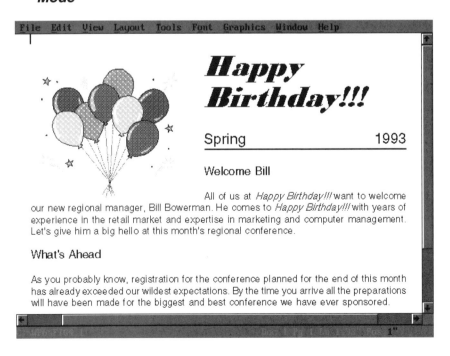

would get when printing, you could not *edit* it in that screen; you had to shift back to Print Preview whenever you wanted to see what your changes would look like. With the Graphics mode, that is no longer a problem.

Notice in the Graphics mode and in the Text mode that the menus (and all the options available) are exactly the same. The major difference is really how the document appears in the Word-Perfect window.

OK. That's two out of the three modes you can now use to view and work with your WordPerfect documents. The last, **Page mode** you see in Figure 4.3, is similar to Graphics mode in that you see just what will print. What you see in the Page mode that you won't see in the Graphics mode (or the Text mode, of course) is headers and page numbers and anything else that has to do with pages.

▼ **Figure 4.3.   A WordPerfect Document in the Page Mode**

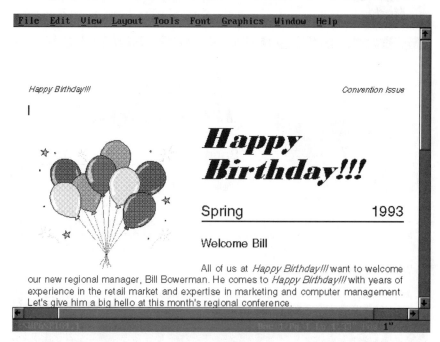

TIP

Many WordPerfect users enter text in the Text mode, then switch over to the Graphics or Page mode when they are ready to format the document for the final printing.

Which mode is for you? Here is a summary of each and when it is best to use it. In the next lesson, we'll get to how to switch back and forth painlessly!

WordPerfect Mode	*What you see*	*When you might want to use it*
Text	Any text that is entered plus on-screen codes for graphics and such.	Fast entry of text-only documents without regard for specific formatting features.
Graphics	Any text that is entered plus on-screen codes for graphics and such.	When including graphics in a document and special fonts for design effects.
	All format changes appear as defined including fonts and graphics.	
Page	Any text that is entered plus on-screen codes for graphics and such.	When including graphics in a document and special fonts for design effects. Absolutely everything that is part of the document will show on the screen exactly as it will print and can be edited as such.
	All format changes appear as defined including fonts and graphics.	
	All margin settings, headers and footers, and page numbers.	

CHECK YOURSELF

1. What are the three views or modes of WordPerfect 6.0?
2. What is the advantage of the Page mode over the Print Preview option on the File menu?

ANSWERS

1. Text, Graphics, and Page.
2. Though you might see the same information, you can edit in Page mode, but you cannot edit in the Print Preview screen.

Lesson 17: Changing View Modes

Changing from one WordPerfect mode to another is one of the most simple of all WordPerfect tasks. All three are located on the View menu.

To change modes:

1. Use the **Ctrl+F3** key combination [Mouse Moves: **View**]. When you do this, you will see the Screen dialog box as you see in Figure 4.4.
2. Select **T**ext (option 2), **G**raphics (option 3), or **P**age (option 4) and you will automatically enter that mode.

TIP

Want to see something cool? Go into the Graphics mode, exit WordPerfect and then start it up again. Look at that great opening screen!

That's all there is to it. Just make the selection using the keyboard or using the mouse and the document will appear in the selected mode.

▼ *Figure 4.4.* *The Screen Dialog Box*

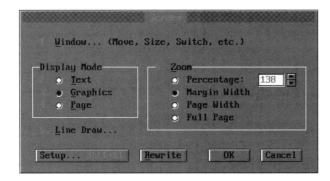

CHECK YOURSELF

▲ What is one way to quickly switch between modes?

ANSWER

▲ Select the mode you want to work in from the **View** menu.

Wow, can you do nice things with WordPerfect! We're not sure, but it's hard to see why you would not do most of your work in the Graphics mode from now on. Why not see what you have as you work? It's more pleasant, your results will be more like you want, and you'll gain more control over your word processing activities. And guess what? From here on in this *Self-Teaching Guide*, all the accompanying screens will be in the Graphics mode, since it's so much more attractive and informative then the Text mode.

PRACTICE WHAT YOU'VE LEARNED

1. Clear your WordPerfect window (**F7,N,N**). Now select **Re-**trieve Image from the **Graphics** menu and double-click on any WordPerfect file that has the .WPG extension (for a Word-Perfect graphic). Describe what it looks like in the Text mode. What does it look like in the Page mode?

2. When would you only want to use the Text mode?

ANSWERS

1. In the Text mode, all you should see is a box. In the Page mode, you will actually see the graphic you retrieved.

2. When the only thing you are entering in a document is text and have no need to see what it will look like before it is printed.

5

Using
Button Bars

The three different views of WordPerfect certainly make a difference in the flexibility it provides you to do the work you need. Another new addition to the WordPerfect arsenal of writing tools is the **button bar**. This is a feature borrowed from WordPerfect for Windows and makes using your new version of WordPerfect for DOS a "snap" (actually a click, to use). In this chapter you'll learn how to:

▲ **Identify a button bar**

▲ **Use a button bar**

▲ **Edit a button bar**

▲ **Create a new button bar**

Important Terms
button bar
Button Bar List dialog box
Button Bar Options dialog box
Edit Button Bar dialog box
Feature Button List dialog box
Macro Button List dialog box
Select Button Bar dialog box

Lesson 18: Using the Button Bar

Wouldn't it be easy to just bypass menus altogether and click on an icon that represents the WordPerfect operation you want to perform? It sure would and you can do it using WordPerfect button bars.

A Bit About Button Bars

A **button bar** is a collection of icons that represent different Word-Perfect features and is usually located across the top of the Word-Perfect window as you see in Figure 5.1.

TIP

Sorry folks, but the only way you can use a button bar is with a mouse. Any mode (Text, Graphics, or Page) is fine, but you need the mouse to do the clicking.

All it takes is a click on the File Mgr (the first button on the button bar) and you'll see the Specify File Manager List dialog box, just as if you pressed the F5 function key or selected the File Manager option from the File menu. Similarly, if you wanted to go into the Text mode, just click on that button. It's the button that's a bit to the right of the center button in Figure 5.1 and is named TextMode. Just a click takes you to that mode.

Buttons are great for the quick switch to another feature you have to make. For example, remember in Lesson 16 we talked

▼ *Figure 5.1.   The Default WordPerfect Button Bar*

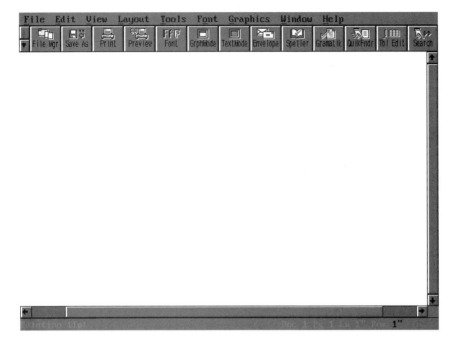

about how some people type in the Text mode and then switch over to the Graphics mode to see how things look? Think how easy that is when you just have to click on one button to go back and forth.

To reveal the button bar on your WordPerfect screen:

▲ Select **B**utton Bar from the **V**iew Mode and the button bar will appear at the top of the WordPerfect window. When the button bar is active, the option on the View menu has a check next to it.

TIP

To use a button bar, just click on the button that represents the operation you want to perform.

You can see in Figure 5.1 that the first button is the one for the File Mgr (for File Manager). The names of buttons are usually abbreviated for space reasons. On the left-hand edge of any button bar are up (▲) and down (▼) triangles. You can see more buttons by clicking on the down triangle, and then return to the other buttons by clicking on the up triangle.

TIP

You'll notice that this figure, and all the others throughout this chapter, is shown in the Graphics mode. Button bars in the Text mode just appear as text and are not very interesting.

These triangle keys (there's one on the left as well) allow you to have more buttons on the button bar than the space in one WordPerfect window allows. Now that you know a bit about the button bar, let's move on to how you can work with and personalize button bars for your particular needs.

CHECK YOURSELF

1. Select the **B**utton Bar from the View menu. What button is to the left of the Envelope button?
2. Describe the icon on the Search button.

ANSWERS

1. The Font button.
2. It looks like two fingers doing the walking for you!

Lesson 19: Editing Button Bars

Button bars are cool, but even more so when you can take advantage of the WordPerfect feature that allows you to edit them to meet your own specific project needs. For example, you might want to add particular buttons to the button bar or delete others—in other words, fine-tune your buttons just as you need them, even changing the location.

When it comes time to edit a button bar, it's done through the Button Bar Setup option on the View menu as you see in Figure 5.2. Using these options you can edit a button bar, select a different

▼ *Figure 5.2.* *The Button Bar Setup Options*

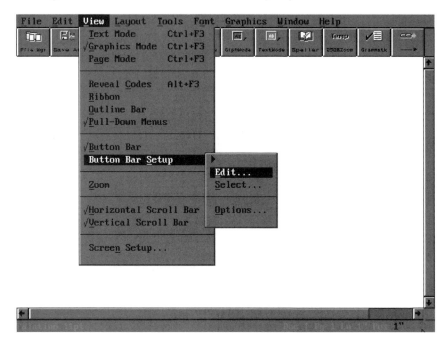

button bar, or change button bar options such as where the button bar appears in the window and how each button appears. We'll start with editing.

To start the editing button bar process:

1. Select Button Bar **S**etup from the **V**iew menu.
2. Select **E**dit and you will see the Edit Button Bar dialog box shown in Figure 5.3.

In the Edit Button Bar dialog box you can see a list of all the buttons that are currently on the button bar named WPMAIN. To the right of the list are six commands you can take advantage of to edit the button bar.

Adding a Button to the Button Bar

The first thing you might want to do is add a new button to the button bar. This means you'll be adding an additional button to an already existing button bar.

▼ *Figure 5.3.* *The Edit Button Bar Dialog Box*

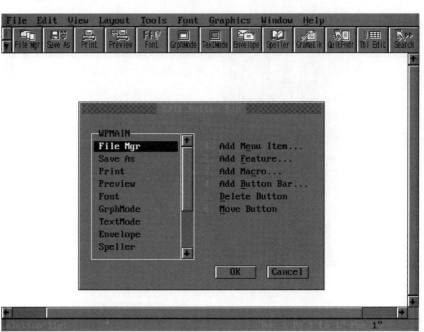

To add a new button to a button bar:

1. Select **A**dd Menu Item (option 1) from the **E**dit Button Bar dialog box and the Edit Button Bar dialog box will ask you to make a selection (or more than one for each button) from the appropriate menu as you see in Figure 5.4. When you do this, WordPerfect considers it to be what you want to add to the button bar. For example, if you wanted a button that would **Re**trieve an image, you would go to the Graphics menu and make that selection as you see in Figure 5.4.

2. Make the addition you want. In our example, we are adding the **Retrieve Image** item to the button bar.

3. Press **F7**. The new item will appear in the list in the Edit Button Bar dialog box and will also appear on the button bar once the Edit Button Bar is dialog box is closed.

TIP

Where will the new button appear on the button bar? Next to the same button it is listed within the Edit Button Bar dialog box.

▼ *Figure 5.4. Adding an Item to a Button Bar*

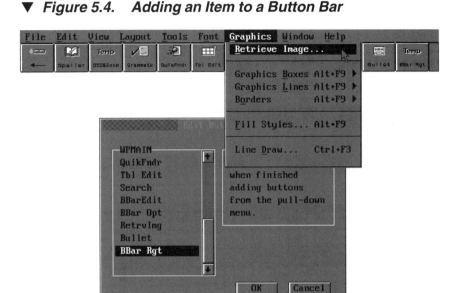

Adding a Feature to the Button Bar

Not all of WordPerfect's features are available from menus and you might want to add something that is located in a dialog box or otherwise inaccessible through simple pull-down or Alt+key activity. That's why WordPerfect created a comprehensive list of features from which you can select.

For example, WordPerfect allows you to move the button bar to the bottom of the screen. As you will see later in this lesson, to do such, you have to go into the Button Bar Options dialog box. You can't access that feature from a menu. But, you can add that feature using the Feature Button List dialog box you see in Figure 5.5.

To add a feature to the Button Bar:

1. Select Button Bar **S**etup from the **V**iew menu.
2. Select **E**dit.
3. Select Add **F**eature (option 3) from the Edit Button Bar dialog box. You'll see the Feature Button List dialog box shown in Figure 5.5. This is an extensive list of *all* the WordPerfect fea-

▼ *Figure 5.5.* *The Feature Button List Dialog Box*

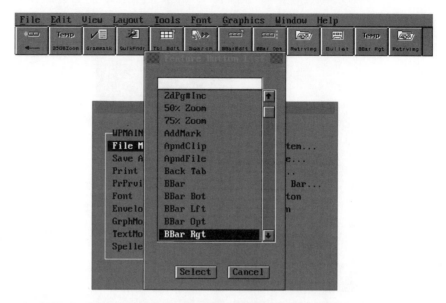

tures, options, and so on that are available and can be added to a button bar.

4. Highlight the feature you want to add to the button bar. In this example (and as you can see in Figure 5.5), **BBar Rgt** is highlighted. This will place a button on the button bar that, when clicked, will place the button bar on the right-hand side of the WordPerfect window.

5. Click on **Select** or press **Enter** and the button will appear on the button bar.

TIP

Remember you can just double-click on any feature and it will become a button.

Adding a Macro to the Button Bar

Macros are stored keystrokes. When you create a macro and create a button to represent the macro, you can then invoke or execute it with a click. Macros can be quite complex, such as searching through a document and generating a table of contents or automatically formatting a graphic. So, being able to do it all with a click is a terrific time-saver, especially when you want to use a particular macro often.

To add a macro to a button bar:

1. Select Button Bar **S**etup from the **V**iew menu.
2. Select **E**dit.
3. Select Add Ma**c**ro (option 3) from the Edit Button Bar dialog box.
4. In the Macro Button List dialog box that appears, select the name of the macro you want to add as a button. All the macros that have been previously created will appear on that list. The macro will then appear on the button bar.

Adding a Button Bar

This option allows you to add a new Button Bar to the existing screen.

To add a Button Bar:

1. Select Button Bar **S**etup from the **V**iew menu.
2. Select **E**dit.
3. Select Add **B**utton Bar (option 4). When you do this, you will see the Button Bar List dialog box, which contains a listing of all the button bars that are available. When you first start WordPerfect, there is only one default button bar available, named WPMAIN.
4. Select the button bar you want to use.
5. Click **Select** and the new button bar will appear in the Window.

Deleting a Button

You might have added a button that you want to remove or you might want to slim down a button bar so that there are fewer buttons to deal with. In both cases, the way to go is through the use of the **Delete** option in the Edit Button Bar dialog box.

To delete a button:

1. Select Button Bar **S**etup from the **V**iew menu.
2. Select **E**dit.
3. Select the button you want to delete from the list in the Edit Button Bar dialog box.
4. Select **D**elete Button (option 5) from the Edit Button Bar dialog box. WordPerfect will ask you to confirm that you want to delete the button.
5. Select **Y**es.

Moving a Button

Finally, you may just not like the way a button bar looks and want to change the order in which the buttons are arranged. The order in which buttons appear on the actual button bar is the same as the order in which they appear in the list in the Edit Button Bar dialog box.

For example, in Figure 5.1, the Save As button is to the right of the File Mgr button. In the list of buttons in the Edit Button Bar dialog box, the Save As button is right below the File Mgr button.

To move a button:

1. Select Button Bar **S**etup from the **V**iew menu.
2. Select **E**dit.
3. Highlight the button you want to move in the Edit Button Bar dialog box.
4. Select Move Button (option 6). When you do this, the Move Button option turns into a paste button.

5. Using the mouse or arrow keys, move the highlighted bar where you want the button relocated in the list of buttons in the Edit Button Bar dialog box.
6. Select **OK**.
7. The button will be pasted in the list (and in the button bar) before the highlighted button.

Creating Your Own Button Bar

This is a create-your-own-button-bar opportunity you won't want to miss. In spite of the fact that WordPerfect starts you off with a mondo button bar full of choices, it just may be too big and too general for your work habits. For example, what if you want a button bar that deals only with graphics? You could delete all the buttons from the main bar that don't deal with graphics, but that's self-defeating, since you may want to use them again in a later work session. Instead, why not create your own button bar?

To create your own custom Button Bar:

1. Select Button Bar **S**etup from the **V**iew menu.
2. Select **S**elect. When you do this, you will see the Select Button Bar dialog box as shown in Figure 5.6.
3. Select **C**reate (option 2). WordPerfect will ask you to assign a name for the new button bar. Do so and click **OK**. Once you assign a name, you'll find yourself in the familiar Edit Button Bar dialog box as shown in Figure 5.7, with the name of the new button bar (Graphics in this case) and with a listing of all the buttons on that button bar. As you can see in Figure 5.7, there are no buttons assigned.

TIP

WordPerfect offers many different predesigned button bars containing buttons for those features that the developers of WordPerfect thought would be most popular. You can use, or edit these, as you need.

▼ *Figure 5.6.   The Select Button Bar Dialog Box*

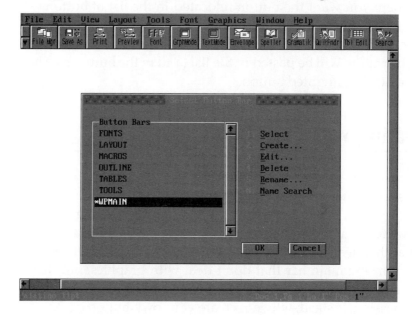

▼ *Figure 5.7.   A Button Bar Named GRAPHICS without Any Buttons*

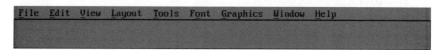

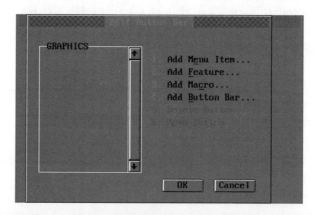

4. Add and edit the button bar as needed using the six Edit Button Bar tools we just reviewed (Add Menu Item, Add Feature, Add Macro, Add Button Bar, Delete Button, and Move Button).

Lesson 19: Editing Button Bars

We created this new button bar with special buttons on it to deal with graphics, and you can see what we have in Figure 5.8.

Using Button Bar Options

Last, but certainly not least, is changing the appearance of buttons and the location of the button bar in the window. All of this is done with the Button Bar Options dialog box shown in Figure 5.9.

To change button bar options:

1. Select Button Bar **S**etup from the **V**iew menu.
2. Select **O**ptions.
3. Click in the position you want the button bar to appear: on the top, bottom, left edge, or right edge of the window.

▼ **Figure 5.8.   The Graphics Button Bar**

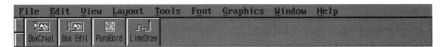

▼ *Figure 5.9.   The Button Bar Options Dialog Box*

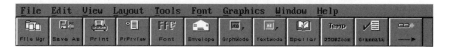

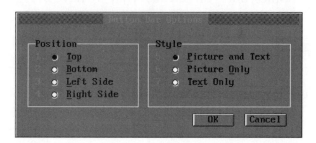

4. Click on whether you want the buttons to be represented by both pictures and text (option 5), pictures only (option 6), or text only (option 7).

In general, both text and pictures convey more information, but they also take up more room in the window.

CHECK YOURSELF

1. Reveal the button bar in the window and delete any button. Now use the Add Feature option in the Edit Button Bar dialog box to replace that item.
2. Add Italics (from the Font menu) to the button bar. What other font options might you add?

ANSWERS

1. You can replace the item in the same place by moving it once the button is in the list of buttons.

2. You could add any of the style features such as italics, bold, or underline.

Button bars are cool and can be a great help in your everyday WordPerfect work. Don't ignore them just because they might seem a bit intimidating at first. The more you use them the more you'll love them!

PRACTICE WHAT YOU'VE LEARNED

1. Create a new button bar named Grammar that consists of the spelling and thesaurus and Grammatik tools that are on the WordPerfect Tools menu.
2. In the Text mode, select the button bar from the View menu. What do you see?
3. What is the difference between the Add Menu Item and Add Feature options in the Edit Button Bar dialog box?
4. What is the easiest way to trim down a button bar so that it better fits your needs?
5. What is the advantage and disadvantage of having buttons represented by both text and pictures?

ANSWERS

1. Be sure to use the **Select** option on the Button Bar Setup.
2. You see the buttons, but they appear only in text and can only be selected using a mouse.
3. The Add Menu Item option allows you to create a button based on a menu item. Since not all WordPerfect features are on menus (such as those in dialog boxes), the Add Feature option offers a list of all WordPerfect features that can then be used to create buttons.
4. Use the Delete Button option.
5. You get the most information but pictures take up a good deal of space in the window.

6

Managing Files

You've already done some pretty fancy things and you're only beginning Chapter 6! As you learn more about WordPerfect, you'll be creating more files, and good housekeeping is an essential part of being a good WordPerfect user. Good housekeeping means that files should be well organized and you should be able to find and recall the ones you need with little trouble.

The goal of this chapter is to teach you how to be a good housekeeper through the use of the List Files options that we touched on earlier in Lesson 9. In this chapter you'll learn how to:

▲ **Use the List File screen to manage your WordPerfect files**

▲ **Distinguish between the Current and Parent directories**

▲ **Use the most important options on the File Manager screen**

▲ **Select multiple files**

▲ **Mark and unmark multiple files**

Important Keys	*Important Terms*
F5	Current <DIR>
	Copy dialog box
	File Manager
	Find Word in Entire Document dialog box
	Find dialog box
	Move/Rename dialog box
	Parent <DIR>
	Print Multiple Pages dialog box
	Search for Filename dialog box

Lesson 20: The File-Management Options

You know that WordPerfect makes extensive use of the function keys that are located either to the left of or above your keyboard. One of these keys, the **F5** function key [Mouse Moves: **File, File Manager**], is your entry into a host of file management tools that are bound to make your word processing activities simpler and more efficient.

The File Manager Screen

The File Manager screen provides you with a series of options for managing files. You can see the screen (such as the one shown in Figure 6.1) by pressing the **F5** function key and the **Enter** key. Let's take a close look at this window and what it has to offer.

Your File Manager screen may look different from the one you see in Figure 6.1 because your default directory is probably different from the one shown here. But all of the features of the File Manager are the same, so it doesn't matter.

To begin with, you see all kinds of summary information in the File Manager window, plus a set of commands on the right side of the screen. For example, across the top of the screen is the name of the current directory and how WordPerfect is sorting files (by file-name in the example) and the date (4-27-93) and the time (12:08p).

▼ *Figure 6.1.* **The File Manager Window**

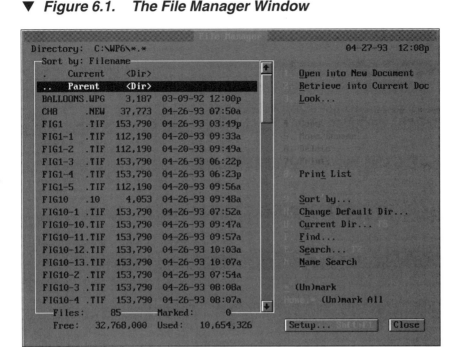

Then there's a ton of information about all the files in the directory as well as the hard drive. For each file, you'll find its name and the date and time it was last modified.

On the bottom of the screen the number of files in the directory is shown (Files: 85), the number that are marked (Marked: 0), the amount of space available on the hard drive (Free: 32,768,000), and the amount of space being used by the files in this directory (Used: 10,654,326).

Generally, you will select (or mark) one or more files to perform some operation on, and then select a command. For example, if you wanted to open a file into a new document, you would highlight the file you want to open and then select **O**pen into New Document (option 1) from the right-hand side of the File Manager. Or, to print the contents of the File Manager screen, just press the **F8** key (Print List).

The center of the File Manager window is where the name (and extension) of all the files in the directory are listed. Along with the name of each file you will also find the size of the file and the date on which the file was most recently revised (very handy for checking when the latest version of a file was created). If a name is followed by <DIR>, it means that it is a directory and not a file.

TIP

The screen is divided into two halves by a vertical line. On the left is the list of files and on the right the list of File Manager commands.

Finally, to the right of the file listing are the different File Manager options that you will learn to work with in the next lesson.

The Current and Parent Directories

Right below the header on the List Files screen are two directory headings, Current and Parent. The Current directory simply lists directories and files in the current directory. The Parent directory serves a different purpose. It allows you to move through different levels of directories quite easily. Highlighting the Parent <DIR> line (using the arrow keys to move there) and pressing the return (or double-clicking it with the mouse) provides you with the name of the next higher level directory (if there is one).

TIP

Moving to a different directory within the File Manager window does not change the directory you are currently working in. To do that, you have to select option H from the File Manager.

For example, let's say you have a directory called *Letters,* which has a subdirectory named *Business,* which in turn has a subdirectory named *Project1.* The tree structure would look something like this:

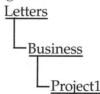

Letters
    └─Business
        └─Project1

If you were in the Project1 subdirectory (and that's what was showing in your File Manager window) and you highlighted the Parent <DIR>, and pressed Enter, the File Manager screen would display the files in the directory named Business. The Parent <DIR> tool is a great one for moving through directories and you can use it to move easily throughout your hard disk.

Lesson 20:
The File-
Management
Options

CHECK YOURSELF

▲ Press the **F5** function key to list the files in the current directory. How many files are there and how much space has been used?

ANSWER

▲ You can find this information along the bottom of the List Files screen.

Lesson 21: Some Important File-Management Options

Here are the top ten options used to manage files. All of these can be performed through other WordPerfect "channels," but you'll find using File Manager to be a great deal easier.

To use any of these options, your first step is to press the **F5** function key and get to the File Manager or select **File Manager** from the File menu.

Opening a File

You learned how to do this in Lesson 9, but just to keep similar tasks (working with files) together, let's review it here. When you open a file from the File Manager, WordPerfect will always open it into a new document window.

To open a file (that of course has been already created):

1. Highlight the name of the file you want to retrieve with the arrow keys or click once with the mouse.
2. Select **O**pen into New Document (option 1) in the command area of the File Manager.

   The file will appear in a WordPerfect window.

TIP

If you want to add an existing document to one that is already in a window, use the Retrieve into Current Document (option 2) **option.**

Deleting a File

When you delete a file, the address or name of the file is removed from the directory that keeps track of the file's location, but this does not mean that all is lost. Many companies offer utilities that can help you recover a lost file, and even the DOS operating system offers UNDELETE, which can be a big help.

To delete a file:

1. Highlight the name of the file you want to delete.
2. Select **D**elete (option 6).

   In its polite way, WordPerfect will ask you to confirm that you really want to delete the file.

TIP

If you do inadvertently delete a file, don't panic. WordPerfect created a backup with a .bk! extension. Look for that in the same directory.

Moving and Renaming a File

Good file management includes being able to rename and move files from one location to another.

To rename a file:

1. Highlight the file you want to rename.
2. Select **M**ove/Rename (option 5).
3. WordPerfect shows you the Move/Rename dialog box (as shown in Figure 6.2) and will ask you to provide a new name and location for the file through the following prompt (including the old name).
4. Supply the new name and location and press the **Enter** key.

Renaming a file can serve several purposes. First, you can rename a file you may want to use again, but for a different purpose. Second, you might want to be a good housekeeper and rename files when others are created so that you can easily distinguish between them.

You can rename a file anything you want as long as that name is currently being used in the same directory and as long as you do not exceed the eight character rule laid down by your operating system.

Lesson 21:
Some
Important File-
Management
Options

▼ *Figure 6.2.   The Move/Rename Dialog Box*

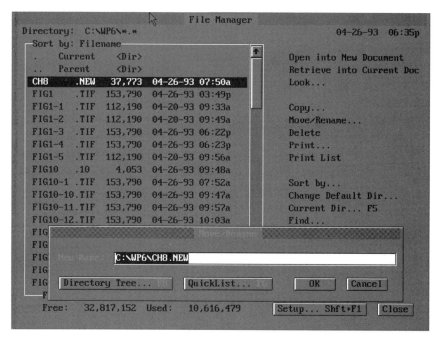

To move a file, you need to provide the location of its new home in the Move/Rename dialog box. You are, in effect, giving it a new name, but the new name determines where it will be moved. For example, a letter created under the filename *c:\letter\doug* can be moved to *c:\business\doug* without the file being renamed or can be moved to *c:\business\springer* with the file being moved and renamed from *doug* to *springer*.

Printing a File

By far, the easiest way to print is by using the Print feature in File Manager.

To print using the File Manager:

1. Highlight the file you want to print.
2. Select **Print** (option 7).
3. If you want to print the entire document, then press the Enter key when you see the Print Multiple Pages dialog box as shown in Figure 6.3, or fill in the range of pages you want to print in the Page/Label Range text box.

If you want to print from a particular page to the end of the document, enter the page and a hyphen and press the **Enter** key. For example, the entry 32- will print from page 32 on.

If you want to print from the beginning of a document to a particular page, enter a hyphen and the page number and press the **Enter** key. For example, the entry -16 will print the first 16 pages.

TIP

Want to print only odd or even pages? Just select that option by clicking in the ♦ or triangles in the Print Multiple Pages dialog box.

Looking at Files

Once you've located a file that you think you want to retrieve, delete, copy, rename, or whatever, you might want to give it a

▼ *Figure 6.3.* ***The Print Multiple Pages Dialog Box***

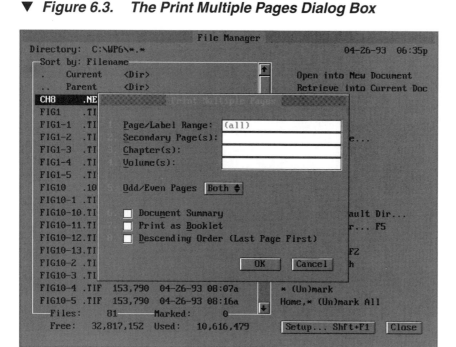

once-over and see if it's actually the file you think you are working with. In other words, how about an easy way to look at the contents of a file before it is opened?

To look at files:

1. Highlight the file you want to see.
2. Select Look (option 3) on the File Manager menu. You see a screen similar to the one showing in Figure 6.4, where you can see the contents of the file named *ch8.new* and information about that file, including its name and the last time the file was modified. Now, you can't do anything to a file that's just being looked at. To modify it in any way you have to first open it. But, this tool is a terrific way to avoid deleting a file that you think contains last year's list of winners in the poker game but really contains this year's salary raise information!

The Look option also provides you with other options as well, as you can see on the bottom of the screen shown in Figure 6.4.

▼ *Figure 6.4.* *Looking at Files*

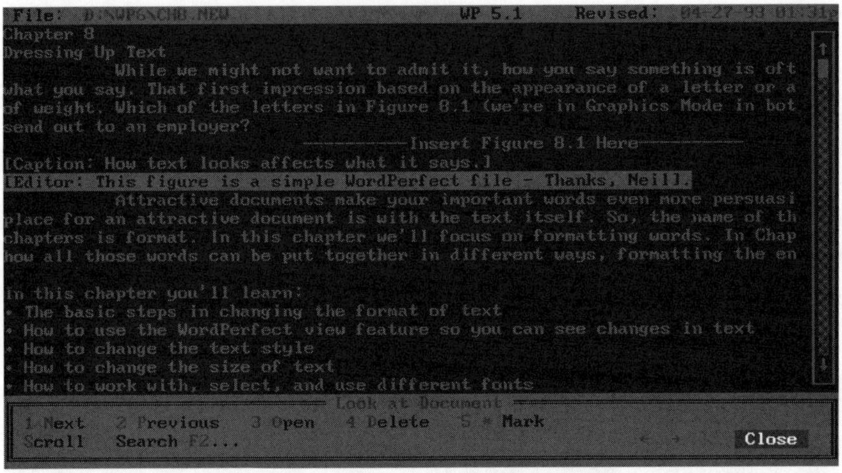

Here you can select from several different numbered commands such as:

▲ Next (option 1), which will provide a look at the next document.

▲ Previous (option 2), which will provide a look at the previous document.

▲ Open (option 3), which will open the file you are looking at in a Window of its own.

▲ Delete (option 4), which will delete the file you are looking at. Be careful!

▲ * Mark (option 5), which will mark the file for another operation, such as copy or delete. You can mark multiple files.

Changing Directories

A place for everything and everything in its place. That's the official good housekeeping motto. Files are things that need to be kept in their place, and their place is usually a subdirectory organized by the type of file. So, for example, you might have a directory called letters, one called jobs, one called applications, and so on.

To switch to any directory using the File Manager:

1. Select Current Dir (option U) in the File Manager window. When you do this, you'll see the Specify File Manager List dialog box.
2. Enter the name of the directory you want to switch to.

Be sure to include the entire path such as *c:\letters* or *c:\wp\letters\salary* or whatever the full name of the directory is.

If there is no such directory (you made a boo-boo), WordPerfect will ask you if you want to create a new directory with the name that you provided. This is a quick way to create a new directory without having to return to the operating system level.

3. Press **Enter**.

You might notice that there's another option in the File Manager window that deals with directories as well. That's option H (Change Default Dir). When you use option U, you change the *current* directory. But when you use option H, you change the *default* directory. Every time you use the F5 key to access the File Manager, it goes right to the default directory.

TIP

Use option U to change directories and option H to set a new default directory.

Lesson 21: Some Important File-Management Options

Copying Files

You already know how to move a file, but what about making a copy of one? Say, for example, you need to copy the file named *doug.ltr* from a directory on your hard drive onto a floppy disk.

To copy a file:

1. Highlight the name of the file you want to copy.
2. Select **C**opy (option 4) from the File Manager. When you do this, WordPerfect will show you the Copy dialog box you see in Figure 6.5.
3. Provide the destination for the file to be copied to.
4. Press **Enter**.

Once you copy a file, the copy will appear in the new location and the original will remain in the location it was copied from. The Copy option in the File Manager is the way many people back up their WordPerfect disks onto a floppy disk without leaving WordPerfect.

Finding Information in Files

Hmm. Where is that letter about the new building? Can't remember the name of a file. That happens to all of us. Thank heaven for WordPerfect's Search feature, option F, in the File Manager.

▼ **Figure 6.5.** *The Copy Dialog Box*

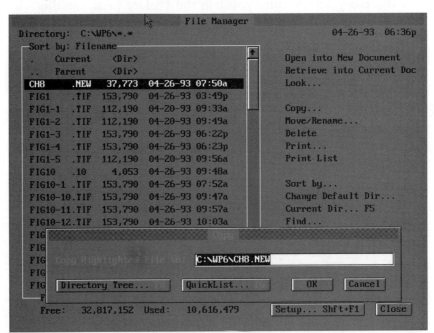

TIP

When you search, try to give WordPerfect as much information as you can. The more it knows, the faster WordPerfect will find the files.

To find files by providing a sample of text in the file:

1. Select Find (option F) from the File Manager. You'll see the Find dialog box as you see in Figure 6.6.
2. WordPerfect provides you with a variety of options to use for searching.
   a. Select Name (option 1) to search by a filename.
   b. Select Document Summary (option 2) to search through the document summary.
   c. Select First Page (option 3) to search through the first page of a document (often the title page).
   d. Select Entire Document (option 4) to search through the entire document.
   e. Select Conditions (option 5) to create a conditional search.

▼ *Figure 6.6.   The Find Dialog Box*

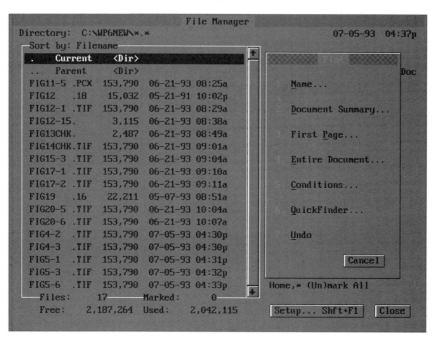

f. Select **Q**uickFinder (option 6) to use the QuickFinder options.

g. Select **U**ndo (option 7) to undo any search operation.

3. Once you select an option, WordPerfect will ask you what you want to search for. For example, in Figure 6.7, you can see how **E**ntire Document (option 4) was selected. You need to supply WordPerfect with a word pattern in the Find Word in Entire Document dialog box.

4. Select **OK**.

WordPerfect will search for the string of characters and then list only those files in the List Files menu that contain files with those characters.

Now, you can use Look (option 3) to look at each file until the specific one that is desired is found.

Finding Files by Name

You can also search for a particular file by the name of that file. If you have a relatively short list of files on your screen, you can probably just eyeball the list until you find what you want.

▼ *Figure 6.7.* *The Find Word in Entire Document Dialog Box*

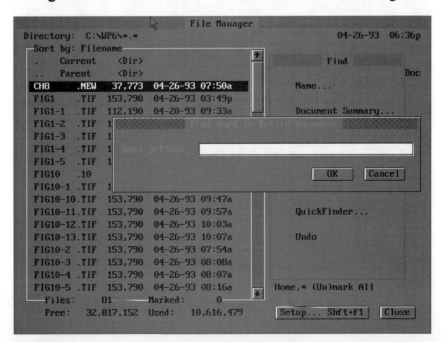

If you have a very long list, press **E** for Search and you'll see the Search for Filename dialog box. WordPerfect will ask you to enter the name of the file you are looking for and will automatically highlight it. You can then perform any of the other List Files menu options, such as delete or copy.

Lesson 21:
Some
Important File-
Management
Options

Selecting Multiple Files

Finally, WordPerfect allows you to perform certain options on more than one file. You can select multiple files by starring them using the asterisk (*) key. Each time you select a file, an asterisk is placed to the left of the file. When you then go ahead and perform a File Manager menu option, WordPerfect will ask if you want to perform the option for all files, such as:

    Copy marked files?

or

    Delete marked files?

You then indicate yes or no. If you respond yes, WordPerfect will perform the option on all the marked files.

TIP

To unmark an individual file, just highlight it and press the * key again. To unmark all marked files, use the Home,* key **combination.**

CHECK YOURSELF

1. Which specific File Manager commands would you use to:
    a. rename a file from log.day to log1.day?
    b. find the string of characters "return" in a file?
    c. retrieve the file named "xyz" into a new document?
2. What would be the exact sequence of commands to make a copy of a file named "toys" on the floppy disk in drive A?

ANSWERS

1. (a) Copy (option 5), (b) Find (option F), (c) Open into a New Document (option 1).
2. F5, Enter, (Select the file named toys), 4, A: Toys

Managing files is not exciting and won't make you a better writer, but it will certainly help you save the time you need to practice becoming a better writer. There are some other management tools that are important to learn about, and that's now where we move to—searching and finding text.

PRACTICE WHAT YOU'VE LEARNED

1. Provide three examples when the File Manager Search feature would be helpful.
2. How does the Look option on the File Manager work and why is it a valuable feature? When would you use it, rather than retrieving the entire document?
3. Here are some word patterns that you might Search for, using the Search File Manager option. Discuss why some would be useful to search for, while others might be a waste of time.
   a. the
   b. the foundation of the
   c. to take

ANSWERS

1. When you want to view a file without retrieving it into memory, print a set number of pages, or switch directories.
2. Using option 3 on the File Manager screen allows you to view a document but not edit it. You would use it when you want to see the contents of a file but do not want to change it in any way.
3. A search for words such as *the* can be futile, since it occurs not only as its own word but also as part of so many others. Always search for the most information you can.

Searching Through Documents

You might very well know what it is you want to edit but have some difficulty trying to find it—especially if your documents are long. WordPerfect provides several tools that help you search through a document to find characters, words, phrases, or whatever you are looking for and then provides you with another set of tools to change it. In this chapter you'll learn how to:

- ▲ **Search forward and backward in a document for text**
- ▲ **Search for reveal codes**
- ▲ **Search and change text in one step**

Important Keys	**Important Terms**
Alt+F2	replace
F2	search
Shift+F2	Search Codes dialog box
	Search and Replace dialog box
	Search dialog box

Lesson 22: Searching for Text

"Where did I leave my keys?" Ever go through that on the way out of the house in the morning? How about, "Where is that reference to the new product in the final report I prepared for Sam?" Sort of the same thing. You have to look for something, and until you find it, you're sort of stuck right where you are.

Searching Forward

WordPerfect to the rescue again. Using the **F2** function key, WordPerfect provides you with a quick and powerful tool that allows you to find any set of characters that are part of the text it is searching. And, you can **search** either forward (from a point in the document to the end of the document) or backward (from a point in the document to the beginning of the document).

TIP

The F2 **function key begins the forward search process. The** Shift+F2 **key combination begins the backward search process.**

To initiate a search:

1. Press the **F2** function key [Mouse Moves: Edit, Search] to see the Search dialog box as you see in Figure 7.1.
    WordPerfect is waiting for you to provide the text you want to search for.
2. Type the string of characters you want to search for.
3. Press **F2** again and WordPerfect will search for the string of (up to 85) characters you provided.

▼ *Figure 7.1.* *The Search Dialog Box*

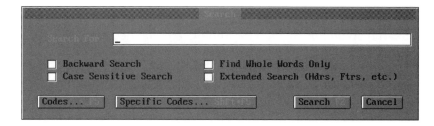

TIP

WordPerfect will search from the location of the cursor throughout the document and not the entire document.

If WordPerfect cannot find what you told it to search for, it will give you the

```
Not Found
```

message. This means that you told WordPerfect to search for something that isn't there.

TIP

Press the F2 key to begin the search process, not the Return or Enter key, otherwise WordPerfect will search for the characters you provide plus a carriage return.

Searching Backward

Searching backward for a string of characters involves the exact same process, except you use the **Shift+F2** key combination; then WordPerfect provides the Search dialog box you saw in Figure 7.1, but the Backward Search option is already selected. When you provide the characters you want to search for and then press the **F2** function key, WordPerfect will search backward through the document to find what you are trying to locate.

TIP

The Search command is great for finding text that needs to be edited.

Repeating Searches

WordPerfect always remembers what you searched for last. If you want to repeat the search to find the same set of characters throughout a document, just press the **F2** key twice to search forward for the same text or the **Shift+F2** key combination to search backward.

Some Search Reminders

Here are some ways to speed up your searches:

First, try to search for as much information as you can, without going overboard. For example, if you want to find the word *different*, don't search for the letter *d*, or even *di*, since many words begin with *d* (*dad, dope, delicious*) or *di* (*distance, dill, diligent*). Rather, search for as much of the word as uniquely identifies it, such as *diff*. Now you might get difference or differential, but the odds on your having those words in your document are slimmer than having general *d* or *di* words.

TIP

WordPerfect remembers exactly what you searched for. If you want to search for the same thing, no need to reenter the text. Just press the F2 function key twice.

Second, WordPerfect will search for letters and such that may be a part of another word. For example, if you have it search for the set of characters *the*, you may find it stopping on *them*, *their*, or *themselves*. If you want to search for the word *the*, then include spaces in the search. The extra space before and after the word makes all the difference. The first case (the) would find all the words with the characters *t,h,e* such as *thematic*, *these*, and *theory*. The second case (the) would find only those with a space before and after the characters *the*.

Third, WordPerfect also distinguishes between upper and lowercase. For example, *max* will find *Max*, but *Max* will not find *max*. The solution? Always search in lowercase unless you need an exact match. In that case, use the Case Sensitive Search option you see in the Search dialog box shown in Figure 7.1.

Searching for Reveal Codes

Characters are not the only thing you can search for in a WordPerfect document. You can also search for reveal codes. This is especially handy when it comes time to find out where you inserted a particular code (such as the code for a header or footer).

For example, in Figure 7.2, you can see how the code for a header [Header A: Every Page...] was entered in the Search dialog box. How do you enter a code to then search for it? Easy. Just select Specific Codes from the Search dialog box or go right into searching for codes by using the **F5** function key.

To search for a header, you would search for the reveal code [Header A]:

1. Press the **F2** function key [Mouse Moves: **E**dit, Sear**ch**] to see the Search dialog box.

▼ *Figure 7.2.   Entering a Reveal Code in the Search Dialog Box*

File Edit View Layout Tools Font Graphics Window Help

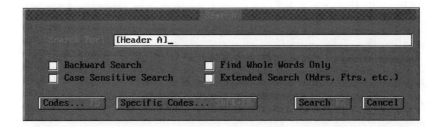

2. Press the **F5** function key to select **Codes** . You'll see the Search Codes dialog box as shown in Figure 7.3.
3. Highlight the code [Header A] using the arrow keys.
4. Select **Select**.

TIP

To insert a code in the Search dialog box, you can just double-click on it with the mouse.

WordPerfect will attempt to find the header using the information you provided as shown in Figure 7.2.

TIP

People use the F2 search feature for many different purposes. One of these is to mark test where you have finished working and want to begin next time. Just use a unique set of characters, such as *xxx*

▼ *Figure 7.3.* **The Search Codes Dialog Box**

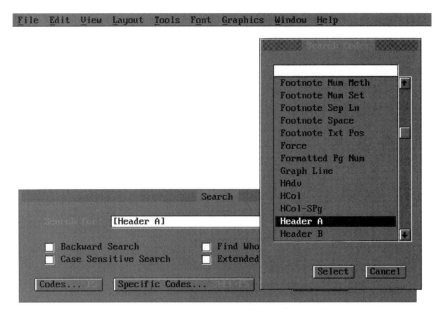

(which are never part of a word), and search for that next time you begin working.

CHECK YOURSELF

1. Enter the first 13 letters of the alphabet on a clean WordPerfect screen with a carriage return after each one. Now search forward for the letter *D*. Go to the end of the 13 characters and search backward for the same letter.
2. In your screen full of 13 characters, turn on the reveal codes screen (**Alt+F3**) and search for any **[HRt]** carriage return codes. Continue to search until you have found them all.

ANSWERS

1. You can search forward (**F2**) or backward (**Shift+F2**). WordPerfect will always find the first occurrence of what you tell it to search for.

2. **[HRt]** are placed at the point where you press the **Enter** key, such as at the end of a paragraph. Notice that WordPerfect places the cursor after the code when the search is completed.

Lesson 23: Replacing Text

Being able to search for text and find it quickly is extremely useful. Being able to search for it and then replace it is one of the most useful WordPerfect tools available.

Searching for and Replacing Text

Here's the rule. Anything that you search for can be replaced by anything else! For example, if you entered the boss's name as *Bill Bower* rather than *Bill Bowar*, just search for the first version (*Bower*) and **replace** it with second (*Bowar*).

Better yet, why not just type shorthand for particular words or phrases and replace them? For example, you may be writing a report that uses the word *database* quite often. Why not just type the characters *db* and then search and replace them with *database*?

To search and replace:

1. Use the **Alt+F2** key combination [Mouse Moves: **S**earch, **R**eplace] to begin the search and replace operation, and you will see the Search and Replace dialog box you see in Figure 7.4.

TIP

The Alt+F2 **key combination begins the search and replace process.**

If you want to search and replace without confirmation at each occurrence, you need do nothing. If you want to confirm each potential change, select **Confirm Replacement**.

2. In the **Search For:** box, enter the text (*db* in this example) or reveal codes (**F5**) that you want to search for and replace.

▼ *Figure 7.4.* *The Search and Replace Dialog Box*

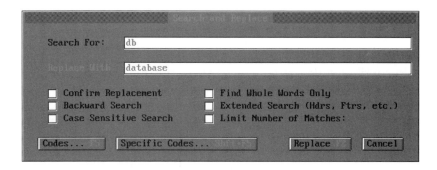

3. Press the **Tab** key or click in the **Replace With:** text box.
4. In the **Replace With:** box, enter the new text (*database* in this example) or reveal codes (**F5**).
5. Press **F2**.

WordPerfect will search through the entire document and replace text or reveal codes as you designate.

TIP

Want to search and replace in only part of a document? Create a block (Alt+F4 or use the mouse) and then use the Alt+F2 key combination. The search and replace will take place only in the blocked area.

Once you complete the search and replace process, WordPerfect will tell you how many occurrences of what you were searching for were found and how many replacements were made.

Some Search and Replace Reminders

Just some notes so that your search and replace efforts are successful. First, know when to confirm or not to confirm the replacement. You don't need to stop at every occurrence of text to check on whether you want it replaced if (and this is a big if) the text is unique to the document. In other words, in our example of *db*, it's unlikely that there are other words with those characters. On the other hand, you definitely want to confirm each replacement if you are searching for text such as *the*. Otherwise, you will end up changing all the *th*'s in your document to *t*'s and end up with words such as *teir, te, tat, tink,* and so on.

Second, always search for as much information as you can so you can avoid your worst nightmare: replacing text incorrectly and not being able to reverse the process. Don't ever search for one character and replace it with another without confirmation. Imagine spelling Mr. Jones's name as *Mr. Jines*. OK, you say, I can just search for the *i*'s and replace then them with *o*'s. Oops! Now all the *i*'s in all the words in the document become *o*'s. Then you try to search for all the *o*'s and change them back and you find that even the *o*'s you didn't affect before (in words such as *on, top,* and *town*) are now something they shouldn't be. What a mess!

Third, always save your document before you perform any substantial search and replace. That way, if you replace incorrectly, you can always go back to the document that was saved before your error.

CHECK YOURSELF

1. In your earlier list of 13 characters, replace the letter *a* with the text letter *b*.
2. Enter a paragraph of text copied from any page in this book. Use the **F2** function key to change the word *the* to *tha*. Now change all the *a*'s to *e*'s. What were some of the unintended effects of trying to erase your error?

ANSWERS

1. You can see how WordPerfect follows your search and re-place instructions to the letter. Be careful that you only search for exactly what you want to find.
2. You probably have a mess! Changing vowels is always dangerous. Remember to save your document before a search and replace operation. That way, if you do make an error, you can easily go back to where you just were.

Searching for text to find it and searching and replacing text are skills that you will use constantly in your WordPerfect activities. So, you're an editor and can fix words to appear as they should and say what they should. Now on to making your WordPerfect documents appear as they should. In the next chapter, you'll learn about dressing up both text and documents.

PRACTICE WHAT YOU'VE LEARNED

1. Enter the following paragraph:
   There are few people who find that WordPerfect does not meat there needs for word processing chores. Almost everyone, whether a beginner or an advanced user can benefit from the features that wp has to offer.

   a. Use the Search tool to find the word *meat* and edit it to read *meet*.

   b. Using the Search and Replace tool:
   find *there* and replace it with *their*
   find the word *word processing* and replace it with *word-processing;*
   find the text *wp* and replace it with *WordPerfect.*
2. Why should you save a file before you do a Search and Replace through a large document?
3. If you want to search for the two characters *Ti*, what will WordPerfect do if you ask it to find *tI*? *TI*? *ti*?
4. Under what conditions should you confirm the replacement of text?
5. Why would you never search for the letter *a* and replace it with the letter *o* in a misspelling such as *mather*?

ANSWERS

1. Remember that when you search you should try to provide as complete and accurate information as is possible.

2. This way, if you accidently replace incorrectly, you will not have lost all your work. Just go back to the original file.

3. WordPerfect will only find all occurrences of letters *t* and *i*, unless you indicate Case Sensitive Search and it will mark upper- and lower-case exactly.

4. When you have any doubts that more occurrences of text than what you want to replace exist and should not be changed.

5. Because every other *a* in a document will be replaced, and you cannot then replace every *a* with an *o* to correct your error.

Dressing Up Text

Although we might not want to admit it, how you say something is often as important as what you say. That first impression based on the appearance of a letter or a report carries a lot of weight. Which of the letters in Figure 8.1 (we're in Graphics mode in both) would you rather send out to an employer?

Attractive documents make your important words even more persuasive, and the starting place for an attractive document is with the text itself. So, the name of the game for the next two chapters is format. In this chapter we'll focus on formatting words. In Chapter 9, we'll focus on how all those words can be put together in different ways, formatting the entire document. In this chapter you'll learn how to:

▲ Change the format of text

▲ Use the WordPerfect View feature so you can see changes in text

▲ Change the text style

▲ Change the size of text

▲ Work with, select, and use different fonts

Important Keys	**Important Terms**	
Ctrl+F8	case conversion	PrevPage
F6	Close	Print Preview
F8	Convert Case dialog box	Thumb 8
Shift+F8	FacingPgs	Thumb 32
	Font dialog box	thumbnail sketches
	FullPage	Zoom100%
	GoToPage	Zoom200%
	initial font	ZoomIn
	NextPage	ZoomOut

▼ **Figure 8.1.** **How Text Looks Affects What It Says**

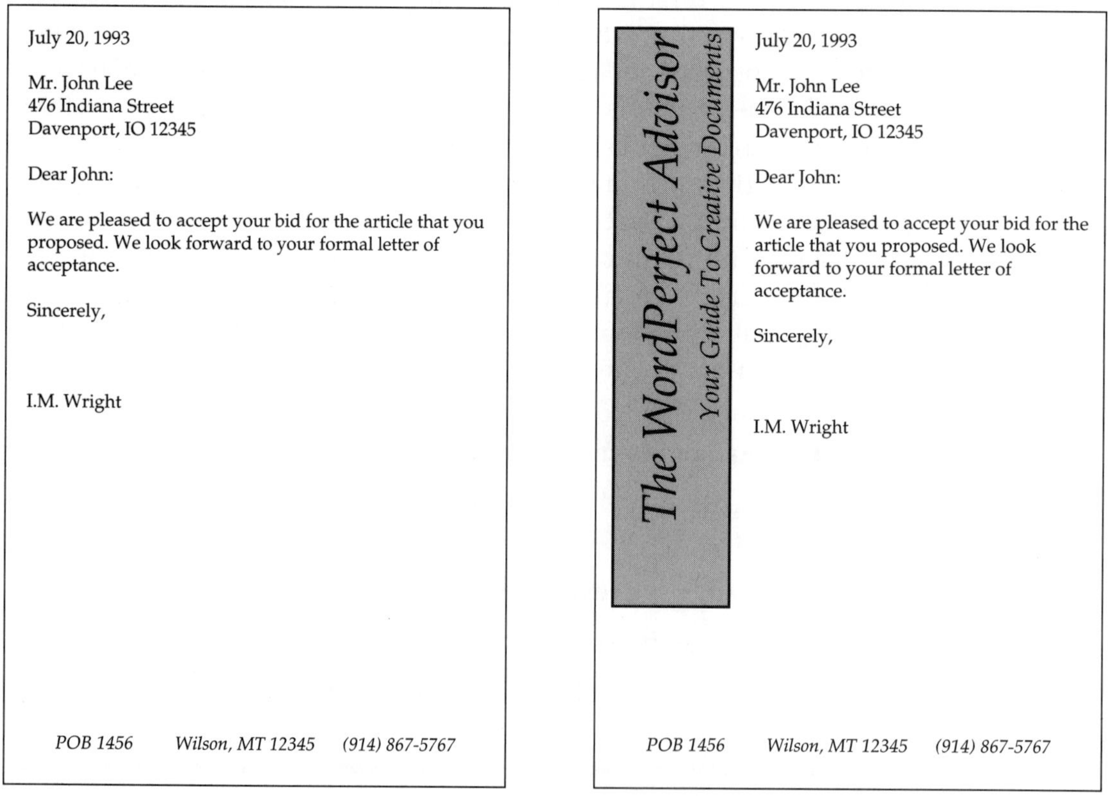

July 20, 1993

Mr. John Lee
476 Indiana Street
Davenport, IO 12345

Dear John:

We are pleased to accept your bid for the article that you proposed. We look forward to your formal letter of acceptance.

Sincerely,

I.M. Wright

POB 1456   Wilson, MT 12345   (914) 867-5767

The WordPerfect Advisor
Your Guide To Creative Documents

July 20, 1993

Mr. John Lee
476 Indiana Street
Davenport, IO 12345

Dear John:

We are pleased to accept your bid for the article that you proposed. We look forward to your formal letter of acceptance.

Sincerely,

I.M. Wright

POB 1456   Wilson, MT 12345   (914) 867-5767

Lesson 24: Working with Text

Lesson 24: Working with Text

WordPerfect allows you to modify the size, appearance, and font that make up your finished documents. There are two different methods to do this. Let's look at each one with some very simple examples before we move on to the many options that the Font dialog box has to offer.

Formatting Text as It's Entered

Formatting text as it is entered involves entering the special WordPerfect code that begins the format change.

To format text as it's entered:

1. Enter the command to turn the formatting on.
2. Enter the text you want formatted.
3. Enter the command to turn the formatting off.

TIP

Text can be formatted before it is entered by entering the reveal code before you begin typing.

Let's look at two examples where WordPerfect makes modifications especially easy to use by identifying two keys just for format changes.

Boldfacing Text as It's Entered

To boldface text that you have not yet entered:

1. Press the **F6** function key [Mouse Moves: **F**ont, **B**old] to turn on bold.
2. Enter the text.
3. Press the **F6** function key [Mouse Moves: **F**ont, **B**old] to turn off bold.

When you do this, the [Bold On] reveal code is entered before the boldfacing begins and the [Bold Off] reveal code is entered after the boldfaced text. **Boldfacing is a powerful way to emphasize something you want to say. It stands out!**

Underlining Text as It's Entered

You won't be surprised to find that WordPerfect also set aside another function key (**F8**) just for underlining.

To underline text that you have not yet entered:

1. Press the **F8** function key [Mouse Moves: F**o**nt, **U**nderline] to turn on underline.
2. Enter the text.
3. Press the **F8** function key [Mouse Moves: F**o**nt, **U**nderline] to turn off underline.

When you do this, the [Und On] reveal code is entered before the underlining begins and the [Und Off] reveal code is entered after the underline text. <u>Underlining emphasizes text but is also used to indicate text that is to appear in *italics*.</u>

The **F6** and **F8** function keys are the only ones predefined to format text.

Formatting Text After It's Entered

The other way to make changes in text format is to follow these general steps:

1. Select the text that has already been entered using the Block feature we covered in Lesson 12.
2. Select the format command you want to use to change the text.

Let's look at the same two format codes again, but use this method for formatting text.

Boldfacing Text After It's Entered

To boldface text that is already entered:

1. Enter the text you want to boldface.
2. Block the text (**Alt+F4**) or use the mouse to drag and create a block you want to bold.
3. Pres the **F6** function key [Mouse Moves: **F**ont, **B**old] to turn off bold.

Only the text that was selected (highlighted) will appear in boldface.

Underlining Text After It's Entered

To underline text that is already entered:

1. Enter the text you want to underline.
2. Block the text (**Alt+F4**) or use the mouse to drag and create a block you want to underline.
3. Press the **F8** function key [Mouse Moves: **F**ont, **U**nderline]. Only the text that was selected (highlighted) will be underlined.

Before or After? That Is the Question

And the answer depends on the way you like to work. Some people like to plan things out and have them formatted as the work continues. Others like to go back and then format. The latter group feels that going back after all the text is entered gives them a chance to see the big picture. Our recommendation is to go with the "format-after-text-is-entered-strategy," since experience with creating lots of new documents seems to show that you never really know exactly what it is you want until you can see what you've produced. This is especially true now that WordPerfect 6.0 offers a Graphics mode where you can see just what is happening.

If you're typing someone else's work, however, it may be a different story. In that case, you'll probably want to enter format changes as you go along so that you don't forget to make the changes.

The Font Dialog Box

Boldfacing (**F6**) and underlining (**F8**) are the only two immediately available function key operations for formatting text. But by no means is that all that WordPerfect can do. First, there is a whole set of font changes you can make as shown on the Font menu in figure 8.1, from Bold to Underline to Outline to Small Caps.

If you press the **Ctrl+F8** key combination, you'll see the Font dialog box as shown in Figure 8.2, which is like font central control. Options galore are available here.

The Font dialog box is separated into different areas, all of which control the appearance of some font quality.

At the top, you can see the name of the currently installed printer (which in this case is the NEC LC890). The fonts that

▼ *Figure 8.2.   The Font Dialog Box*

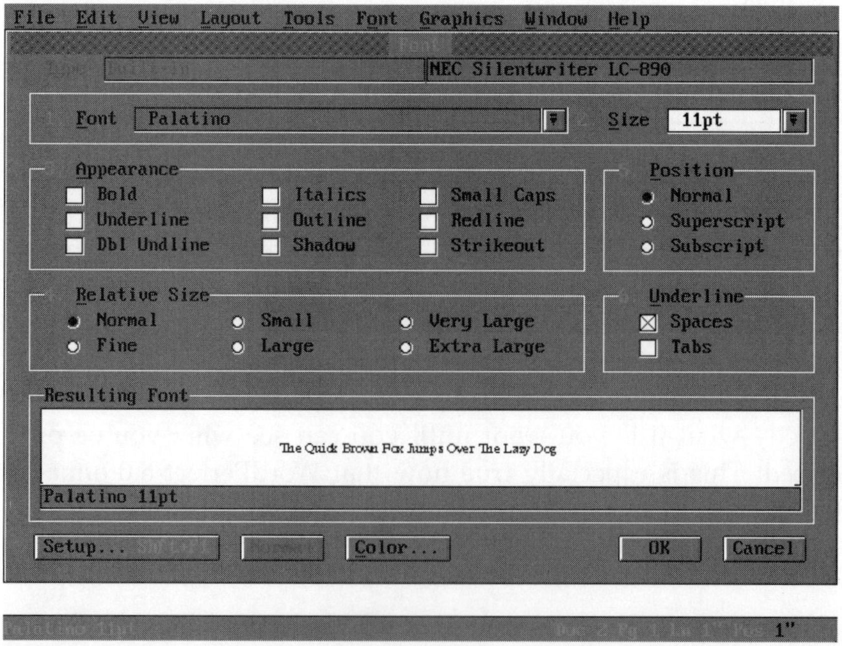

WordPerfect will have available to print with is a function of the printer you are using. In Chapter 17, you'll learn more about how to select and add a printer to your WordPerfect printer files.

Changing Fonts

The first box at the top of the Font dialog box deals with the font itself (option 1) and the size of the font (option 2). Both of these selections can be easily changed, much as in any WordPerfect dialog box. Either enter the number of the option you want to work, click on it with the mouse, or use the **Tab** key to move to that area.

To change the font and the size of the font:

1. Use the **Ctrl+F8** key combination [Mouse Moves: F**o**nt, F**o**nt] to see the Font dialog box.
2. Enter the value 1 to move to the Font options or click on it with the mouse. When you do this, you will see a list of fonts that are available from which you can choose as shown in Figure 8.3.

▼ **Figure 8.3.   Selecting a New Font**

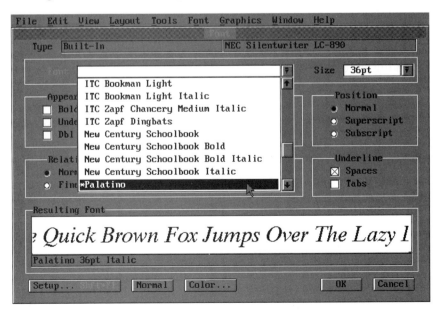

3. Using the arrow keys, move down to the font you want to select and press **Enter**. Or, use the mouse and double-click on the
name of the font you want to select.

TIP

**Want to know what fonts look like before you return to the docu-
ment? Look in the Resulting Font area toward the bottom of the Font
dialog box.**

4. Press **Enter**.

The font you have selected will then become the active font in
the current document.

TIP

**You can always check what font is active by examining the reveal
codes (Alt+F3), where you will find the reveal code representing that
font, such as [Font: Palatino].**

Changing Font Size

To change the size of the font, select **Size** (option 2) and enter a value. In Figure 8.2, the size of the font is in points. A point is $1/72$ of an
inch, so a 36-point font (as you see in Figure 8.2) is $1/2$ of an inch tall
and a 12-point font (usually what you use to write letters and
memos) is $1/6$ of an inch tall. In some cases, again depending on the
printer you are using, you can enter values ranging from 1 to 400
points, whereas for other printers, all that is available is a fixed
number of fonts of a particular size.

To change the size of a font:

1. Use the **Ctrl+F8** key combination [Mouse Moves: Font, Font]
to see the Font dialog box.
2. Enter 2 to move to the **Size** option (or click on it with the
mouse).
3. Enter the new size.

4. Press **Enter** or click **OK**. The new font size will be in effect from the location of that reveal code [Font Size:] in the document until the font size is changed again.

Seeing How Things Look

One last comment before we turn our attention to each of the different options on the Font menu to see how they can enhance the appearance of your text.

Since what you enter on your screen is not exactly the way that the printed document may look, you can be at a disadvantage. After all, you make all these format changes and would really like to find out how the finished product will appear. You can use the various view options we discussed in Chapter 4, but they don't give you a full-page view.

One way is to actually print the document. Printing, however, is sometimes the least productive way to spend your time trying to find out how something looks. For one thing, it takes time. It also wastes paper.

Wouldn't you know that WordPerfect has an answer: the **Print Preview** option available through the **Shift+F7**, **Print Preview** [Mouse Moves: **File**, Print Preview] combination. Although this is a printing function, we're covering it here because you may want to use it to see the effects of format changes in your document as you make them. When you select this option, you'll see your document as it will actually appear when printed. For example, in Figure 8.4, you can see a preview of the letterhead shown in Figure 8.1. If you're not impressed by this, go back to your quill pen!

The Print Preview option shows you how your document will appear when printed, but what it shows might be limited by the capability of your monitor.

The Print Preview Options

At the top of Figure 8.4, you can see a button bar that acts just like the ones we described in Chapter 5. The **Print Preview Button Bar**

▼ *Figure 8.4.* *A Print Preview Look at a Document*

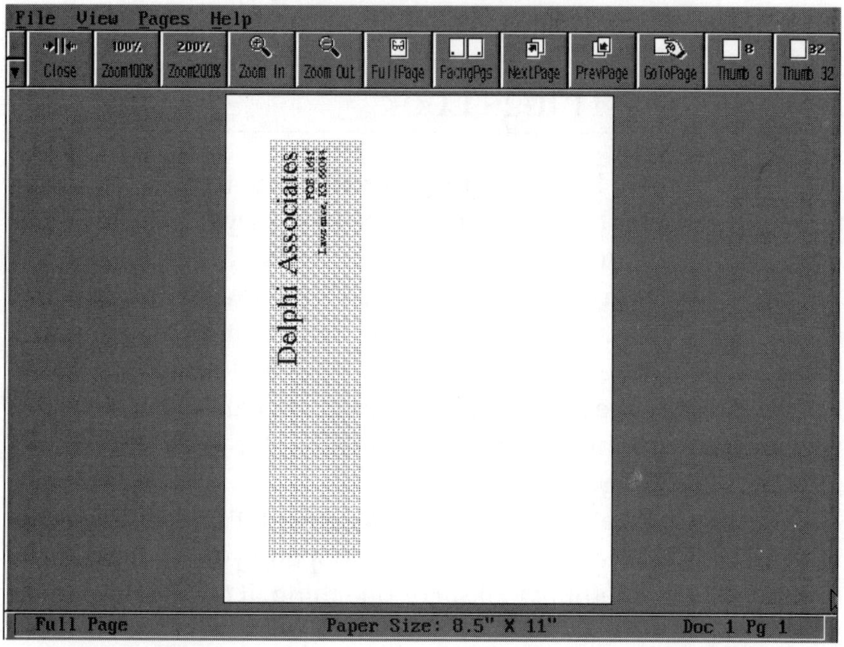

is full of options that you can use to help view your documents. Keep in mind that the Print Preview Button Bar can be edited as any other button bar, so you can easily customize it to fit your needs.

The buttons you see in Figure 8.4 (from the left to the right) do the following. You can select these options by clicking on one using the mouse, or by using the View or File menu. When you use any of these options, note that WordPerfect considers the current age the one on which the cursor is located.

The **Close** option closes the Print Preview window and returns you to your document.

The **Zoom100%** (Zoom 100%) option provides you with a 100% image of the page or pages.

The **Zoom200%** (Zoom 200%) option provides you with an image two times the page or pages.

The **ZoomIn** (Zoom In) option allows you to select (using the mouse to drag and create an area) and magnify the text in that area, as you see in Figure 8.5; the text you see in Figure 8.5 was magnified several times. ZoomIn is a great button to use when you want to examine very small text that is not readable on the Print Preview screen.

TIP

When you zoom in, WordPerfect tells you how much you have zoomed. In Figure 8.5, the image has been magnified 734%, which is more than seven times its original size.

The **ZoomOut** (Zoom Out) option allows you to return to normal magnification (which is 100%).

The **FullPage** (Full Page) option lets you preview the full page.

The **FacingPgs** (Facing Pages) option allows you to preview the page that is facing the one on which the cursor is currently located.

The **NextPage** (Next Page) option allows you to preview the next page in the document. For example, if the cursor is on page 21 and you select Next Page, then the Print Preview screen will show you page 22. If there are no pages beyond 21, that's the page you will see.

▼ *Figure 8.5. Zooming in on Text*

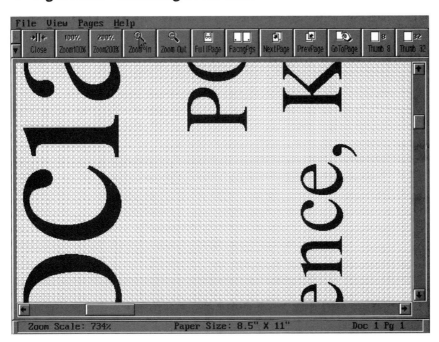

The **PrevPage** (Previous Page) option allows you to preview the previous page in the document. For example, if the cursor is on page 3 and you select Previous Page, then the Print Preview window will show you page 2.

The **GoToPage** (Go To Page) option provides you with the GoTo Page dialog box, where you enter the page you want to go to and WordPerfect takes you there.

TIP

You can also use the Ctrl+Home **key combination to get to the GoTo dialog box, which accomplishes the same thing.**

Finally, and a very cool addition to WordPerfect 6.0, you can have the Print Preview feature generate what is know as **thumbnail sketches** of pages. The **Thumb 8** and **Thumb 32** options generate small replica of the exact pages as they would appear when printed, such as you see in Figure 8.6.

▼ *Figure 8.6.   An 8-Page Set of Thumbnail Sketches*

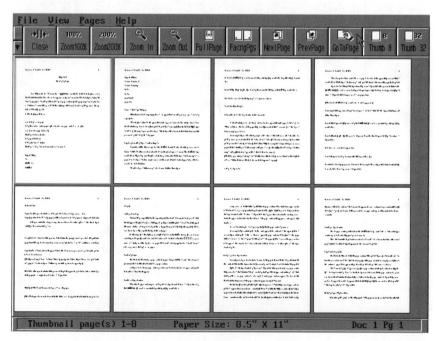

You can't do any editing in the Thumbnail (or in any Print Preview window), but using Thumbnails is a great way to get an overall impression of what a document looks like.

You can select the number of thumbnails you want in two different ways. First, you can click on the **Thumb 8** or **Thumb 32** buttons in the Print Preview screen. Or, you can select **Thumbnails** from the **View** screen in the Print Preview window and select 1, 2, 4, 8, 16, 32, or some other number. Once you select the number you want (either using the mouse or keyboard strokes), you'll see the thumbnails.

TIP

The number of thumbnails you produce is limited by the number of pages in a document. If you have only four pages in a document, WordPerfect will not be able to generate six thumbnail sketches.

Once you finish with the Print Preview screen, just use the **F7** key to select **C**lose from the **E**dit menu to return to the original document.

CHECK YOURSELF

1. Enter the following two sentences and save it under the name *ch8*.

    WordPerfect allows you to change the appearance of text and make your documents much more impressive than they might otherwise be. One of the main tools for accomplishing these changes is through the use of the Font menu.

    a. Boldface the word *WordPerfect* and the phrase *Font menu*.
    b. At the end of the paragraph, enter a reveal code for boldface (**F6**), then enter a new sentence, and then enter the final reveal code (**F6** again).

2. Recall the filename *ch5* and use the **Shift+F7,V** key combination to view the text as it will appear when printed. Experiment with some of the options at the top of the view screen and see what happens to the screen.

ANSWERS

1. On many monitors, you can see the boldfacing and underlining that WordPerfect does. On others, you may have to resort to reveal codes or Print Preview to see where these features begin and end.
2. It takes a while for WordPerfect to deliver a View Document screen, since it is a graphics screen (you can't work on it like you do in the regular text screen).

Lesson 25: Changing the Size of Text

You can easily change the size of a font, but WordPerfect provides you with another tool to work with the *relative size* of a font. You can see these options in the Relative Size area of the Font dialog box you see in Figure 8.2. They are Normal (the default), Fine, Small, Large, Very Large, and Extra Large. What do they mean? Let's find out.

Working with Different Text Sizes

You'll soon see how to change to Fine or Very Large relative size, but how does WordPerfect know what small or fine or large means? Since different printers support different fonts (such as Helvetica, Palatino, and so on), WordPerfect couldn't possibly be designed to have absolute definitions of these different sizes. Instead it does the most logical thing. It predefines these different size options *relative* to the standard font that your printer uses.

For example, when you select the Large option, the text that WordPerfect produces will be 120 percent of the initial font that your printer is using. You can see, in the following chart, the size option on the font menu, the preset percentages, the key combination, and an example of each.

The initial font is the reference point that WordPerfect uses to generate other sizes of fonts on the Font menu.

Option	Percent	Key Combination	Example
Normal	100%	Ctrl+F8,3,Normal	Normal
Fine	60%	Ctrl+F8,3,Fine	Fine
Small	80%	Ctrl+F8,1,3,Small	Small
Large	120%	Ctrl+F8,1,3,Large	Large
Very Large	150%	Ctrl+F8,1,3, Very Large	Very Large
Extra Large	200%	Ctrl+F8,1,3, Extra Large	Extra Large

As we mentioned earlier, font sizes are generally measured in points. If you are using a font that is 10 point (Normal), the Large option on the size menu will produce a font that is 120 percent larger than 10 point or 12 point. Likewise, the Fine option will produce 6-point (or 60 percent of 10 point) type.

One more note before we go on. The Relative Size options are relative sizes, as you already have learned. When you get into working with fonts (Lesson 26), you'll see how you can set the absolute size of a font. The flexibility with which you can do this is a function of the features your printer offers.

CHECK YOURSELF

1. What happens if you first highlight text and then press the **Ctrl+F8** key combination?
2. How big would Very Large 10-point type be?

ANSWERS

1. You will see the Font dialog box.
2. 15 points.

Lesson 26: Changing the Appearance of Text

You've seen how simple it is to change the selection and size of text. It's just as simple to work with appearance in the appearance area of the Font dialog box. Difference is that differences in size run along a single quantitative dimension (from small to big). Differences in appearance are qualitative in nature. **Boldface** text is quite distinct from Outlined text, for example.

Working with Different Appearance Options

Here's the handy chart for this lesson, showing you the appearance options available in the Font dialog box.

Bold
Underline
<u>Double Underline</u>
Italic
Outline
Shadow
SMALL CAPS
Redline
~~Strikeout~~

It's simple to apply a new appearance to text. You can either make your selection and then enter the text (and then deselect the appearance option), or you can create a block of text and then select the option from the appearance area of the dialog box. In either case, you get the same result.

If you are working with a mouse, you will find the appearance options on the Font menu.

When to Use What?

These are nine very useful options for changing the appearance of text, as you see in the chart. But, when to use what? Some of these options have straightforward applications (such as <u>underline</u>), while others are probably nothing short of decorative (like shadow). In any case, here's a brief description of what each one should be used for.

TIP

Try not to overdo the combination of different sizes and appearance changes. Otherwise, your text can lose its message.

Boldfacing is the most common way to emphasize text, such as special words that need to be stressed or particular points you want to make.

Traditionally, underlining is used to indicate that a word should appear in italics when typeset or to appear in a foreign language (muchacha, l'amour) or scientific terms (e.g., Doppler effect, antigens).

Double underlining? Double the fun!

Italics are used for foreign language and such, as mentioned above. Sometimes they are also used to offset quotes, such as the beginning of this quote from Hamlet: *What a piece of work is man! How noble in reason. In apprehension . . .*

Outline and Shadow? Strictly to jazz up your presentation.

SMALL CAPS ARE OFTEN USED IN THE CREATION OF CHARTS AS WELL AS SUBTITLES IN A DOCUMENT. Its use makes the text a little more apparent than all caps, which may be overkill.

Redline is an extremely useful tool, especially if your project has more than one author. When text is added to a document by another author, it can be redlined to stand out from the other text. It appears on your screen as dimmed text. This way, the first author knows what has been added.

Strikeout is the editor's dream tool. When you change the appearance of text using the Strikeout option, ~~WordPerfect places a series of hyphens through each letter.~~ This material is to be deleted from the document.

CHECK YOURSELF

▲ Create some text and italicize it. What do the reveal codes look like?

ANSWER

▲ [Italic On] and [Italic Off]

Changing the Position

The next set of options that WordPerfect provides concerning fonts is working with the position of location of text relative to normal text. The Position of text refers to whether it appears as Normal

Lesson 26: Changing the Appearence of Text

(the default), Superscript (which appears above the line) like this R^2, or subscript, which appears below the line like this R_{xy}.

In all three cases, you can change the position of text by selecting the appropriate option in the **P**osition area of the Font dialog box. As with other font changes, you can make the change before you enter text, or block the text and then select the change.

TIP

It's often easier to block and then select the change, since you need not worry about turning reveal codes off once you are finished.

Underlining

Last, several underline options (option 6) in the Font dialog box exist. You can select to underline words and spaces such as is being done here, or just words (and no spaces) as is done here, or even tabs and spaces and words, which is done at the beginning of this paragraph (where a tab appears).

As with any other format change, the key is in starting the change where you want it to appear and recognizing that the change stays in effect until you turn it off. If you do want to work with underlining, keep in mind that for changes in tabs or spaces to work, the Underlining option in the appearance area of the Font dialog box must first be selected.

Working with the Initial Font

When you install WordPerfect, you have a selection of fonts from which you can select an **initial font**. WordPerfect automatically selects a font for you to get you started, and as you will shortly see, you can easily change that. The available fonts from which you can select your initial font are determined by your printer, and the initial font becomes the default font, the one that will always be used unless another one is specified.

Selecting a New Initial Font

There are several levels of WordPerfect dialog boxes you have to go through to select a new initial font, so follow carefully.

To select a new initial font (using the Print option or the File menu):

1. Use the **Shift+F7** key combination [Mouse Moves: File, Print] to see the Print dialog box.
2. Press **S** for **S**elect.
3. Select **E**dit (option 3).
4. Select **F**ont Setup (option 6).
5. Select: Select Initial **F**ont (option 1).
6. Finally! Now select Font (option 1) and select the font you want to be the initial font that WordPerfect uses when it begins a new document.
7. Now select the **S**ize (option 2) of the initial font.
8. Press the **F7** key five times to return to the original document.

Whatever initial font you select, it will be in force until you change it. All of your new documents will automatically use that font. And the selection of the initial font will alter the way your type appears on your monitor screen as well. For example, if you select a 20-point type as your initial font, since these are larger (in both height and width), fewer characters will fit on each line.

The Case Conversion Tool

Last font trick in this lesson. WordPerfect has a neat way to change text either to all uppercase or to all lowercase.

To use Case Conversion:

1. Block the text you want to convert.
2. Use the **Shift+F3** key combination [Mouse Moves: Edit, Convert Case] to see the following options—Uppercase, Lower Case, Initial Caps—in the Convert Case dialog box.
3. Select the conversion you want.

TIP

Uppercase text and small caps (available through the Ctrl+F8,3, Small Caps **key combination) are different from each other and should not be used for the same purpose.**

Lesson 26:
Changing the
Appearance
of Text

TIP

If when you pressed the Shift+F3 **keys, you found yourself on a blank screen, it's because you forgot to block text. Select some blocked text and start over.**

CHECK YOURSELF

▲ Change the initial font to any other font your printer has available. Recall the file named *ch8* (or create a new one) and then use the View feature to see the difference in how the fonts appear.

ANSWER

▲ The number of initial fonts from which you can select depends on your printer's capabilities.

Lesson 27: Combining Format Changes

WordPerfect does not restrict you to just one format change in any of the dimensions of size, appearance, or fonts. For example, you can combine size and appearance. But, oh my. What a mess we can make when we start using these new toys without any discretion.

Welcome to Font Junk

For example, look at the text in Figure 8.7. This is your basic font junk, and it certainly doesn't look very attractive, let alone get the message across. Combining size and appearance options is as easy as boldfacing the text and selecting the option, but you have to be careful not to go overboard.

Any font size, font appearance, and font type can be combined together, but remember to be judicious in combining these alternatives.

Lesson 27: Combining Format Changes

▼ ***Figure 8.7. Font Junk!***

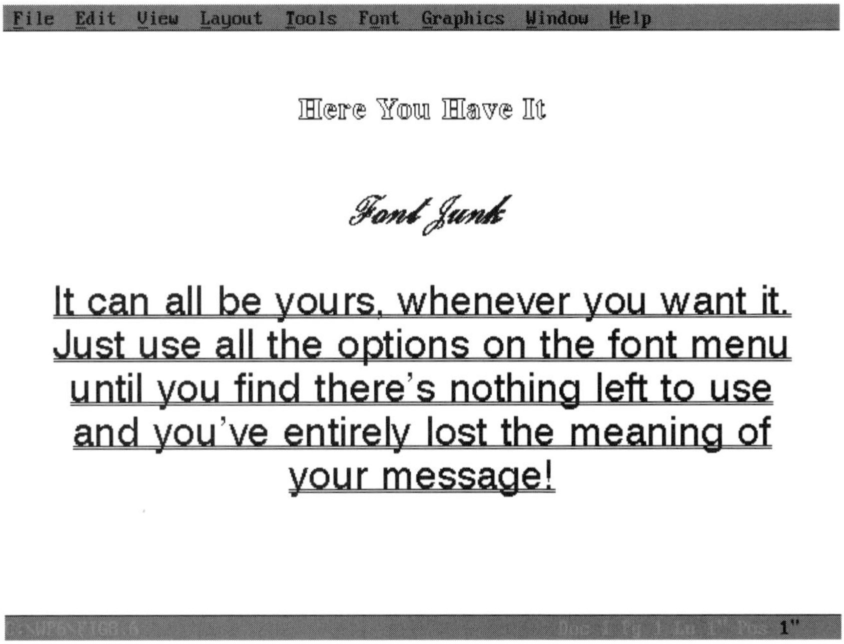
File Edit View Layout Tools Font Graphics Window Help
Here You Have It
Font Junk
It can all be yours, whenever you want it. Just use all the options on the font menu until you find there's nothing left to use and you've entirely lost the meaning of your message!
1"

Hints on Combining Different Fonts

- ▲ Use only one font in any one document such as Times, New York, Palatino, and so on. If you need to mix, read a graphics design book that contains charts that show which families go together, such as New York and Helvetica.
- ▲ Change sizes to fit the message. If you want to get someone's attention, use a large font for titles, banner, and so on.
- ▲ Use tools such as italics and shadow options sparingly. You lose the power of these tools if you use them too much.

CHECK YOURSELF

▲ Enter the following text:

This is an example of using more than one format feature.

Block the entire sentence and then underline it. Now boldface the word **format**. Examine the reveal codes to see where the format codes are placed.

ANSWER

▲ Reveal codes always show you exactly what format changes will occur and when.

Now that you're an expert on changing the way text appears, it's time to turn to the second half of the format toolbox and begin learning about the way that you can work with complete documents, including changing margins, numbering pages, changing line spacing, and more, and more, and more.

PRACTICE WHAT YOU'VE LEARNED

1. What is the definition of an initial font?
2. Discuss some of the advantages and disadvantages of first entering text and then working with format changes.
3. What are two reasons why the View Document feature is useful?
4. Write down the set of reveal codes that accompanies each of the following format changes:
   Redline
   Small Caps
   Italics
   Fine
   Superscript
5. When WordPerfect makes font sizes such as Fine and Large available, how big are these and how is the size determined?
6. How many different fonts are available on your printer and when would you want to change from one initial font to another?
7. When would you use the Case Conversion option?
8. Use as many different fonts and sizes and other changes to create the ugliest document you can (no kidding!). Now that you've had your fun, take the same content and use the tools you learned about in this chapter to create text that is appealing and communicates the message effectively.

ANSWERS

1. It's the default font that WordPerfect will always use unless told otherwise.

2. On the one hand, you get the text down rapidly without having to be concerned with the way things look. On the other, you want to see things as they evolve, and being able to preview them with font changes already made is one good way to do this.

3. You can look at the effects of overall format changes in the document and also view changes in font appearance.

4. [Redln On] [Redln Off]; [Sm Cap On] [Sm Cap Off]; [Italic On] [Italic Off]; [Fine On] [Fine Off]; [Suprscpt On] [Suprscpt Off].

5. Fine is 60 percent of the size of the initial font and Large is 120 percent of the initial font's size. These are relative sizes based on the size of the initial font.

   The number of fonts is a function of the printer you are using with WordPerfect.

6. You may want to switch initial fonts for a particular project.

7. To change from upper- to lowercase or lower- to uppercase.

8. Yikes! Is that ever ugly!

Dressing Up Lines

Well, you've seen (and we hope learned) how to work with the size and appearance of text as well as different fonts. Although words are the most important part of a letter or a report, you also need to pay attention to the format of the entire document. That's where working with lines and pages comes in and that's what Chapter 9 is all about.

Once you combine what you learned about formatting text with formatting documents, you'll be ready to take on any task and present your words, sentences, paragraphs, and pages as very impressive finished documents. In this chapter you'll learn how to:

- ▲ **Set left and right margins**
- ▲ **Use different types of justification**
- ▲ **Space lines of text**
- ▲ **Set a tab**
- ▲ **Use different types of tabs**

Important Keys	Important Terms
Alt+F6	center justification
F4	double indent
Shift+F4	full justification
Shift+F6	full, all lines
Shift+F8	hanging indent
Shift+Tab	left justification
Tab	left indent
	Line Format dialog box
	Margin Format dialog box
	right justification
	tabs

Lesson 28: Working with Lines

A line of WordPerfect text consists of the characters (which make up words) that lie between the left and the right margins. Since the line is the basic unit of a page, WordPerfect offers a variety of different adjustments you can make to change the way that lines, and therefore the entire document, appear.

Many of the features discussed in this chapter are changed through the use of the **Shift+F8,1** key combination [Mouse Moves: Layout, Line], which produces the Line Format dialog box shown in Figure 9.1. This is also the screen that you will begin with for many of the features discussed in this chapter.

Setting Left and Right Margins

When you first start up WordPerfect, the left and the right margins are set to a default of one inch of space between the left-hand edge of the paper and where printing begins and one inch of space between the end of the line and the right-hand edge of the paper. You can confirm this by moving your cursor all the way to the left-hand margin (use the **Home**, ← key combination) and you will see the **Pos** marker in the lower right-hand corner read as 1 inch. If it does not, you are either not all the way over or you are working in units other than inches.

▼ *Figure 9.1.   The Line Format Dialog Box*

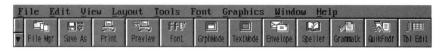

To change the left or the right margin settings (or both):

1. Use the **Shift+F8,2** key combination [Mouse Moves: **Layout, Margins**] to access the Margin Format dialog box you see in Figure 9.2.
2. Select **L**eft Margin (option 1) to change the value of the left margin and press the **Enter** key or click **OK**.
3. Select **R**ight Margin (option 2) to change the value of the right margin and press the **Enter** key or click **OK**.
4. Press the **F7** function key, record the changes, and return to document you are working on.

The amount of text that fits on a line depends on the margin settings and the font you are using. A larger font will allow less text on any one line than a smaller font, given the same margin settings.

In Figure 9.3, you can see two pages, both containing the same text. One has the left and right margins set at 1 inch and 1 inch, respectively. The one on the right has the margins set at 1 inch and 3 inches, respectively. You are, of course, not surprised to see that the smaller the margins (the less space between text and the paper edge), the less information fits on the page.

▼ *Figure 9.2.* *The Margin Format Dialog Box*

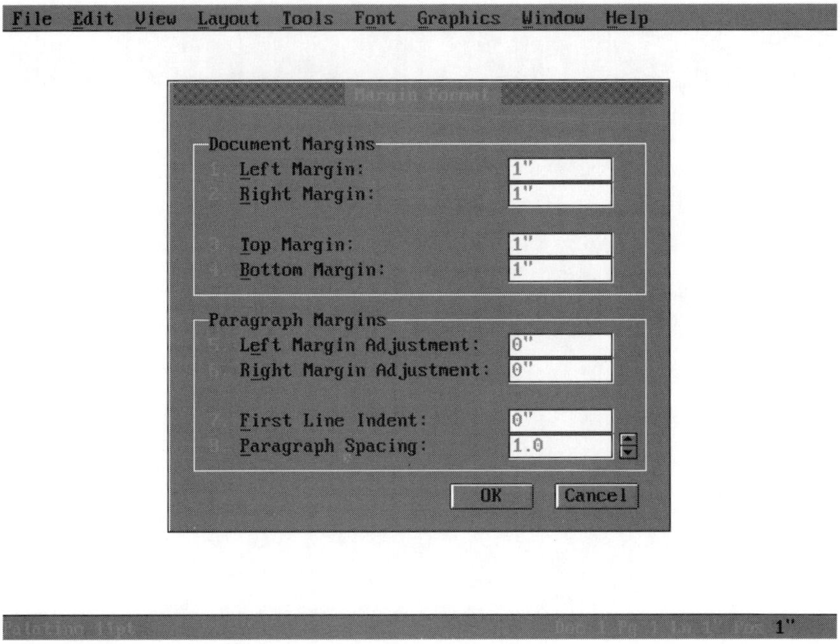

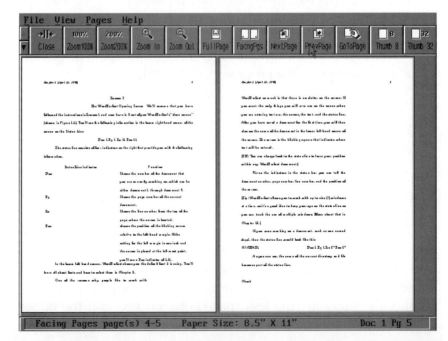

▼ *Figure 9.3.* *Using Different Margin Settings*

TIP

You can also change the top and bottom margin in the Margin Format dialog box. Just select the top or bottom margin and make the changes. More about this in Lesson 30.

Wherever the cursor is located in a document when you make changes in the left or right margin (or both of course), it's from that point on that the margins will be changed in the document.

TIP

Any margin change goes into effect where the reveal code is located and continues until another margin change is made.

Checking Your Margins

You can easily check the position of your margins in a document. The quickest way is to use the reveal codes key combination (**Alt+F3**) and look for the left and right margin indicators ({ }) on the line that separates the document window from the reveal codes window.

TIP

If you want to see the exact value of a margin setting, use the arrow keys and place the cursor on the reveal code. What looks like [Rgt Mar], for right margin, becomes [Rgt Mar: 3"], indicating the right margin setting is 3 inches.

Indenting Paragraphs

Almost anyone who writes needs to indent text at one point or another. The advantage to using WordPerfect and using indents is that you can insert an indent code into a document without worrying about changing the margin settings.

You can indent material in three ways :

▲ from the left margin (called a **left indent**)
▲ from the left and right margins (called a **double indent**)
▲ all lines but the first one indented from the left margin (called a **hanging indent**)

Using a Left Indent

A left indent indents all of the lines in a paragraph from the left margin.

To insert a left indent:

1. Place the cursor at the location where you want the indent to begin.
2. Press the **F4** function key [Mouse Moves: Layout, Alignment, Indent].
3. Enter the text you want indented.
4. Press the **Enter** key to return to the left margin setting.

TIP

You can also select any of the three types of indents before you enter a paragraph of text and the following paragraph will be indented.

For example, in Figure 9.4, you can see how the first paragraph has a left indent.

TIP

Remember that WordPerfect considers a paragraph to be any text that ends in a hard carriage return (or a [HRt] reveal code).

Using a Double Indent

A double indent indents all of the lines in a paragraph an equal distance from both the left and the right margins.

▼ *Figure 9.4.* *Different Types of Paragraph Indents*

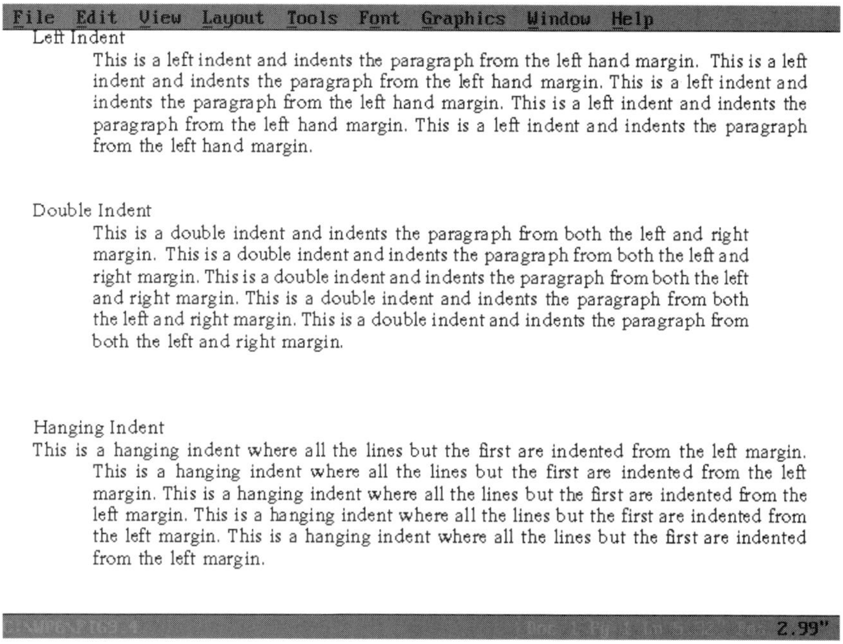

File   Edit   View   Layout   Tools   Font   Graphics   Window   Help

Left Indent
    This is a left indent and indents the paragraph from the left hand margin. This is a left
    indent and indents the paragraph from the left hand margin. This is a left indent and
    indents the paragraph from the left hand margin. This is a left indent and indents the
    paragraph from the left hand margin. This is a left indent and indents the paragraph
    from the left hand margin.

Double Indent
        This is a double indent and indents the paragraph from both the left and right
        margin. This is a double indent and indents the paragraph from both the left and
        right margin. This is a double indent and indents the paragraph from both the left
        and right margin. This is a double indent and indents the paragraph from both
        the left and right margin. This is a double indent and indents the paragraph from
        both the left and right margin.

Hanging Indent
This is a hanging indent where all the lines but the first are indented from the left margin.
    This is a hanging indent where all the lines but the first are indented from the left
    margin. This is a hanging indent where all the lines but the first are indented from the
    left margin. This is a hanging indent where all the lines but the first are indented from
    the left margin. This is a hanging indent where all the lines but the first are indented
    from the left margin.

2.99"

To insert a double indent:

1. Place the cursor at the location where you want the indent to begin.
2. Use the **Shift+F4** key combination [Mouse Moves: **L**ayout, **A**lignment, **I**ndent].
3. Enter the text you want indented.
4. Press the **Enter** key to return to the left margin setting.

For example, in Figure 9.4, you can see how the second paragraph has a double indent.

Using a Hanging Indent

A hanging indent indents all of the lines in a paragraph from the left margin, except for the first one, which remains aligned with the left margin.

To insert a hanging indent:

1. Place the cursor at the location where you want the indent to begin.

2. Press the **F4** function key and then the **Shift+Tab** key combination [Mouse Moves: Layout, **A**lignment, **H**anging].
3. Enter the text you want indented.
4. Press the **Enter** key to return to the left margin setting.

For example, in Figure 9.4, you can see how the third paragraph has a hanging indent.

Justifying Text

The text in this book is fully justified. *Justified* refers to the way that text aligns itself along the right and left margins. WordPerfect provides you with five different justification options, all of which are available in the Line Format dialog box. Figure 9.5 shows you the different types of justification.

You won't see the effects of justification on your monitor screen in Text mode, but you will in Graphics or Page mode. You can also use the Print Preview option in the File menu or print out a hard copy.

Left Justification aligns text along the left-hand margin and is sometimes called unjustified. **Center Justification** aligns each line of text an equal distance from the left and right margins. It's like using the **Shift+F6** key combination to center a line of text before it is entered or after it is blocked. **Right Justification** aligns text along the right-hand margins and is sometimes called ragged left. **Full Justification** aligns text along both the left and the right margins. **Full, All lines** will fully justify all the lines of text, even the last one (as you see in Figure 9.5).

When you use the **Shift+F8,1,2** key combination [Mouse Moves: Layout, **J**ustification], you can select the type of justification you want to use. As you can see in Figure 9.6, you make the selection you want under the justification option.

No matter where you place a justification code, WordPerfect will justify the entire paragraph of which it is a part, since WordPerfect automatically places such codes at the beginning of the paragraph. If you don't want WordPerfect to place codes automatically, you can turn this function off in the Setup (**Shift+F1**) window under Environment. The initial (or default) justification setting is full. If you do not change the justification setting, then all of your documents will be fully justified.

▼ *Figure 9.5.* *Different Types of Justification*

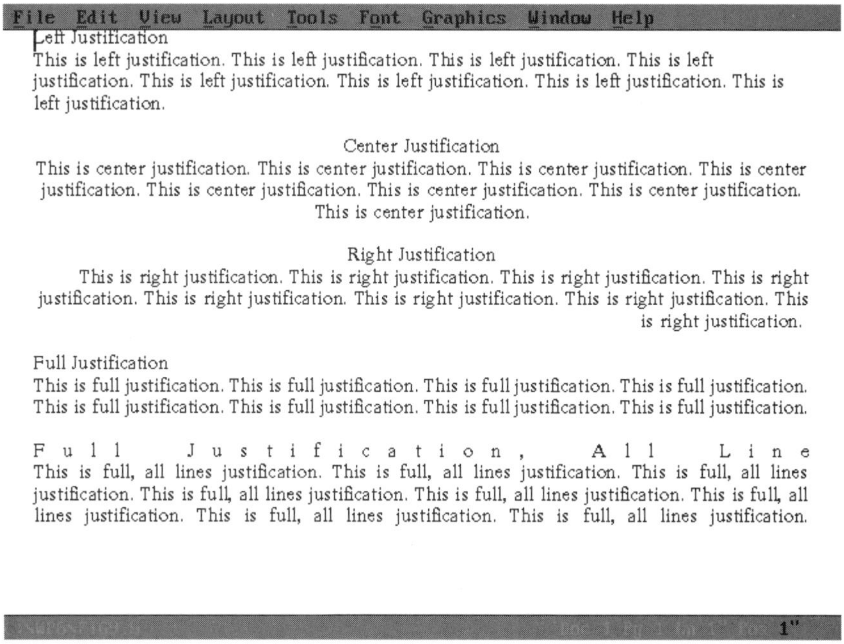

File Edit View Layout Tools Font Graphics Window Help
Left Justification
This is left justification. This is left justification. This is left justification. This is left
justification. This is left justification. This is left justification. This is left justification. This is
left justification.

Center Justification
This is center justification. This is center justification. This is center justification. This is center
justification. This is center justification. This is center justification. This is center justification.
This is center justification.

Right Justification
This is right justification. This is right justification. This is right justification. This is right
justification. This is right justification. This is right justification. This is right justification. This
is right justification.

Full Justification
This is full justification. This is full justification. This is full justification. This is full justification.
This is full justification. This is full justification. This is full justification. This is full justification.

F u l l   J u s t i f i c a t i o n ,   A l l   L i n e
This is full, all lines justification. This is full, all lines justification. This is full, all lines
justification. This is full, all lines justification. This is full, all lines justification. This is full, all
lines justification. This is full, all lines justification. This is full, all lines justification.

1"

▼ *Figure 9.6.* *Different Line Justification Options*

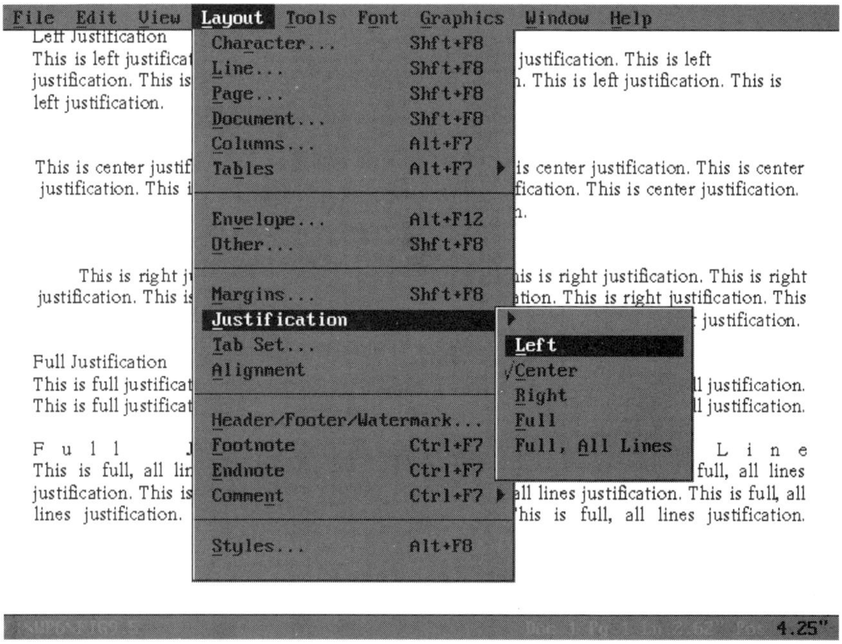

File Edit View **Layout** Tools Font Graphics Window Help
Left Justification   Character...   Shft+F8
This is left justifica| Line...   Shft+F8   justification. This is left
justification. This is| Page...   Shft+F8   n. This is left justification. This is
left justification.   Document...   Shft+F8
                       Columns...   Alt+F7
This is center justif| Tables   Alt+F7   ▶ is center justification. This is center
justification. This i| fication. This is center justification.

                       Envelope...   Alt+F12
                       Other...   Shft+F8

This is right ju| is is right justification. This is right
justification. This is| Margins...   Shft+F8   tion. This is right justification. This
                       Justification   ▶   t justification.
                       Tab Set...   **Left**
                       Alignment   √Center
Full Justification   Right   ll justification.
This is full justifica| Full   ll justification.
This is full justifica| Header/Footer/Watermark...
F u l l   J| Footnote   Ctrl+F7   **Full, All Lines**   L i n e
This is full, all lin| Endnote   Ctrl+F7   full, all lines
justification. This is| Comment   Ctrl+F7 ▶ all lines justification. This is full, all
lines justification.   his is full, all lines justification.

                       Styles...   Alt+F8

4.25"

Flush Right

If you want to align only one line of text against the right-hand margin, there is no need to use the Right Justification option. Just use the **Flush Right** (**Alt+F6** key combination) [Mouse Moves: **L**ayout, **A**lign, **F**lush Right]. The cursor will move to the right edge of the screen and as you enter text, it will move to the left. Flush right is perfect for entering text that is set apart, such as an author's name accompanying a quotation:

Nobody ever goes there anymore, it's too crowded.

Yogi Berra

The author's name is flush with the right-hand margin.

Spacing Lines

The last thing we'll learn is how to change the number of spaces between lines. WordPerfect is preset to no spaces between lines.

To change spacing:

1. Use the **Shift+F8,1,3** key combination [Mouse Moves: **L**ayout, **L**ine, **S**pacing].
2. Select Line **S**pacing.
3. Enter the number of spaces you want between the lines.

How big is a space? That depends on the size of the font you are using. WordPerfect will place the equivalent of one blank line of text between lines of text if line spacing is set at 1. If it is set at 2, it will place the equivalent of two, and so on.

Since WordPerfect allows you so much control and precision in your work, you can place two spaces between each line (called double spacing) or three, or four, or even two and one-half if that's what you need. Remember to use the Print Preview option before you print it so that you can see the effects that line spacing has on your document.

TIP

Reports, and especially documents that will be read by someone else, are double spaced.

Working with lines is the first step to formatting a document the way that you want it to appear. After you make any format changes, it's a good idea to use the **Alt+F3** key combination to check and see that the reveal codes are in place.

CHECK YOURSELF

▲ Enter the following text and do the following.

You can set margins, justify text in a variety of ways, and adjust line spacing as you need. You can set margins, justify text in a variety of ways, and adjust line spacing as you need. You can set margins, justify text in a variety of ways, and adjust line spacing as you need. You can set margins, justify text in a variety of ways, and adjust line spacing as you need.

   a. Set the margins to 1 and 2.75 inches.
   b. Right justify the text.
   c. Set the line spacing at two spaces between each line.
   d. Then right justify.

ANSWER

▲ Margins, line spacing, and justification are all related to one another in such a way that changing one can affect the impact that the other changes have as well.

Lesson 29: Working with Tabs

One time-saving feature that you'll find very valuable is **tabs**. These are settings that save time by allowing you to define positions along a WordPerfect line where you can stop every time by just the push of a key. When you press the **Tab** key, the cursor scoots over to this spot.

Tabs are extremely useful for accomplishing such word processing tasks as entering columns of text or figures in a way that the entries are neatly aligned (and can be imported to other applications). If it were not for tabs, you would have to use the space bar to continually space over to where you want your text to be entered. Using tabs, all you need to do is just press one key.

There are four different types of tabs that we'll discuss: left, decimal, center, and right. Let's discuss how tabs are set and then turn to each one of these with an example.

Setting a Tab

Once again, we're using the Line Format dialog box you see in Figure 9.1. Only this time, we use the **Shift+F8,1,1** key combination [Mouse Moves: **Layout, Line, Tab Set**] to produce the Tab Set dialog box you see in Figure 9.7.

Each of the *L*'s in Figure 9.7 represents a left tab setting. As you can see, a tab is set for every one-half inch. This is the WordPerfect

▼ *Figure 9.7.   The Tab Set Dialog Box*

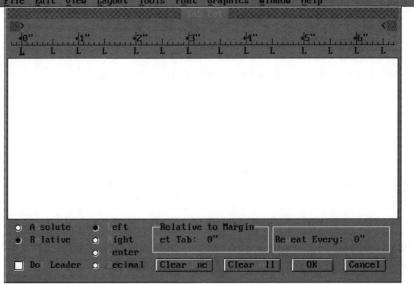

default setting for tabs. If you press the **Tab** key, the cursor will stop at each one-half inch all the way across the monitor screen and insert a [Tab] reveal code at each place the key is pressed.

To set a new tab, follow this one step: In the Tab Set dialog box, use the spacebar to move the cursor to the location where you want the new tab placed, and press the letter **L**.

To clear all the tabs and set new ones:

1. Press the **Shift+F8,1,1** key combination [Mouse Moves: Layout, Line, Tab Set].
2. Select Clear **A**ll to erase all the previous tab settings.
3. Use the → key to place the cursor in the location you want a tab to appear and press **L**.
4. Enter the value corresponding to the tab you want to set. This value can range from 0 inches to 54.5 inches.
6. Press **F7** to exit the Tab Set dialog box.
7. Press **F7** to return to the document.

Don't use a tab to indent for a paragraph. Instead, use the **F4** key to indent.

For example, in Figure 9.8, you can see where these steps were followed and the number 1.5 was entered so that a tab was set at one and one-half inches from the left margin. Each time that the Tab key is pressed (at the beginning of a new line), the cursor will move one and one-half inches to the right.

TIP

WordPerfect will also insert a tab code into your document where any tab changes begin. To return to the document after you set a tab, press the F7 key three times.

Setting Multiple Tabs

In Figure 9.8 you see how you can set a single tab that the cursor will move to each time the Tab key is pressed. You might, however, need to set more than one tab. For example, you might want to enter text every 1.25 inches beginning at 1.5 inches from the left margin.

▼ *Figure 9.8.* *Setting a New Tab*

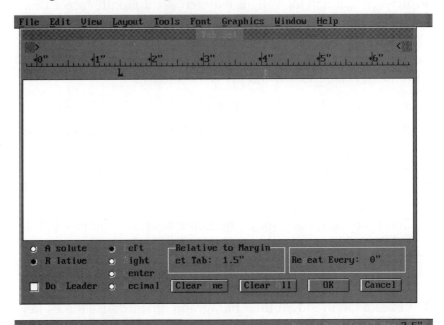

To set multiple tabs:

1. Press the **Shift+F8,1,1** key combination [Mouse Moves: **L**ayout, **L**ine, **T**ab Set].
2. Select **Clear All** to clear all the tabs in the Tab Set dialog box.
3. Select the **Set Tab** box.
4. Enter the value where you want the Tab setting to begin (1.5 in this example).
5. Select the **Repeat Entry** text box.
6. Enter the repeat value (1.25 in this example).
7. Press **F7** or **Enter**.

The completed Tab Set dialog box looks like the one shown in Figure 9.9.

Using Different Types of Tabs

You already know that WordPerfect offers you four different types of tabs. You saw in Figure 9.8 how WordPerfect placed an *L* to rep-

▼ *Figure 9.9.* *Tab Settings Beginning at 1.5 Inches and Appearing Every 1.25 Inches*

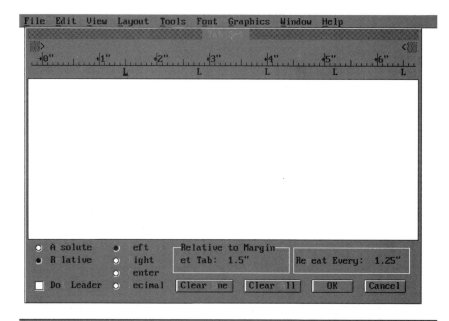

resent a left tab. The letter that corresponds to the type of tab you are using will appear on the Tab Ruler.

When you want to set a tab other than the default Left type of tab, just move to the position along the Tab Ruler where you want the tab set and enter the corresponding letter. For example, if you want a decimal tab at 2.25 inches, then place the cursor at 2.25 inches and press the **D** key.

The Left Tab (L)

When you use a left tab and begin typing, the text appears on the screen and moves one character at a time to the right of the tab position. For example, in Figure 9.10, the first tab setting is a left tab. The next character will appear to the right of that and so on.

▼ *Figure 9.10.* *Different Types of Tab Settings*

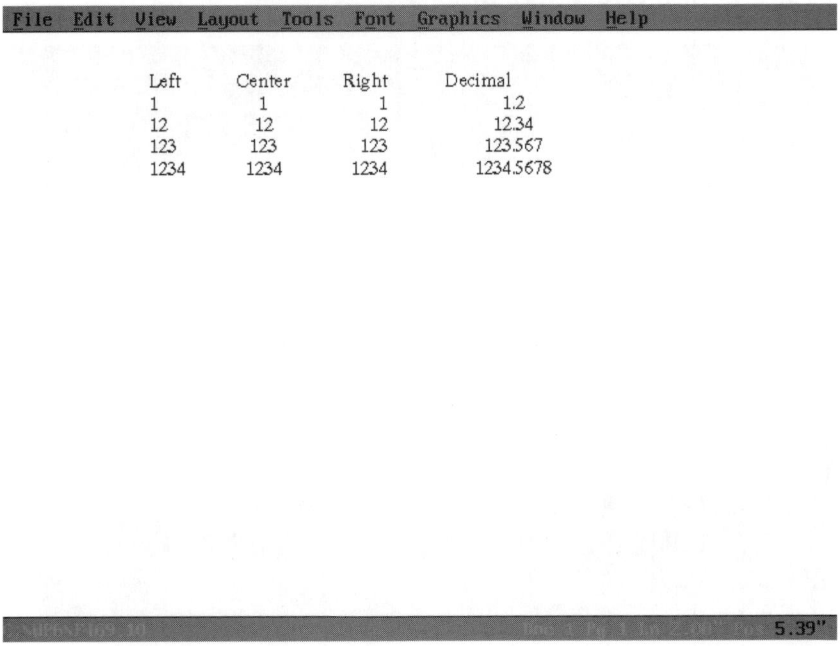

File	Edit	View	Layout	Tools	Font	Graphics	Window	Help

Left	Center	Right	Decimal
1	1	1	1.2
12	12	12	12.34
123	123	123	123.567
1234	1234	1234	1234.5678

5.39"

The Decimal Tab (D)

When you set a decimal tab and begin typing, the text appears to the left of the tab position until you press the decimal point. The information then appears to the right. This is the key to entering numerical information (such as dollars and cents) and keeping things neat. You can see in Figure 9.10 that the length of the value (number of decimal places) does not matter. WordPerfect will always align things along the decimal point (which is entered as a period, of course).

TIP

To change the character that the text aligns itself on from a period (.) to any other character, use the Shift+F8,6,1 **key combination and enter the new character you want to use in the Character Format dialog box.**

The Center Tab (C)

When a center tab is used, text is centered under the location of the tab setting as shown in Figure 9.10. It's just like using the **Shift+F6** key combination to center a line or block of text. The only difference is that this centering takes place each time you press the **Tab** key and only for the text located by that tab setting.

The Right Tab (R)

As the left tab aligns text to the left, the right tab aligns it to the right. As you type, you will see the text move to the left until you are finished.

TIP

The left margin setting is the point at which the first tab stop will be located. So, you can't have the place where the tabs begin to be less than that setting.

A Few Hints on Tabs

▲ A tab setting stays in force until you reset it. In other words, if you change to right tabs at two inches, that's what every tab setting that follows will be unless you change it otherwise.

▲ Don't use a tab if you want to indent a paragraph. Use the Indent (**F4**) function key instead. That way, you can reset tabs as needed and not worry about paragraph settings.

▲ To delete a set of tab setting, just place the cursor after the [Tab Set] reveal code and hit the **Backspace**. All the tab settings will be removed and if no others are present, the default will be in force.

▲ If you have special tabs (decimal or right) set and want to ignore those settings, use the **Home+Tab** key combination. WordPerfect will treat it as a regular left tab and enter characters to the right of the tab location.

CHECK YOURSELF

▲ Switch to a new document screen (the **F7,N,N** key combination will do it).
   a. Set three tabs at .75 inches beginning at inch 3.0.
   b. Set a decimal, right, and left tab at the three settings and enter the following text:
   12.38 boy girl
   123.80 boys girls
   1238.00 boys girls

ANSWER

▲ You don't have to use the (.) as the character on which the text aligns. WordPerfect allows you to designate any character in the decimal format, such as *, &, or #.

Now that you're familiar with making changes in text and lines, it's time to move on to bringing it all together in the formatting of pages. Words and lines all combine to create pages and in the next chapter you'll learn about using headers and footers, page numbering options, how to start a new page, and more.

PRACTICE WHAT YOU'VE LEARNED

1. What margin settings would you use for the following documents? Why?
   a. newsletter
   b. business letters
   c. term paper
2. Align the following set of numbers into three columns at 12, 24, and 36-column positions using left decimal.
   1,2,3
   12,23,34
   123,234,345
3. What are some examples where you would want to right justify text? Center text?
4. Enter the following paragraph:

This is the first time that I have used WordPerfect and I find that it fits my needs quite well. I have used other word processors before, but none this powerful.

Use the block and copy feature to copy the block over until a complete page of text is present. Set the left and right margins to two inches. Now print out a copy and see how these margin settings affect the format of the document.

5. Provide an example of when it is appropriate or desirable to single- or double-space lines in a document.

ANSWERS

1. The margin settings that you use depend on the type of material that you are including. The more graphics that are included, the more space you want on the borders so that graphics show up and work effectively.

2. 1   2   3
    12   24   36
    123   234   345

3. Right justify text in formal documents. Center text that are titles or for special effects, such as the last paragraph in a story.

5. Double spacing is most appropriate when a draft of a document or a manuscript is to be read by someone else (or even yourself). Single spacing should be used for final documents, including business letters, reports, etcetera or when space is a consideration.

10

Dressing Up Pages

Now that your text and lines are stunning(!), let's turn our attention to the final chapter on using WordPerfect format tools to enhance the appearance of your documents. This chapter deals with dressing up pages and working with such things as page numbers, adjusting page margins, using headers and footers, and more. When you finish the chapter, you'll be ready to make anything you want to say look as if it really says it! In this chapter you'll learn how to:

▲ **Begin a new page**

▲ **Use the various number pages options to set a new page number in a new style**

▲ **Center a page horizontally**

▲ **Create a header or footer**

▲ **Edit headers and footers**

▲ **Create and use document summaries and comments**

Important Keys	*Important Terms*
Ctrl+Enter	Create Paper Size/Type dialog box
Ctrl+Ins	Document Summary dialog box
Shift+F8	Header A dialog box
	Margin Format dialog box
	Page Format dialog box
	Page Number Position dialog box
	Page Format dialog box
	Page Numbering dialog box
	Paper Size/Type dialog box
	document comment
	document summary
	footer
	header
	page format
	paper size

Lesson 30: Working with Pages

Text, lines, paragraphs, and now pages. You've worked your way up and are doing a great job.

This chapter deals with the pages that make up your document. You already learned how WordPerfect recognizes a sentence (from period to period) and a paragraph (from [Hrt] to [HRt]). A page is defined by the margins you see at the top and the bottom of the document, which you learned to set in Lesson 28. WordPerfect assumes that you are using 8.5-inch by 11-inch paper.

Remember all the time we spent learning about Line and Margin options in the Format dialog box? As you saw in Figure 9.1, that dialog box allows us to work with Lines, Margins, Pages, and more. The **Shift**+**F8,2** key combination will provide you with options that allow you to work with the top and bottom margins in a page. Since the top and bottom margins are one of the most noticeable facets of page design, let's turn our attention to that feature.

To set the top and bottom margins of a document:

1. Use the **Shift**+**F8,2** key combination [Mouse Moves: **L**ayout, **M**argins] to get the Margin Format dialog box.

2. Select **T**op Margin (option 3).
3. Enter the new value for the top margin and press **Enter**.
4. Select **B**ottom Margin.
5. Press the **F7** function key to return to the document.

In WordPerfect you do not directly set the size of a page. Rather, the page is defined by the difference between the size of the paper that you set (more about that in a moment) and the top and bottom margins you define.

For example, if you define the top margin at 2 inches and the bottom one at 2 inches, then the printing area on your sheet will be 11 inches minus 4 inches (2 inches for each margin), for a total printing area of 7 inches by 8 inches (which is the width). For example, in Figure 10.1, you can see one page with the default top and bottom margin settings, and a second page one (on the right) with a 3-inch top and bottom margin setting. (We're showing you this in the Print Preview screen.) Notice that everything, even the header on the page on the right, starts three inches down from the top of the paper.

▼ **Figure 10.1. Two Different Pages with Different Top and Bottom Margin Settings**

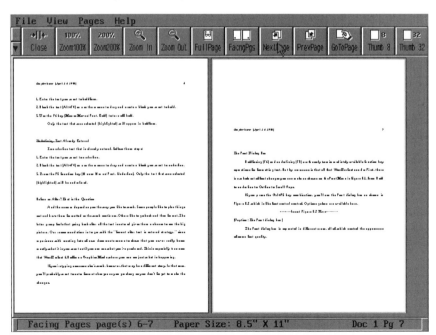

TIP

When you set margins, keep in mind that the size of the font that you use determines the height of a line and that will also contribute to how much text appears in a page.

Setting the Paper Size

The other part of how much fits on a page is the size of the paper that you use. That, in combination with the top and bottom margin settings, will determine the area of the page that is printed.

Paper Size is set through the Page Format dialog box you see in Figure 10.2. When you make that selection (**Shift+F8,3,4** or [Mouse Moves: **L**ayout, **P**age, Paper **S**ize]), you'll see the Paper Size/Type dialog box with the current paper size in use highlighted. It is here you can add new paper sizes.

▼ *Figure 10.2.* *The Paper Size / Type Dialog Box*

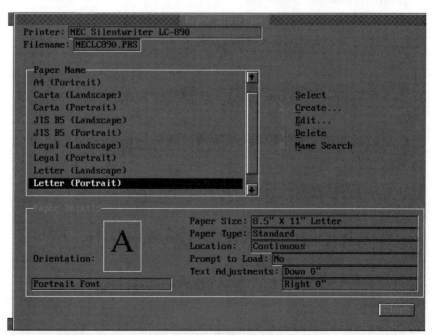

TIP

Use the Shift+F8,3,4 **key combination to set the paper size.**

To print envelopes and add that definition to your list:

1. Select the **Paper Size/Type** menu using the **Shift+F8,3,4** key combination [Mouse Moves: **L**ayout, **P**age, Paper **S**ize/Type].
2. Select **C**reate (option 2). When you do this, you will see the Create Paper Size/Type dialog box as shown in Figure 10.3.
3. Enter a new name for the paper size. In this example, it's *Envelope*.
4. Press **Enter**.
5. Select Paper **S**ize.
6. Select the size of paper you want to use. In this example, it's *Size 11 Envelope*.
7. Select **OK**.

The newly created paper size/type will be available in the Paper Size/Type dialog box to be selected when you need it.

▼ *Figure 10.3.   The Create Paper Size/Type Dialog Box*

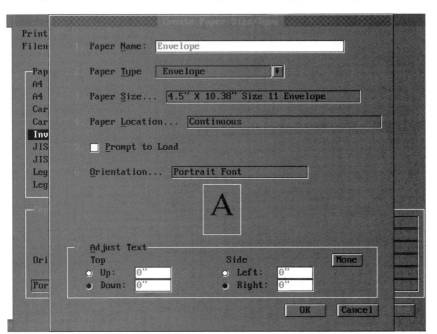

After you select the size, you may also want to consider other options in the Create Paper Size/Type dialog box. Here's what they do.

Paper Type refers to the kind of paper you will be using such as standard paper, envelopes, card stock, and so on.

Paper Size allows you to select one of the predefined sizes or design your own size.

Prompt to Load refers to whether you want WordPerfect to prompt you when you load this particular paper form. This may be the case when you are using single sheets of special paper and need to insert them one at a time.

Paper Location addresses where the paper is stored. Continuous means you are using a dot matrix printer with continuous forms.

TIP

If your laser printer offers multiple trays, use different paper types in different trays. You can then print drafts using paper in the lower tray and letters on your stationery from the upper tray.

Orientation allows you to select whether you want the print to appear along the horizontal or vertical edge of the paper.

The **Adjust Text** is used to move text up and down the page.

TIP

The Paper Size reveal code must be the first one on the page for WordPerfect to recognize the change.

Working with Page Numbers

Almost any document has the pages numbered. With Word-Perfect, you can make page numbers appear almost any way you want in anyplace on the page. Let's explore these possibilities.

Starting a New Page

You're writing a report that has five separate parts. You shouldn't be surprised when you find that the last page of Chapter 2 is only one-half page long. Do you start Chapter 3 in the middle of that page? Of course not. You need to go to the top of the next page. One way to do that is just to repeatedly hit the **Enter** key until you get to the top of the next page.

Another way (and the right way we might add) is to use the **Ctrl+Enter** or **Ctrl+Ins** key combination, which inserts a solid double line like this, ═══on your screen and starts you at the top of a new page. This is called a **hard page break** and should be used whenever you want to begin a new page.

Numbering Pages

WordPerfect will not assign a page number to a page unless you tell it to do so. Unlike other word processors, the default for WordPerfect is no page numbers. But if you decide to use page numbers, you have a wide choice of where the page number will be located and how it will appear.

Location of Page Numbers To work with page numbers, you need to begin with the Page Numbering dialog box shown in Figure 10.4 using the **Shift+F8,3,1** [Mouse Moves: **L**ayout, **P**age, Page **N**umbering] key combination.

Here, you can control the following attributes of page numbers.

To control where a page number will be located on any one page, select Page Number **P**osition (option 1). When you do this, you will see the Page Number Position dialog box shown in Figure 10.5 showing you the various locations where you can locate the page number. Just enter the choice, and the page number will appear on each page in that location.

For example, if you select option 3, then each page will be numbered in the upper right-hand corner. If you select option 4, then on the even pages the page number will be placed in the upper left-hand corner and on the odd pages it will be placed in the upper right-hand corner (like the numbering you see in many books). The page numbers will appear in the same font and size as the rest of the text. Now on to other options in the Page Numbering dialog box.

▼ *Figure 10.4. The Page Numbering Dialog Box*

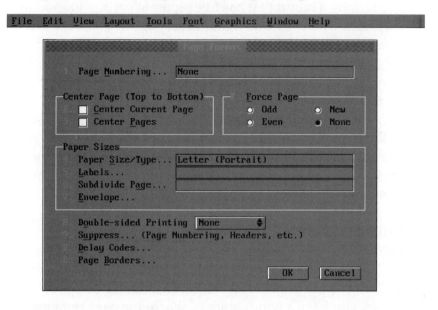

▼ *Figure 10.5. The Page Number Position Dialog Box*

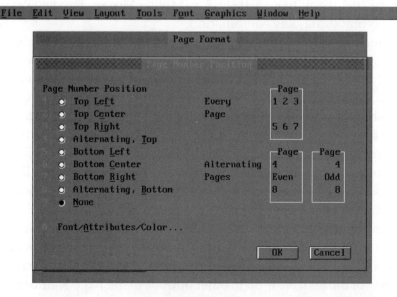

Assigning a New Page Number   Now, why would you have to start a document with page 5, 52, or 71 rather than page 1? Don't they all start with the number 1? Most of the time. But, what if your assignment is Chapter 4, which starts with page 52?

When you select Page Number (option 2) in the Page Numbering dialog box (and you see the Set Page Number dialog box as shown in Figure 10.6) you can assign any page number that you want (**New Number**) and WordPerfect will begin numbering starting with that page number. Keep in mind that starting with a new page number is not enough to make page numbers appear. You have to tell WordPerfect *where* you want the page numbers to appear as we just discussed.

It's also here in **Numbering Method** where you can indicate whether you want page numbers printed in upper- or lowercase Roman numerals (i, ii, iv, viii or I, II, IV, VIII) or numbers (1, 2, 4, 8) or upper or lower levels (A, B, C or a, b, c). Arabic numerals (called *Numbers* in WordPerfect) are the default. Roman numerals are often used for what's called front matter (such as a table of contents, dedication, etc.). If you want all of the numbers in the document to appear as Roman numerals, then you must set this right at the be-

Lesson 30:
Working
with Pages

▼ **Figure 10.6.   The Set Page Number Dialog Box**

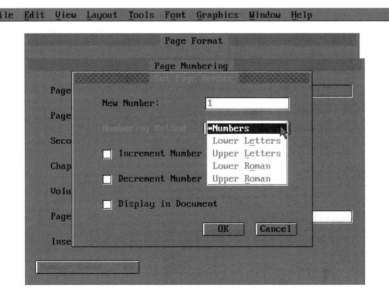

ginning of your document. When you set the new page number, you either use Arabic or Roman numerals.

Inserting a Page Number

Want a page number quick? Just use the **Shift+F8,3,1,7** key combination and the actual page number of the document (as you defined it or the Arabic default) will appear in your document.

When the Formatted Page Number (which looks like this [Formatted Pg Num]) reveal code is inserted into a document, whatever the current page is (check the status line) will appear when the document is printed.

TIP

Use the Formatted Page Number feature to add the current page number to a header.

Page Numbering Styles

WordPerfect will see to it that the page number will be printed if you give it a location. A nice touch, however, is some additional text to accompany just the page number. For example, you might want the number on page 47 to appear as *Page 47* or *-Page 47-* or *Page -47-* or even • • 47 • •.

To add something (anything you can type) to a page number, select Page Number **F**ormat (option 6) in the Page Numbering dialog box, and enter the text you want to use with the page number, then press **Enter**. WordPerfect will automatically enter the code for the page number. In Figure 10.7 (this is the Page Preview view at 200%) you can see how the page is formatted to appear as This is [Page #1]. You can see how this is specified in the Page Numbering dialog box in Figure 10.8.

Centering Pages Top to Bottom

Almost everything begins with a title page. And title pages are usually centered both from the left and right margins as well as from the top and bottom margins. Instead of fooling around with counting lines and trying out different top and bottom margin settings, WordPerfect allows you to center horizontally the contents of any one page.

Lesson 30: Working with Pages

▼ *Figure 10.7. Using the Page Number Format Feature to Assign Text with a Page Number*

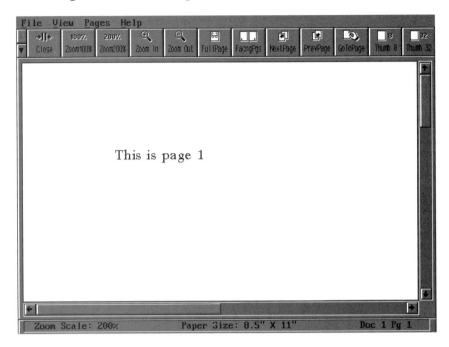

▼ *Figure 10.8. Text Along with a Page Number*

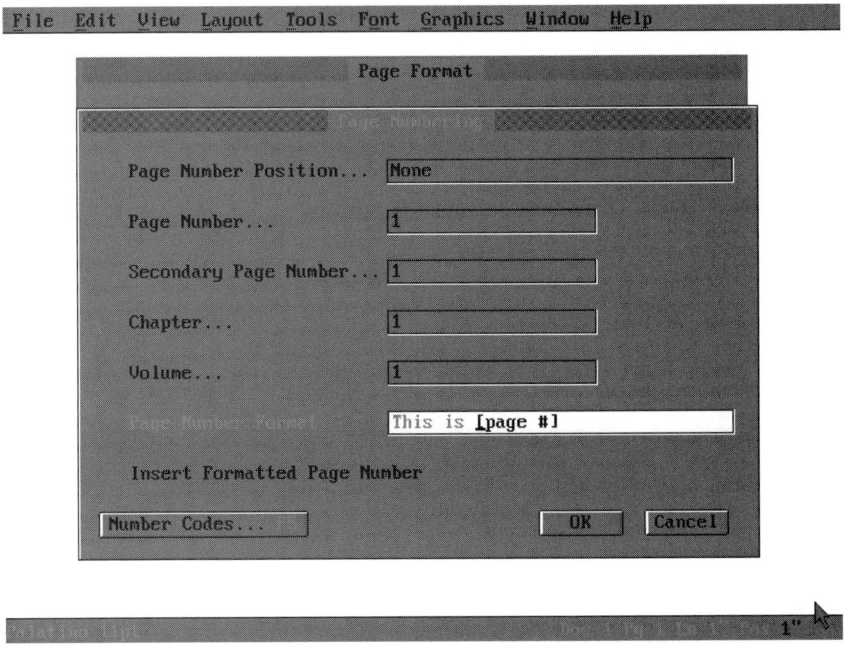

To center the current page horizontally:

1. Place the cursor at the beginning of the page you want to center.
2. Use the **Shift+F8,3,2** key combination [Mouse Moves: Layout, Page, Center Current Page] and respond **Yes** to the prompt.

TIP

If you want to center the text on all pages, select Center Pages (option 3) in the Page Format dialog box.

All of the text on the page will be centered from the top and bottom margins. If you want to center the text horizontally, equal distance from the margins, create a block and then use the **Shift+F6** key combination to center the lines.

CHECK YOURSELF

1. Set the paper size for an index card (3 inches by 5 inches). Now enter more text than can fit in the size you defined. What happens?
2. What is the exact set of keystrokes you would use to start numbering pages, beginning with the Roman numeral xii?

ANSWERS

1. WordPerfect will go on to another page the exact same size as you defined and begin to enter text there.
2. Shift+F8,3,1,2,2,0,1,12,F7,F7,F7,F7,F7

Lesson 31: Creating Headers and Footers

Headers and Footers are user-defined text that are exactly alike except for one thing. **Headers** appear at the top of a document and **Footers** appear at the bottom. In both cases, they allow you to add information to a document, and you can even sneak in some very creative ideas like page numbers or graphics.

Creating a Header or Footer

Headers and footers are created through the Format dialog box that you originally saw in Figure 9.1. Since headers and footers are created and edited the same way, we'll create a header as an example. You create a footer using the same steps.

To create a simple header:

1. Use the **Shift+F8,5,1** key combination [Mouse Moves: Layout, Header/Footer, Watermark, Headers]. When you do this, WordPerfect will ask you whether the header you are about to create will be Header A or Header B.
2. Select option 1 in the dialog box for header and then select option 1 or A for Header A. You'll see the Header A dialog box shown in Figure 10.9.

▼ *Figure 10.9. The Header A Dialog Box*

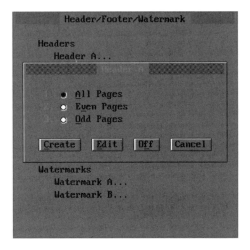

3. Now you have to select the frequency with which you want the header to appear from the Header A dialog box.

   All Pages (option 1) will print a header on every page.

   Even Pages (option 2) will print the header on only even-numbered pages.

   Odd Pages (option 3) will print the header on only odd-numbered pages.

   For this example, we'll select option 1 so the header prints on every page. Select **A**ll pages.

4. Press **Enter**. When you do this, you see a window that looks much like any WordPerfect window except that in the lower left-hand corner, you can tell it is a Header A window. This is the window in which you will create the header.

5. Enter the text as you would like it to appear in the header. As with any other text, you can format it any way you want.

6. Press the **F7** function key to return to your WordPerfect document.

Once you're out of the Header screen, the header is then ready to appear on whatever pages you've decided.

WordPerfect allows you to put two headers or two footers on each page. Keep in mind that if you want multiple headers or footers, you have to leave room for each of them, otherwise they'll run into each other.

TIP

Make headers and footers smaller than the text, by about 20 percent. For example, 10-point text should have 8-point headers and footers. Otherwise, the header or footer information takes on the same degree of importance as the text.

You can see in Figure 10.10 how a header appears when complete (we're in the Page mode). You may also notice that we incorporated a page number into the header, an extremely helpful piece of information. Here's how we added it.

Lesson 31: Creating Headers and Footers

▼ Figure 10.10. A Sample Header with the Current Page Number Inserted

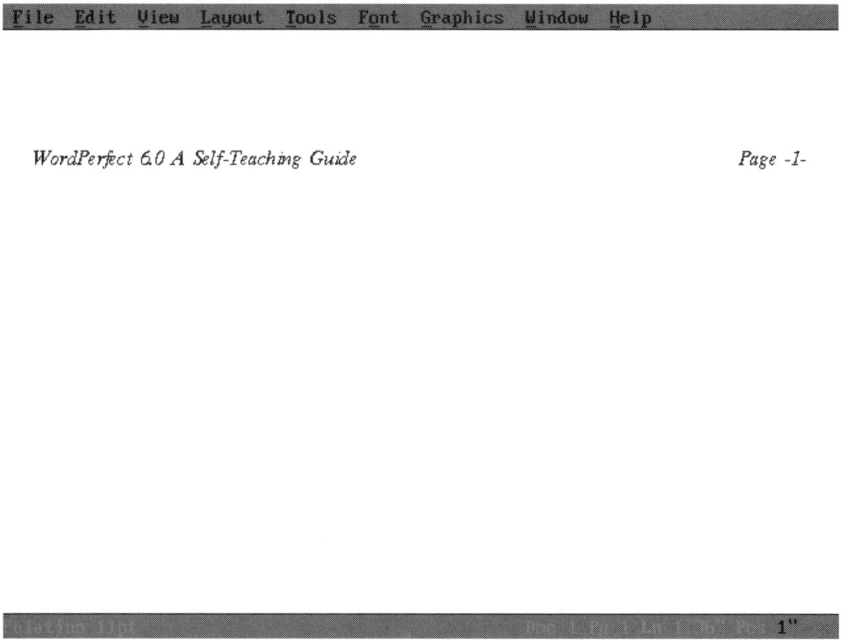
File Edit View Layout Tools Font Graphics Window Help
WordPerfect 6.0 A Self-Teaching Guide
Page -1-

Inserting Page Numbers into Headers

One nice time-saving trick is to insert the page number in a header by using the Page Number format option in the Page Numbering dialog box you see in Figure 10.8.

To create a header, if you are on page 34, that looks something like this:

WordPerfect 6.0: A Self-Teaching Guide Page -34-

1. Use the **Shift+F8,5,1,1, Enter** key combination [Mouse Moves: **L**ayout, **H**eader/Footer, **Watermark**, **H**eaders, **A**ll Pages, **Enter**] to get to the header screen.
2. Enter text *WordPerfect 6.0: A Self-Teaching Guide.*
3. Use the **Alt+F6** key combination to move to the right margin and enter the page number.
4. Enter the text **Page -**.
5. Use the **Shift+F8,3,1,7** key combination to insert a page number in the header.

6. Enter the text -.
7. Press **F7** until you return to your document. The header, as it was created, is shown in Figure 10.10.

Special Headers

You can do all kinds of neat things with headers, including placing WordPerfect graphics in them. Even though you won't be learning about graphics until Chapter 19, we thought it would be fun for you to see what you can do.

For example, in Figure 10.11, here's the same header as in Figure 10.10 with a graphic line running below it. Makes for a nice touch.

You can do even better by actually inserting a graphic into a header, perhaps your company logo. We'll do that later in Lesson 50.

Editing Headers and Footers

You might have noticed in the Header A dialog box (in Figure 10.9) is the option for editing a header. When you make this selection,

▼ **Figure 10.11.   A Header with a Graphic Line Added**

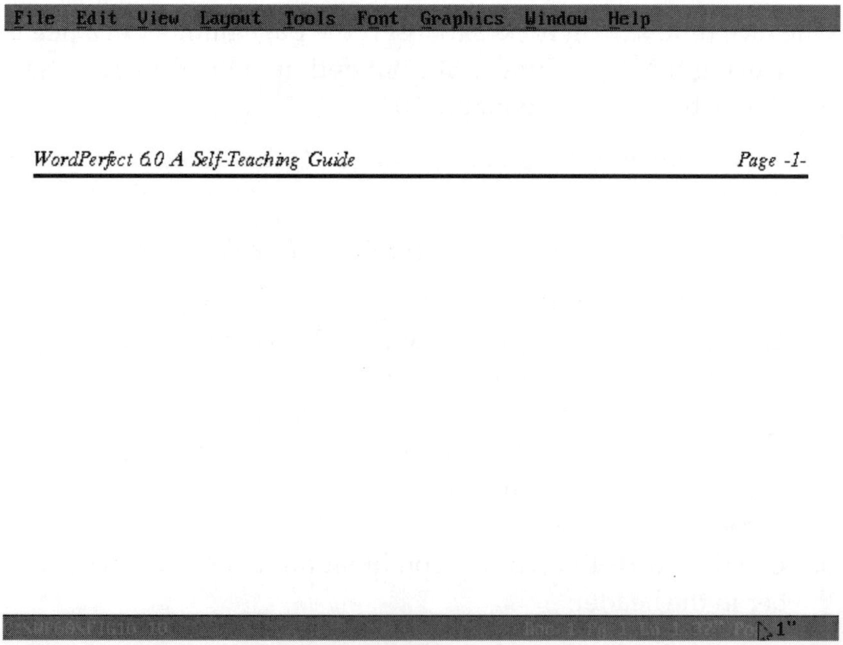

File   Edit   View   Layout   Tools   Font   Graphics   Window   Help

WordPerfect 6.0 A Self-Teaching Guide   *Page -1-*

WordPerfect will place you back into the same header window you used to create the header in the first place. You will see the contents of the header, and you edit as you would any other WordPerfect document. Press **F7** to get back to the original document, and rest assured that whatever changes you made are now part of the header.

CHECK YOURSELF

1. Create the following header to appear on every page. The * represents the current page.
    WordPerfect 6.0: A Self-Teaching Guide Chapter 17, Page *
    What will the header show when the document is printed?
2. Create the following footer in a new document.
    Footer A
        Now Edit the footer using the Edit option discussed in this lesson to read as follows: The * represents the current page.
    Footer A (Page *)

ANSWERS

1. WordPerfect 6.0: A Self-Teaching Guide Chapter 17, (the current page number)
2. You go through the same process to create a footer as you do a header.

Lesson 32: Summarizing Documents

Now that we're done with most of the changes to be made in words, lines, and pages, let's finish up with the WordPerfect feature that allows you to insert comments on a manuscript (like those little yellow post notes) and also produce a document summary so that important information about the document is available to you and anyone else who might need to work with it.

Creating a Document Comment

You're zipping along, and you get to a point where you have to check whether the abbreviation for *Maine* is *MA* or *ME*. You could place a note in the text itself, such as ****look for state abbreviation****, but that would become part of the printed document. You don't want that. Instead, you create a document comment that will appear on-screen but will not be printed.

To create a document comment:

1. At any location in the text, use the **Ctrl+F7,2,1** key combination [Mouse Moves: **L**ayout, Co**m**ment, **C**reate] and you'll see a new WordPerfect window with *Comment: Press F7 when done* in the lower left-hand corner of the status line.

TIP

Use the Ctrl+F7,2 **key combination to create a document comment.**

2. Enter whatever text you want to include in the comment.
3. Press the **F7** key and the comment is inserted. Figure 10.12 shows you how a comment is inserted and appears on-screen.

TIP

Because comments you create will not appear in a document when it is printed, you will not see comments on the Print Preview screen.

You can enter as many document comments as you like. Each time you enter one, a [Comment] code will appear as a reveal code. The only drawback to comments is that the screen can become filled up with these comments. But if you don't mind, it's a great way to remind yourself of what you may otherwise forget.

TIP

If you want to get rid of the comment, just delete the reveal code.

▼ *Figure 10.12.   A Comment Inserted in Text*

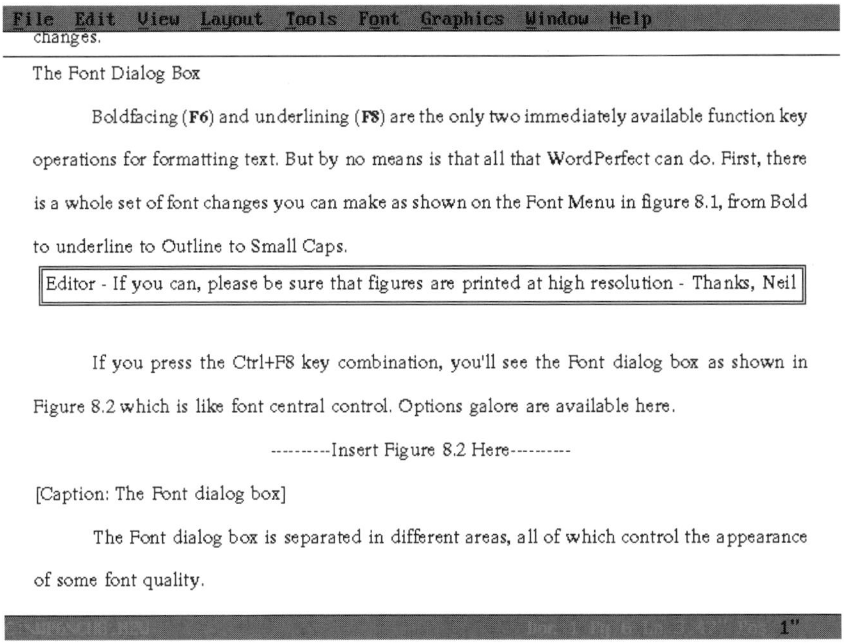

File   Edit   View   Layout   Tools   Font   Graphics   Window   Help

changes.

The Font Dialog Box

Boldfacing (**F6**) and underlining (**F8**) are the only two immediately available function key operations for formatting text. But by no means is that all that WordPerfect can do. First, there is a whole set of font changes you can make as shown on the Font Menu in figure 8.1, from Bold to underline to Outline to Small Caps.

Editor - If you can, please be sure that figures are printed at high resolution - Thanks, Neil

If you press the Ctrl+F8 key combination, you'll see the Font dialog box as shown in Figure 8.2 which is like font central control. Options galore are available here.

----------Insert Figure 8.2 Here----------

[Caption: The Font dialog box]

The Font dialog box is separated in different areas, all of which control the appearance of some font quality.

1"

Creating a Document Summary

Document summaries provide important information for whomever will be seeing the document at a later point in time and helps you organize and locate documents. They are a part of the document, just as normal text is, but don't appear on the document screen.

To use the Summary option:

1. Use the **Shift+F8,4,4** key combination [Mouse Moves: Layout, Document, Summary] to produce the Document Summary dialog box you see in Figure 10.13.
2. Fill in the information that is relevant to the document such as the date it was revised, a descriptive name, and so on. You can move from field to field using the mouse or Tab key.
3. Press the **F7** function key until you return to the original document.

Anytime you want to see the summary, from anywhere in the document, use the **Shift+F8,4,4** key and you'll see it on the screen.

▼ *Figure 10.13.* *The Document Summary Dialog Box*

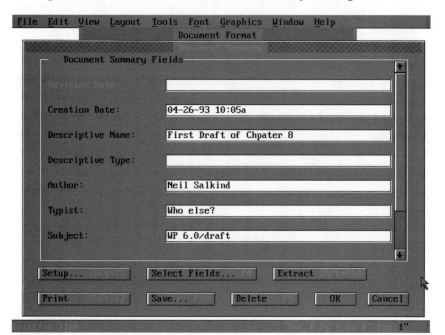

TIP

To delete a document summary, retrieve the summary to see it and then select Delete **or press the** F9 **key.**

CHECK YOURSELF

▲ Insert a document comment into an existing page and print that page (**Shift+F7,2**). Why doesn't the comment show on the hard copy as it does on the screen?

ANSWER

▲ Comments do not show on printed copies, which makes them excellent for notes for other people to read.

Finally! The pages look beautiful. Now we can move on to checking the content of our documents using the spell checker and the thesaurus. While they are no substitute for being able to spell and for understanding the difference between a synonym and a homonym, both are invaluable for helping you produce professional documents.

Lesson 32:
Summarizing
Documents

PRACTICE WHAT YOU'VE LEARNED

1. Design the title page of a report and center the entire page.
2. If you have more than one header (or more than one footer) on the same page, what must you be particularly careful of?
3. Provide an example of a situation where you would use both Roman and Arabic numerals.
4. Enter a paragraph of text and then copy and paste it until you have a full page of text.
   a. Set the top and bottom margins at 2 inches.
   b. Assign the page number 45 in the center top position.
   c. Print out the page.
5. Provide three examples of how a graphic can be used in a header.

ANSWERS

1. Most document title pages are centered vertically.
2. That they do not overlap one another.
3. The front matter of a book, Roman numerals (such as i, iv, etc.) are used. In the text of the book, Arabic numbers are used.
4. Take one operation at a time and use the Print Preview feature to check as you go.
5. As the header itself, as a centered part of a header, or as a focal point for the header that accompanies text.

Spell Checker and Thesaurus

Enuff bad speling can ruin yur day. Maybe your spelling skills are not that bad, but no matter. Everyone needs a little spell check once in a while, and WordPerfect offers you the perfect tool to help correct the type of spelling errors you see in the first sentence in this paragraph.

WordPerfect also offers a built-in thesaurus, a dictionary of words that have the same meaning (synonyms) and words that have the opposite meaning (antonyms), right at your fingertips. Both of these tools alone won't qualify you for a National Book Club Award, but they will help you hand in reports and papers that are not filled with needless spelling mistakes. In this chapter you'll learn how to:

- ▲ Understand what the spell checker can and cannot do
- ▲ Start the WordPerfect spell checker
- ▲ Check words, pages, and documents
- ▲ Check spelling from floppy disks
- ▲ Use the thesaurus
- ▲ Find the right word even without a document!

Important Keys	Important Terms
Alt+F1	common word list
Ctrl+F2	head word
	Irregular Case dialog box
	main dictionary
	main word list
	Speller dialog box
	thesaurus
	Thesaurus dialog box
	Word Not Found dialog box
	Writing Tools dialog box

Lesson 33: Using the Spell Checker

How the Spell Checker Works

When you ask WordPerfect to spell check a document, it stops at every single word in the document and compares each of the words to the set contained in the WordPerfect main dictionary.

This one file contains 200,000 words (yikes!), divided into two different lists. The first list that WordPerfect checks is the **common word list**. If it cannot find the word there, then it switches over to the **main word list**. WordPerfect continues to check each word in the entire document and provides you with several options should a match not be available in the dictionary. Let's turn to those options now since they are the heart of the WordPerfect spell check system.

Before we begin, a few important words of caution. The WordPerfect spell checker really doesn't check your spelling as much as it does your typing. For example, if you enter the phrase *Their are too* instead of *There are two*, WordPerfect would give you an *A* in spelling but you would flunk freshman English. The lesson? Don't rely on WordPerfect to tell you what forms of homophones (words that sound the same but have a different meaning like *too, to,* and *two*) to use. Also, WordPerfect will not stop to check one-character words such as *a*.

Checking Words, Pages, and Documents

You can check the spelling of an individual word, a page, or an entire document or even from the location of the cursor to the end of a document. You begin by using the **Ctrl+F2** key combination [Mouse Moves: Select **T**ools, **W**riting Tools, **S**peller] and you'll see the Speller dialog box shown in Figure 11.1.

TIP

For you to check the spelling of a document, the document must first be active (on your screen).

To check spelling:

1. Decide on what you want to check.

    If you want to check an individual word, place the cursor on the word or on the space that follows the word.

▼ *Figure 11.1.   The Speller Dialog Box*

File Edit View Layout Tools Font Graphics Window Help

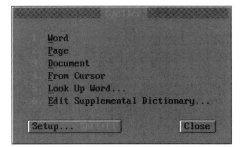

If you want to check the current page, place the cursor on that page.

If you want to check the entire document, place the cursor anywhere in the document.

TIP

The Alt+F1 **key combination will also take you to the Writing Tools dialog box from which you can access the Speller.**

2. Now that you've placed your cursor in the appropriate place, use the **Ctrl+F2** key combination to produce the beginning spell check screen shown in Figure 11.1.

Depending on what you want to check (word, page, or document), select the appropriate option (1, 2, or 3).

3. Make the appropriate selection. You'll see a ***Please Wait*** message in the center of the WordPerfect window, telling you that WordPerfect is working. Although this is a very fast spell checker, give it some time to get started. Long and complex documents take time to check.

4. WordPerfect will then stop on each word in the text that it does not recognize. For example, in Figure 11.2, you can see how WordPerfect stopped on the word *Enuff*. WordPerfect highlights it and then lists all the possible options in the word lists contained in the dictionary. In this example, WordPerfect has the correct suggestion, *enough*.

Other Options

When WordPerfect stops and offers you alternatives, your first course of action is to see if the correct spelling is among those listed. If so, press the letter that corresponds to the correct spelling and the selected word will be inserted in the document. The incorrect spelling will automatically be deleted. In Figure 11.2, pressing the letter **A** would substitute the word *enough* for the word *enuff* in the document.

Once you make a selection, WordPerfect will not stop again on that same misspelling should it occur again. Instead WordPerfect will recognize the misspelling and automatically correct it.

▼ *Figure 11.2.* *Starting the Speller*

Enuff bad spelling can ruin yur day.

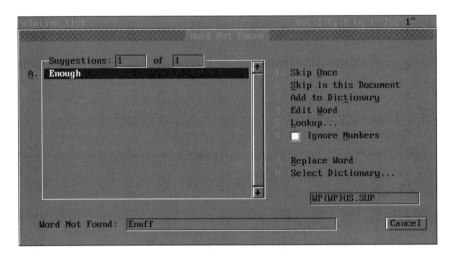

If the word you need is not in the Suggestions box, you'll have to edit the word. Let's look at that, and other options right now.

As you can see in Figure 11.2, WordPerfect offers you eight options during a spell check.

Skip Once (option 1)—skips the particular word only once. This should be used when you want to skip a word that is spelled correctly but is not recognized, such as a proper noun like a name. The next time WordPerfect encounters this word, it will stop once again.

Skip in this Document (option 2) tells WordPerfect not to stop on this word again throughout the entire document. Every time that the Speller encounters the word, it will not stop.

Add to Dictionary (option 3) tells WordPerfect to take this unrecognized word and add it to the supplemental dictionary that WordPerfect has already created. Now's the time to add words that you may use on a regular basis but do not appear in WordPerfect's main dictionary. For example, if you are studying a particular discipline that has its own jargon, or misspell an unrecognized word consistently, you want to add those to your spell checking tool chest. Another good candidate to be added are those proper nouns that WordPerfect will no longer have to stop on.

Edit Word (option 4) allows you to turn off the spell checker until you get a chance to correct the word through editing from the keyboard. When you select this option, you'll see:

```
Editing Misspelled Word: Press F7 or Enter to Exit
```

on your WordPerfect screen. Edit the word as you need to and press the **F7** key and you'll be returned to the Word Not Found dialog box. You will have to decide what you want to do with the word (Skip Once, etc.).

When you are in the Edit mode, you can use the left and right arrow keys to move from one line to the next and to other parts of the document, even if WordPerfect did not stop there to check. You cannot use the up and down arrows to move around the document.

Lookup (option 5) shows you why WordPerfect is so understanding! It not only helps you correct spelling errors when you make them but allows you to ask for WordPerfect's help when you try to find out how to spell a particular word. When you select this option, WordPerfect displays the prompt:

```
Word or Word pattern:
```

on your screen.

WordPerfect is asking you to enter the word you want to spell (as best you can). WordPerfect will then do its best to find as many close matches as are in the dictionary and allow you to select the one you might want to use. You still have to make the final decision, but at least you have some good solid clues to go on.

All well and good, but how are you supposed to approximate the spelling of a word that you can't spell? WordPerfect to the rescue again. Do the best you can and include a question mark (?) to substitute for a letter you are not sure of and an asterisk (*) to substitute for more than one letter.

For example, if you enter the word pattern *t?n*, WordPerfect will show you *tin*, *ton*, *ten* and *tanzanian*! If you enter *t*n*, then WordPerfect will show you all the words that start with the letter *t* and end with the letter *n*, such as *tin*, *ton*, and *ten*, but also *tatterdemalion*, *terpsichorean*, and *tetrabromophenolphthalein*. Yep, they're all there.

TIP

You can always use the Look Up option with a blank screen and just enter the word as best you can. That way you can get help on spelling words not necessarily in the context of a paper or a report.

Ignore Numbers (option 6) does just that. Every time WordPerfect stops for a word that contains a number (such as Room 6A or 123 Main Street), it skips on to the next unmatched word. For example, it makes no sense to check the spelling of all the zip codes in a mailing list. Even if they are wrong, WordPerfect won't be able to tell you anyway.

Replace Word (option 7) will have WordPerfect replace the highlighted word in the document with the suggestion that WordPerfect thinks best fits. Or you can just select the letter of the word (or click on it using the mouse) that you want to substitute.

Select Dictionary (option 8) allows you to select from a specific dictionary you create or one that is prepared by some commercial company and focuses on medical or legal terminology. You can create as many dictionaries as you like.

TIP

WordPerfect automatically checks headers and footers in a document as it checks through the text, but it does not check comments.

Checking Blocks

To check the spelling of the words in a block of text:

1. Block the text you want to spell check.
2. Press the **Ctrl+F2** key combination [**Mouse Moves:** Select **T**ools, **W**riting Tools, **S**peller].

WordPerfect will then begin to check the spelling in the selected text and offer you the same six options that it would if you were checking the entire document.

Double Words and Irregular Cases

WordPerfect has two other special sets of options it will show you in two particular circumstances. The first set is for when you have entered a double word such as in the sentence:

    This is the the one that has the only attach-
ment of its kind.

When WordPerfect recognizes this occurrence, it shows you the Duplicate Word Found dialog box shown in Figure 11.3.

In this dialog box, Options 1 and 2 cause WordPerfect to skip the double word in the document and make no corrections. For example, you might have created columns with entries such as

1 1 2 3 3 2
3 2 2 2 3 3

WordPerfect would stop on the first set of 1's.

TIP

WordPerfect recognizes doubles only when they are separated by spaces. If you use tabs, WordPerfect doesn't recognize the two as being the same.

Option 3 deletes the second entry.
Option 4 allows you to edit the entry.

▼ *Figure 11.3.   The Duplicate Word Dialog Box*

to

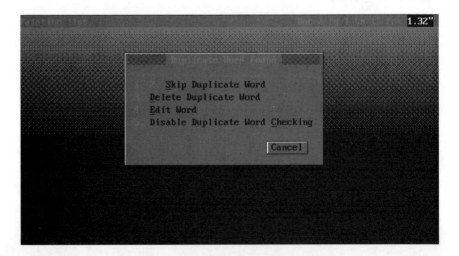

Option 5 disables WordPerfect's checking of double words for the rest of the spell check operation.

The second set of options is when you make what WordPerfect thinks is a capitalization error. WordPerfect shows you the Irregular Case dialog box shown in Figure 11.4 and checks for five kinds of errors.

FAt instead of fat
fAt instead of Fat
fAT instead of Fat
faT instead of Fat
iS instead of Is (only for two-letter words)

When WordPerfect encounters an irregular case (such as what you see in the first part of the preceding examples), it prompts you with the options in the dialog box shown in Figure 11.4.

These are very similar to the options we just described in the case of double words appearing. When you find an irregular case, select the option you want to use.

Unlike straight spell checking, WordPerfect will stop on every occurrence of an irregular case. For example, it will stop on FIgure

Lesson 33:
Using the Spell
Checker

▼ *Figure 11.4.* **The Irregular Case Dialog Box**

to Figure to

1.1 *and* FIgure 3.4. It doesn't remember the correction from time to time, especially since the words are spelled correctly.

Finding Information About Documents

You might need to have information about a particular document such as the number of words, pages, or whatever. Among the Writing Tools dialog box (use the **Alt+F1** key combination or select **T**ools, **W**riting) is option 4, **D**ocument information. Select that, and as you can see in Figure 11.5, you'll find tons of information such as number of paragraphs, average word length, and more.

CHECK YOURSELF

1. Enter the following sentence and begin the spell checker.
   There are two many places too visit.
   What words did the speller stop on and why?
2. Under what conditions would you not want to delete the double occurrence of a word?

▼ *Figure 11.5.   Getting Document Information*

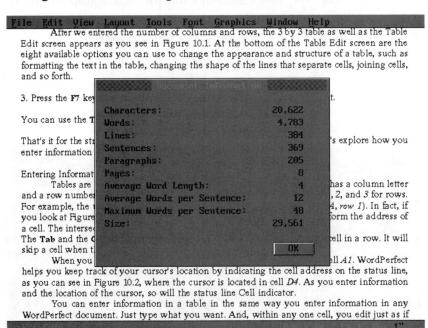

ANSWERS

1. It won't stop on any words, since it recognizes them all as being spelled correctly. The point is that they are not being used correctly. Spell checkers only check spelling, not usage.
2. When numbers appear in columns or when you want the words to appear again!

Lesson 34: Using the Thesaurus

It's right on the tip of your tongue, but you just can't seem to come up with the word, term, expression, statement, utterance (all from the WordPerfect thesaurus!).

How the Thesaurus Works

The thesaurus operates, in many ways, like a dictionary. You place the cursor on or after the word for which you want to find a synonym or an antonym, and WordPerfect searches through its thesaurus to find other words that are similar (or dissimilar).

WordPerfect searches through the 10,000 headwords it contains and generates as many options as possible.

To use the thesaurus:

1. Place the cursor on, or immediately after, the word you want to find an alternative for.
2. Use the **Alt+F1,T** [Mouse Moves: Tools, **Writing** Tools, Thesaurus] to see the Thesaurus screen shown in Figure 11.6. For example, in Figure 11.6, you can see how the thesaurus was used to find a substitute for the word *increased*.

    First, you can see the word *increased* highlighted and the accompanying (*v*), which indicates it's a verb. It could also be a noun (*n*) or an antonym (*a*), all of which you see on the same screen, but you have to scroll down to see all the options.

    Second, the alternatives that WordPerfect generates are organized into groups. The word *increased* is a headword, or one that can be accessed directly through the thesaurus. It's one of those 10,000 that we mentioned earlier. Next are reference

▼ *Figure 11.6. Using the Thesaurus and the Thesaurus Dialog Box*

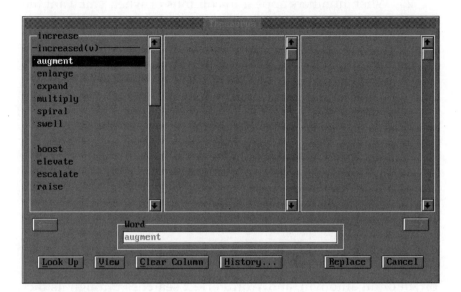

words marked with a bullet (•) such as *augment, enlarge*, and so on. If you highlight a bulleted word (such as *expand*) and press **Enter**, that word then becomes a headword for another set of possibilities as you see in Figure 11.7.

To switch from column to column and assign letters to words in a list, use the right and left arrow keys. Use the up and down arrow keys to see the complete list that cannot be shown because of screen limitations.

3. Select the word you want to use from the list on the thesaurus screen (Press **R** for **R**eplace or click on **R**eplace), and WordPerfect will replace the highlighted word in the document. But that's not all the thesaurus feature can do.

The Thesaurus Options

At the bottom of the thesaurus screen is a set of four options from which you can select.

▼ *Figure 11.7. Finding Other Possible Words for Substitution*

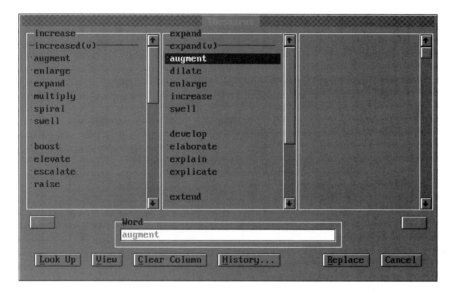

Replace will simply replace the highlighted word with the word of your choice. When you select this option, WordPerfect will ask you to indicate the letter of the word you want to substitute. Remember, if there are no letters next to the word, use the arrow keys to move the column of letters over there.

View allows you to return to the original document so you can take a look at the context within which the word appears. You might find that one synonym (or antonym) works better than another. You can scroll through the text as needed and then press the **F7** key to return to the Thesaurus screen.

Look Up does just that. WordPerfect will provide you with additional synonyms for a particular word.

Clear Column lets you clear the column in the Thesaurus dialog box if the information in that column is irrelevant. Perhaps none of the words fit, and since WordPerfect only allows a total of three columns, you might need space for an additional column. Look and see what you want from a column and then delete it so that you can view other alternatives.

History provides you with a screen showing you the history of what words have been examined.

Wrong Word?

Even though WordPerfect has the most comprehensive thesaurus available, it may not be able to find any synonyms or antonyms for the word you identify. If this is the case, WordPerfect will give the message **Word Not Found**.

CHECK YOURSELF

1. Find all the antonyms available for the following words:
   face
   doctor
   pretty
2. Find some synonyms for the following words:
   time
   word
   insurmountable

ANSWERS

1. face (retreat, strip)
   doctor (there are no antonyms)
   pretty (ugly, plain)
2. time (duration, interval, space)
   word (term, expression, statements)
   insurmountable (formidable, hopeless)

Words, words, words. Everything you've done up to now has concentrated on fixing them, displaying them, and making sure they are spelled correctly. Now it's time to consider other WordPerfect features that allow you to work with something beyond words, such as the tables you can use to organize them.

PRACTICE WHAT YOU'VE LEARNED

1. Here's a paragraph that has five spelling errors. Correct each one using one of the options available on the Spell Check menu.

This course wil offer an introduction to the basic prinic-pals of how engines work and what they can due. It will bee ofered each Wednesday nite.

2. Provide examples for when each of the first three options on the spell menu should be used.
3. How can you get WordPerfect to count the number of words in a paragraph that is part of a larger document?
4. What is a homophone and why do you have to be particularly careful to read over any document where you have used the spell checker and the thesaurus?

ANSWERS

1. This course will offer an introduction to the basic princi-ples of how engines work and what they can do. It will be offered each Wednesday night.
2. When you want to check an individual word, a page on which the cursor is located, or an entire document.
3. Create a block and then use the **Ctrl+F3,6** key combination.
4. A homophone is a word that sounds like another word but has a different meaning. The spell checker might not iden-tify this word as being unusual.

Creating and
Using Tables

It doesn't matter what you do. If you need to display information, WordPerfect Tables is the place to be. If you're in school, business, have a hobby, or whatever, using tables can make your work easier and your documents more impressive and effective. In this chapter you'll learn how to:

▲ **Create a table**

▲ **Add rows or columns after a table is created**

▲ **Change the width of a column or the height of a row**

▲ **Change the lines in a table**

▲ **Format cells and columns**

▲ **Convert text to tables**

Important Keys	*Important Terms*
Alt+F7, F7	address
	column
	row
	table edit
	table

Lesson 35: Your First Table!

Just so we can impress you with how easy it is to create a table, let's go through the steps for creating the table that you see in Figure 12.1.

This is a simple table with three rows and three columns. It's a good idea to roughly sketch out your table using paper and pencil before you even begin using WordPerfect to do the job. The sketch does not have to be anything elaborate, but just enough to give you an idea as to the numbers of rows and columns that you will need.

To create any table:

1. Use the **Alt+F7,2,1** key combination [**Mouse Moves:** Select **L**ayout, **T**ables, **C**reate] to begin creating with tables. When you do this, you will see the Create Table dialog box you see in Figure 12.2. The number of columns in the Create Table dialog box is highlighted. In Figure 12.2, the number of columns is 3.
2. Use the mouse or ↓ arrow key to move to the **Rows:** box.
3. Enter the value **3**.
4. Select **OK** or press **Enter** twice. There you have it! The 3 × 3 table you see in Figure 12.1.

TIP

You can use the up ▲ and down ▼ triangles in the Create Table dialog box to increase or decrease the number of rows or columns in a table.

WordPerfect automatically sets you up with single lines between cells and a thick line border around the table. You can edit these, as you will learn later.

Lesson 35: Your First Table!

▼ *Figure 12.1. Creating a Table*

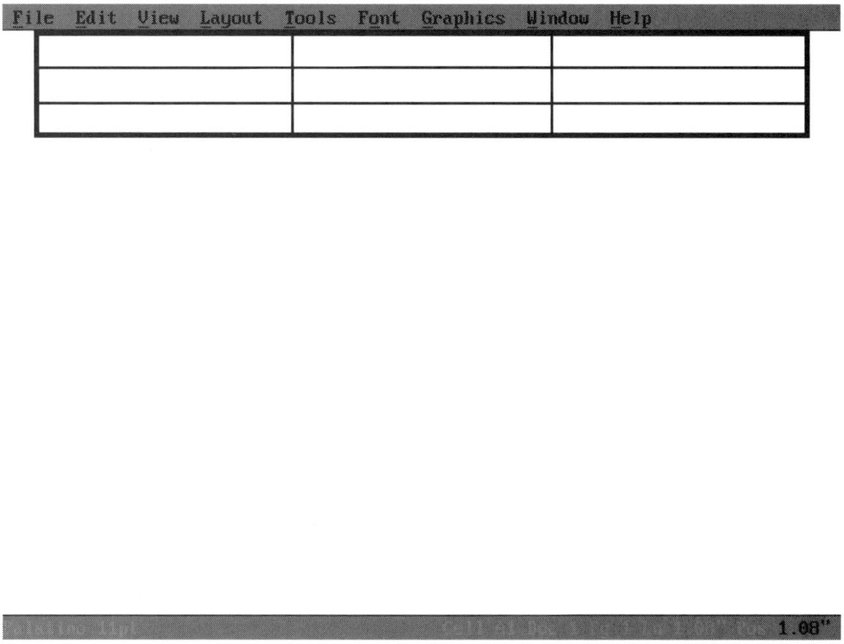
File Edit View Layout Tools Font Graphics Window Help
1.08"

▼ *Figure 12.2. The Create Table Dialog Box*

File Edit View Layout Tools Font Graphics Window Help
Rows:
OK
Cancel
1"

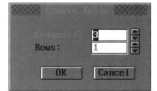

After we entered the number of columns and rows, the 3 × 3 table as well as the Table Edit screen appears as you see in Figure 12.3. At the bottom of the Table Edit screen are the eight available options you can use to change the appearance and structure of a table, such as formatting the text in the table, changing the shape of the lines that separate cells, joining cells, and so forth. You can use the **Tab** key to move from cell to cell.

That's it for the structure of a basic table that has yet to contain any characters. Let's now explore how you enter information into tables.

Entering Information

Tables are made up of **cells,** and cells have **addresses.** Each address has a column letter and a row number associated with it, such as *A, B,* and *C* for columns and *1, 2,* and *3* for rows. For example, the upper left-hand cell in a table will be cell *A1* (for *column A, row 1*). In fact, if you look at Figure 12.4, you'll see how a row and column come together to form the address of a cell. The intersection of *row 3* and *column D* has the address *D3.* When you first create a table, you are in the Table Edit screen as you see in Figure 12.4. Once you press the **F7** key, you are in the regular WordPerfect document window (as in Figure 12.1) and column (A, B, C) and row headings (1, 2, 3) disappear.

TIP

The Tab **key will move you from cell to cell in a row. It will skip a cell when the cell is empty.**

When you create a table, the cursor will automatically be located in cell *A1.* WordPerfect helps you keep track of your cursor's location by indicating the cell address on the status line, as you can see in Figure 12.4, where the cursor is located in cell *D4.* As you en-

▼ Figure 12.3. The Table Edit Screen

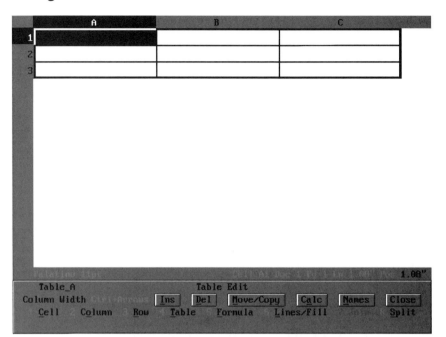

	A	B	C
1			
2			
3			

1.00"

```
 Table_A                          Table Edit
 Column Width                [Ins] [Del] [Move/Copy] [Calc] [Names] [Close]
    Cell    Column    Row    Table    Formula    Lines/Fill        Split
```

▼ Figure 12.4. Rows, Columns, and Cells

File Edit View Layout Tools Font Graphics Window Help

A1	B1	C1	D1	E1
A2	B2	C2	D2	E2
A3	B3	C3	D3	E3
A4	B4	C4	D4	E4
A5	B5	C5	D5	E5

4.4"

ter information and the location of the cursor changes, so will the status line cell indicator.

You can enter information in a table in the same way you enter information in any WordPerfect document. Just type what you want. And, within any one cell, you edit just as if it were any WordPerfect text. Use the left and right arrow keys to move between letters and the Ctrl and Arrow keys to move from word to word.

The cell size will automatically change to accommodate the amount of text that you enter into the cell. It's word wrap all over again. Also, the number of lines will increase, and all cells in that horizontal line of cells will increase in size as any one cell does.

Remember that the base font you are working with will determine how much information fits in any one cell. The smaller the size of the base font, the more information you can fit. Similarly, if you boldface text in a cell, it will take up more room than if the text does not appear in boldface.

To enter text into the table you see in Figure 12.1:

1. Make sure the cusor is in cell *A1*.
2. Press the **Tab** key to move from cell *A1* to cell *A2*.
3. Enter the word *Males* and press the **Tab** key.
4. Enter the word *Females* and press the **Tab** key.
5. Continue to enter text and press the **Tab** key until you have entered all the text into the table.

Copying Tables

If you have created a table that you like and want to use again, you don't have to reconstruct it. Just block the *entire table* as you would any text (using the **Alt+F4** key combination) and then copy it (using the **Ctrl+F4,2** key combination). Place the cursor in the new location, press **Enter**, and a copy of the table will appear.

If you find that you will be using tables a lot and that the basic structure of your tables is the same (except perhaps for differences in information in the tables), then create a table template. This would include everything that does not change from table to table. Just recall it and then edit the table as needed. Don't forget to save it under another name, otherwise your template will take on the name of one of the tables.

CHECK YOURSELF

1. Create a table that has nine rows and nine columns. What is the address of the cell that is right in the middle of the table?
2. Create a three-column table that has six rows.
   a. Label columns B and C as *Wins* and *Losses*.
   b. Enter the names of five different teams, beginning with row two.

ANSWERS

1. Cell 5E
2. Tables can be used for illustrations as well as substituting for WordPerfect's column feature.

Lesson 36: Changing How Tables Look

The table that you saw in Figure 12.1 does the job of displaying information, but with all the WordPerfect table options available, you can do much more. The **Table Edit** window (see Figure 12.3) includes options to add and delete rows and columns and format the table to appear as you would like.

You already know how to create a table, how to enter information (just like any WordPerfect document), and how to move around to edit the text in cells. Let's look at the options on the Table Edit window to see how they work and what they can do for your tables.

The one rule you must remember when working with table options is that you must be in the Table Edit screen, accessed through the **Alt+F7,2,2** key combination [**Mouse Moves:** Select Layout, **T**ables, Edit].

If you have only one table in a document, WordPerfect will automatically place you in the Table Edit window for that table. If you have more than one table, you must place the cursor in the table you want to edit and then use the **Alt+F7,2, 2** key combination to edit that table. WordPerfect will also place you in the Table Edit window for the table that the cursor most closely follows.

Editing Tables

Here we go with a slew of techniques for changing the way that tables appear. The first step is being able to get to the part of the table you want to change.

Moving Around in Table Edit

Remember how you learned about editing documents (and moving around a document using special keystrokes) in Lesson 11? A similar, but different, set of keystrokes are used to move around a table. Here's a table showing you how to move around a table and what keys take you there.

Move	*Keys*
Down one cell	Down arrow key
Up one cell	Up arrow key
Left one cell	Left arrow key or Tab
Right one cell	Right arrow key or Tab
To the beginning of text in a cell	Ctrl+Home, Up arrow key
To the last line of text in a cell	Ctrl+Home, Down arrow key
To the first cell in a column	Ctrl+Home, Home, Up arrow key
To the last cell in a column	Ctrl+Home, Home, Down arrow key
To the first cell in a row	Ctrl+Home, Home, Left arrow key
To the last cell in a row	Ctrl+Home, Home, Right arrow key
First cell in the table	Ctrl+Home, Home, Home, Up arrow key
Last cell in the table	Ctrl+Home, Home, Home, Down arrow key

Don't even try to memorize these different key combinations and what they can do to help you move around tables. Once you begin creating tables and moving around, you'll see how they are much like the same keystrokes you use to move around any WordPerfect document. It takes some time and practice, but just like regular keystrokes, it becomes increasingly easy the more you use WordPerfect.

Adding Rows and Columns

Even the best laid plans sometimes go astray. For example, you might find you need to add a row or a column to a table after the entire table has been created.

To add a row or a column:

1. Use the **Alt+F7,2,2** key combination [**Mouse Moves:** Select Layout, Tables, Edit] to see the Table Edit window you see in Figure 12.4.
2. Place the cursor in the cell either before or after the new location where you want to add a row or column.
3. Select Ins in the Table Edit dialog box and you'll see the Insert dialog box shown in Figure 12.5.
4. Select **C**olumns (option 1) or **R**ows (option 2) depending on what you want to add.
5. Select **H**ow Many and enter the number of rows or columns you want to add.

▼ *Figure 12.5.   The Insert Dialog Box*

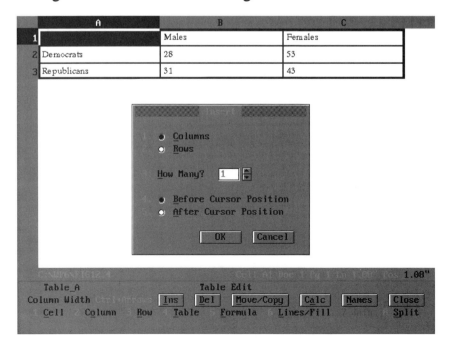

6. Select **B**efore or **A**fter depending on whether you want to insert the row or column before or after the location of the cursor.

For example, in Figure 12.6, 2 columns were added after the location of the cursor.

You can also add a row or column (or more than one) using the block feature.

To add a row or column using the block feature:

1. Block the amount of text you want to insert. If you want to insert one column, block that column in the table where you want the column inserted.
2. Press the **Ins** key and you will see the Insert dialog box.
3. Select **OK**.

TIP

You can block and add only as many rows as are available in the table. If you want to add more rows than are available to block, use the Ins key and indicate the number of rows or columns you want to add.

▼ *Figure 12.6.   Inserting Columns in a Table*

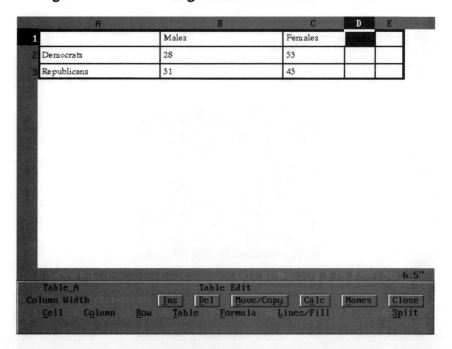

TIP

You can add rows either by using the Ins key directly or by blocking and then using the Ins key.

Deleting Rows and Columns

To delete a row or column (or more than one):

1. Use the **Alt+F7,2,2** key combination [**Mouse Moves:** Select Layout, Tables, Edit] to see the Table Edit dialog box.
2. Place the cursor in the row or column you want to delete.
3. Press the **Del** key and WordPerfect will show you the Delete dialog box as shown in Figure 12.7. Select Columns or Rows or Cells Contents (what's in a cell) and enter how many you want to delete.
4. Select **OK**.

▼ *Figure 12.7.   The Delete Dialog Box*

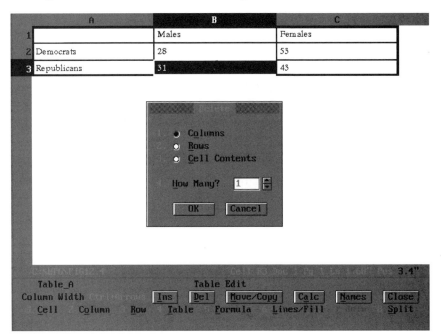

TIP

If you are having trouble deleting or adding rows or columns, you may not be in the Table Edit screen. Be sure to check where you are before you try adding or deleting rows or columns.

Changing the Width of a Column

To change the width of a particular column in a cell:

1. As always, be sure you are in the Table Edit window.
2. Use the **Ctrl+Right Arrow** key combination to increase the width of any one column. Use the **Ctrl+Left Arrow** key combination to decrease the width of any one column. With each push of the arrow key, the column will increase or decrease in size. Remember you can change the height of a column using the **Enter** key and **Backspace** keys but you have to be in the regular WordPerfect document to do this, not Table Edit.

TIP

You cannot save a table in the Table Edit mode. You need to be in the regular WordPerfect document.

The Table Edit Options

In Figure 12.7, you can see the Table Edit screen. The various options listed along the bottom of the screen are the keys to changing the way that a table appears. For example, in Figure 12.8, we used several of these different options to change the appearance of the table that you originally saw in Figure 12.1.

To use any of these options, you must first use the **Alt+F7,2,2,** key combination [**Mouse Moves:** Layout, Tables, Edit] while you have the cursor inside the table that you have created. Then you can select one of eight options. Here's a description of each one of these options and how some of them were used to create the table you see in Figure 12.8.

Lesson 36: Changing How Tables Look

▼ ***Figure 12.8. Using Table Options to Change the Table's Appearance***

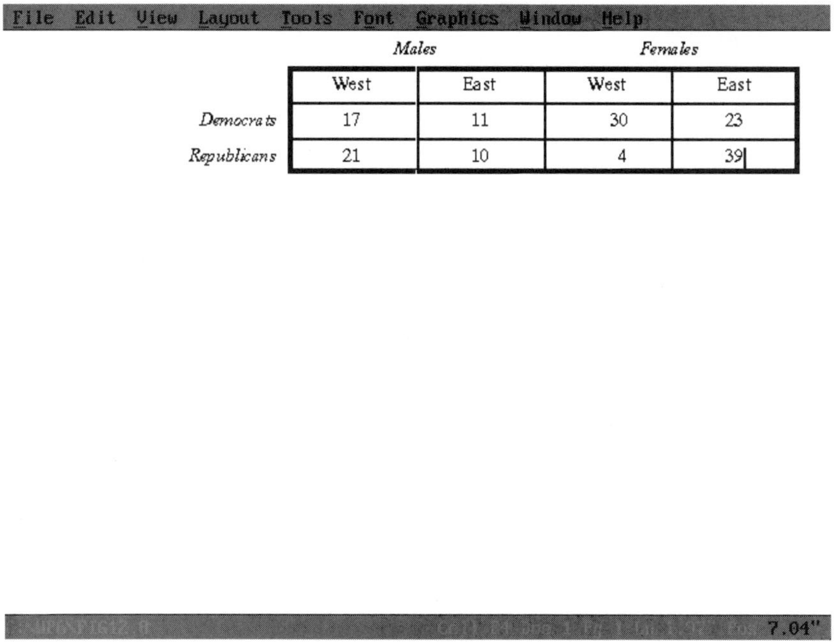
File Edit View Layout Tools Font Graphics Window Help
Males
Females
West
East
West
East
Democrats
17
11
30
23
Republicans
21
10
4
39
7.04"

Working with Cell Format

Cell (option 1) allows you to work with individual cells. When you select this option, you see the dialog box shown in Figure 12.9.

Here you can see how you can work with the attributes of cells including Appearance and Size (options 1, 2, and 3), how characters are aligned in the cell (options 4 and 5), the format for how numbers will appear in the cell including such options as Percent and Currency (option 6), whether you want the columns characteristics to be applied to the cell (option 7), and if the cell should be locked (option 8) where its contents cannot be changed and the values ignored when calculations take place (option 9).

For example, in Figure 12.8, the appearance of particular cells (such as Males and Females) was changed from normal to italic through first blocking those cells and then selecting Italic from the Cell Format dialog box. Text in some cells was also centered justified through the Cell Format dialog box.

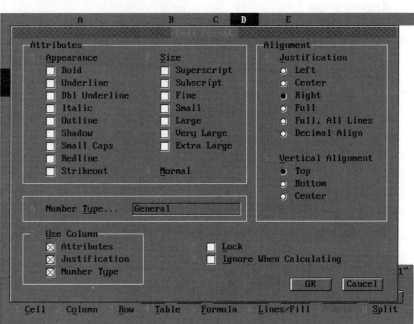

▼ *Figure 12.9.* *The Cell Format Dialog Box*

Working with Column Format

Just as with cells, you can alter much of how information in columns appears through Column (option 2) which produces the Column Format dialog box you see in Figure 12.10.

Attributes (options 1, 2, and 3) can be changed just as with cells. Alignment (option 4) allows you to highlight the first cell in a column, select a column in the Table Edit screen and then center or right justify all the text, adjust the number of digits in the decimal and the distance of the decimal point from the right border of the cell (option 5), the type of number (option 6), and the width of the column (option 7). Even though you can use the Ctrl+→ and Ctrl+← key combination to change the width of a column, option 7 in the Column Format dialog box provides you with a great deal more precision. Here you can specify the exact width to one-hundredth of an inch.

Want to change the width of more than one column? Just block adjacent cells and then use the Width option in the Column Format dialog box.

▼ *Figure 12.10.* *The Column Format Dialog Box*

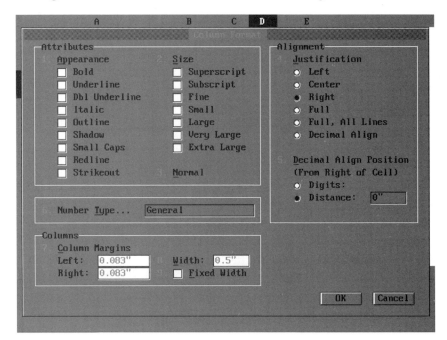

Working with Row Format

Just like columns, rows have their own format options, shown in Figure 12.11.

These are **Row margins** (options 1 and 2), **Row Height** (options 3 and 4), the number of **Lines of Text** that can be used in a row (options 5 and 6), and whether you want a **Header Row** to appear at the top of the table if more than one page is needed to print the entire table (option 7).

Working with Table Format

Table format returns us once again to many of the same options you have seen for cells and columns. But, as you can see in Figure 12.12, you can adjust the Table Position (option P) so the table appears on the left, right, or center of the page. You can also set the exact location of the left-hand border of the table by specifying the exact measurement.

Working with Formulas

Working with Formulas (option 5 in the Table Edit window) gets into the math features that WordPerfect offers, and we'll cover that

▼ *Figure 12.11. The Row Format Dialog Box*

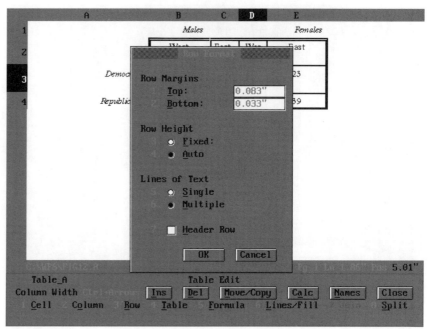

▼ *Figure 12.12. The Table Format Dialog Box*

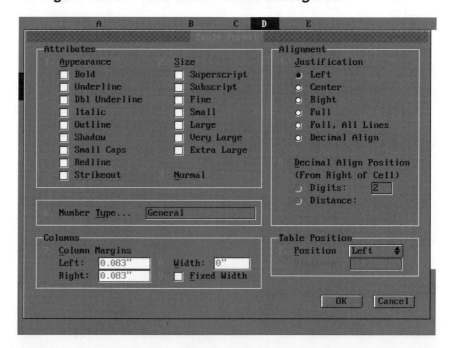

in the next chapter. Using this feature, you can create an actual formula in a table that acts on entries in other cells and returns a value based on the formula. We'll show you how later.

Lesson 36:
Changing How
Tables Look

Working with Lines

Any table that you create will show lines on the WordPerfect screen, and those lines will be part of any hard copy that you print out. You can change the design of those lines, through option 6 in the Table Edit dialog box.

Once you make this selection, you'll see the Table Lines dialog boxes shown in Figure 12.13.

You'll probably notice first that (in the Entire Table area), WordPerfect allows you to work with the entire table (Entire Table) or individual cells and blocks (Current Cell or Block).

In both case, when you select one of the options in the Table Lines dialog box, you will be shown a dialog box where you have to specify what you want for the exact format of the selected cells or the entire table. For example, in Figure 12.8, some cells had the lines removed (such as the cells containing the words Democrats and Republicans).

▼ *Figure 12.13. The Table Lines Dialog Box*

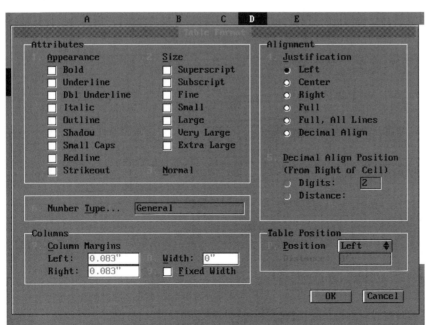

To change a particular line in a cell:

1. Be sure you are in the Table Edit window.
2. Select **L**ines/Fill (option 6).
3. Select the line you want to change. For example, if you want to change the top border of the selected cell or cells, then **T**op (option 5) should be selected. When you do this, you will see, the Line Styles dialog box shown in Figure 12.14.
4. Select the type of line you would like to use. You can see what the different line options look like in Figure 12.15.
5. Select **S**elect (option 1).
6. Select **C**lose.

   The selected cells will then have a line format change.

TIP

The line that forms the border of a cell is treated separately from the lines in a table.

▼ *Figure 12.14.   The Line Styles Dialog Box*

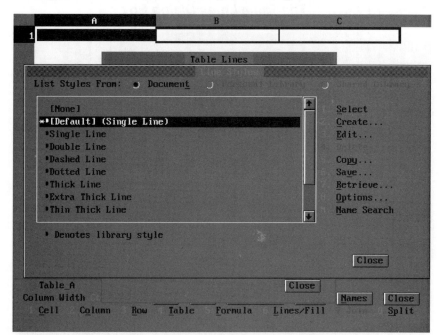

Lesson 36: Changing How Tables Look

▼ ***Figure 12.15. Different Line Styles and What They Look Like***

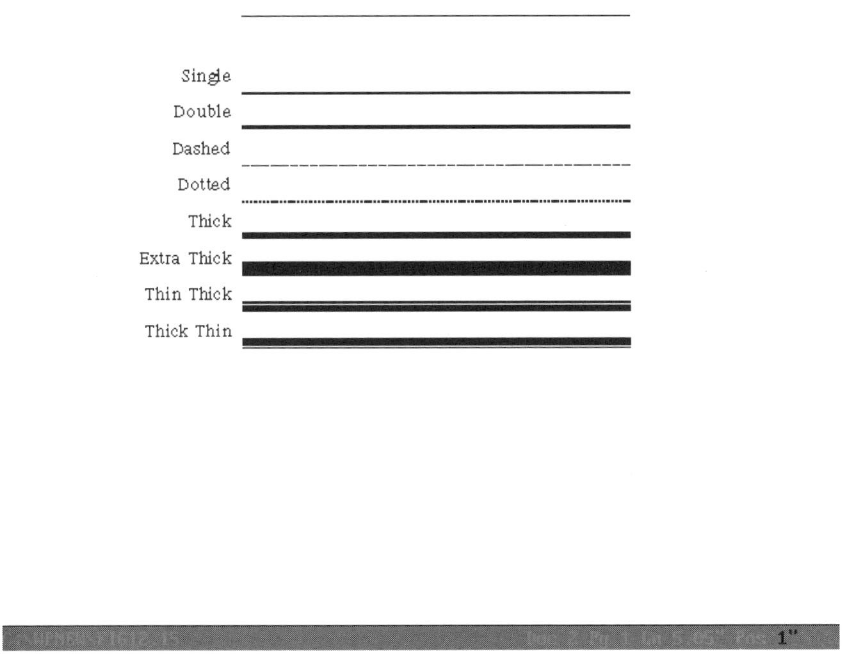
Single
Double
Dashed
Dotted
Thick
Extra Thick
Thin Thick
Thick Thin

Joining Cells

You may create a table that needs to have two adjacent cells combined, or joined, into one. You might do this when you want a particular cell to act as a heading in a column and you would like the header to span two cells. You can see a before and after pair of tables in Figure 12.16.

To join pairs of cells so that the end result is a cell located above and spans the two below it:

1. Use the **Alt+F7,2,2** key combination [Mouse Moves: Select **L**ayout, **T**ables, **E**dit] to see the Table Edit dialog box.
2. Block the cells you want to join.
3. Select **J**oin option (7).
4. Indicate **Yes** when you see the Join Cells? dialog box.

   You can see in Figure 12.16 how two sets of cells were joined.

▼ *Figure 12.16.* *Joining Cells*

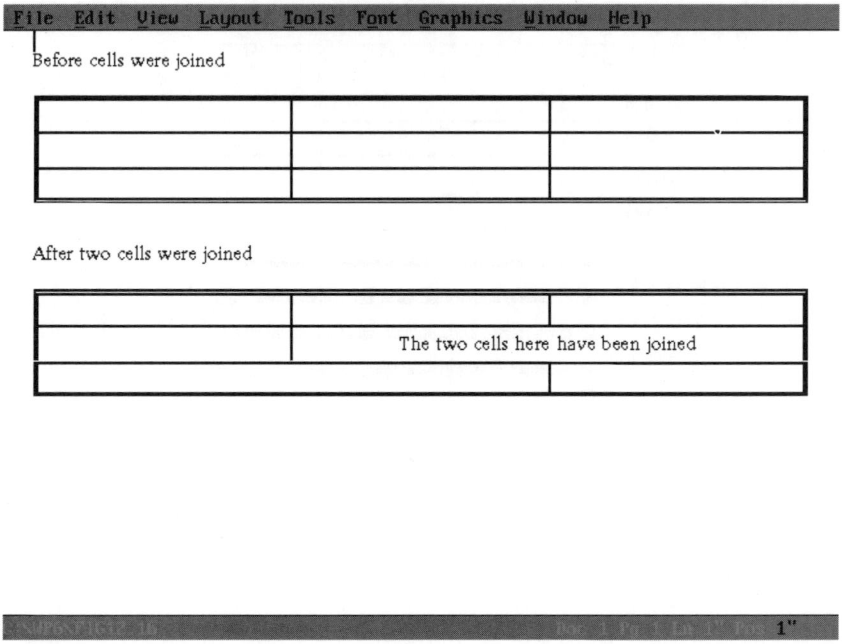

File Edit View Layout Tools Font Graphics Window Help

Before cells were joined

After two cells were joined

	The two cells here have been joined	

TIP

Cells must be adjacent to one another to be joined.

Splitting Cells

Splitting cells is somewhat like the opposite of joining cells, and the steps you take to split cells are very similar.

To split a cell:

1. Use the **Alt+F7,2,2** key combination [Mouse Moves: Select **L**ayout, **T**ables, **E**dit] to see the Table Edit dialog box.
2. Select the cell or column you want to split. In Figure 12.17, cells B2 and B3 will be split.
3. Select **S**plit (option 8) in the Table Edit dialog box.
4. Indicate whether you want to split rows or columns and the number you want to create. In Figure 12.17, we wanted to split a cell into two columns.
5. Press the **Enter** key.

Lesson 36: Changing How Tables Look

▼ *Figure 12.17. Splitting Cells*

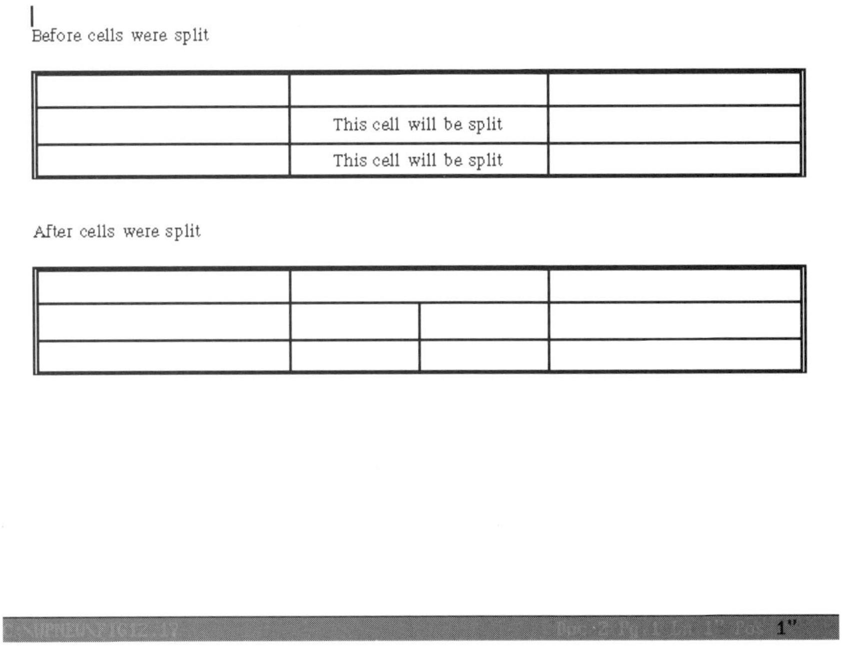
Before cells were split
This cell will be split
This cell will be split
After cells were split
1"

You can see in Figure 12.17 how two sets of cells were split.

Take a look at Figure 12.18 which is a business form used in the collection of debts. That's just one thing you can do with tables once you become familiar with the WordPerfect tools that we covered so far that help you create and format a table. And, with some practice, even complex looking tables are easy to create.

From Text to Tables

One of the most convenient things that you can do with the Tables feature of WordPerfect 6.0 is to take text that has already been entered in a document and then convert it into a table. The only requirement is that the columns of text be separated by tabs and that the rows be separated by carriage returns or that it be in columns.

To convert text into a table:

1. Block the text you want to transform.
2. Use the **Alt+F7,2,1** key combination [Mouse Moves: Select **L**ayout, T**a**bles, **C**reate, 1] to select the Table feature. WordPerfect will show you the **Create Table from Block** dia-

▼ *Figure 12.18.* *An Example of What Anyone Can Do with*
WordPerfect 6.0 Tables

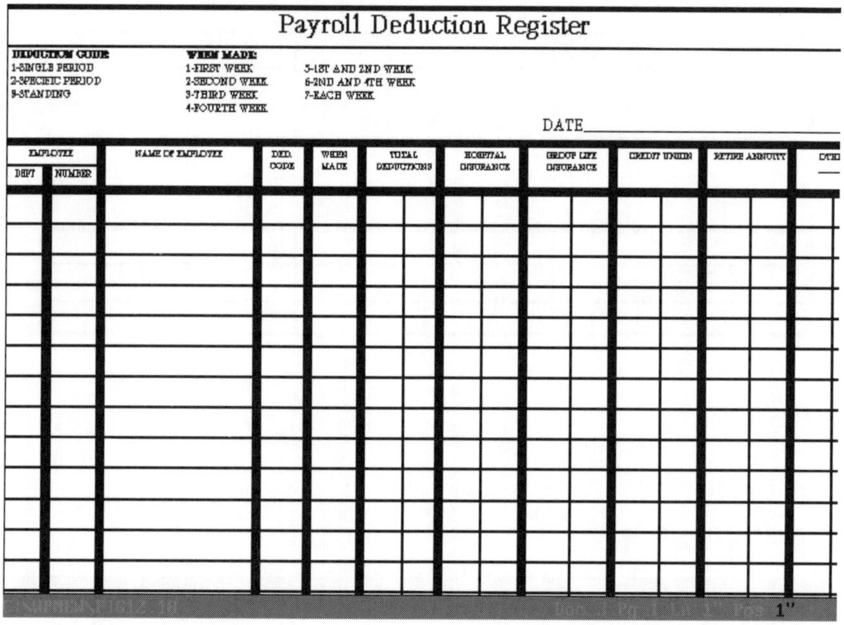

log box. WordPerfect will then ask you whether the data that
you are converting is in the form of tabular columns (option
1—where columns are separated by tabs) or parallel columns
(option 2—where columns were formed).

3. Select **Tabular Text** (option 1).

4. Press return and you'll be in the Table Edit box with your new
table.

Be sure that you use tabs to separate text and end the last line
with a hard return or (a press of the **Enter** key). Otherwise,
WordPerfect will not know where to use the column feature.

CHECK YOURSELF

1. Create a table with four rows and four columns.
   a. Add a column.
   b. Place a dashed line between cells in the entire table.
   c. Delete the outside border around the table.
2. Create a table that has four columns and four rows.
   a. Join the top two rows so there is only one cell in each row.
   b. Split the bottom row so that there are four cells in the bottom row.

ANSWERS

1. Your finished table should look like this.
2. The more you plan out the configuration of your table before you begin, the easier it will be to see how the join and split features can help you create exactly the table you want.

Tables can add more than you can imagine to a document. They can illustrate, illuminate, and inform. Don't overlook how tables can even be used to format material, everything from business forms to stationery, that is not a table but that can best be created using the table tools. With these new uses in mind, we now turn our attention to WordPerfect math, a part of which includes using WordPerfect tables with math.

PRACTICE WHAT YOU'VE LEARNED

1. Under what circumstances would you need to convert text to a table? How can you convert tabled text into straight text?
2. What is the fastest way to add a row to an existing table?
3. What might you see on the bottom of your WordPerfect screen to do any type of table editing?
4. What change takes place in the status line when you edit a table?

ANSWERS

1. When you create the text in another application and want to convert it to a table. Block the text and then copy it into another location.
2. Using the **Ins** key.
3. The Table Edit menu.
4. You see an indicator as to the cell in which you are located.

WordPerfect Math

Preparing a term paper, an annual report, or a business letter may involve more than just text. A job estimate, a budget, and even a project schedule might require the use of numbers. WordPerfect provides you with a set of tools that allows you to perform both simple and complex operations on numbers that are part of a document.

Basic math and **tables math** let you use WordPerfect as if it were a spreadsheetlike electronic ledger with rows and columns. You can then make the calculations you need to find about your next car payment or how much you overspent your budget! In this chapter you'll learn how to:

▲ **Define columns for Math**

▲ **Enter information into Math columns**

▲ **Calculate Math operations**

▲ **Use formulas**

▲ **Use Tables and Math functions**

Important Keys	Important Terms
Alt+F7	basic math
*	Copy Cell dialog box
=	Define Math Column dialog box
+	formulas
/	functions
	math
	Math dialog box
	Move dialog box
	operators
	Table Formula dialog box
	tables math

Lesson 37: Math Basics

Before you can do any fancy math calculations, you first need to be familiar with the basic math steps. This stuff is actually fun, so follow along and do what the book says.

Here's everything you need to know about getting started with WordPerfect Math. There are six basic steps to using WordPerfect Math.

The basic steps are:

1. Placing the cursor where you want math to operate. Math works on tab settings, so you will have to set tabs where you want columns to appear on which math will work.
2. Defining Math columns.
3. Turning Math on.
4. Entering the information you want to work with including special WordPerfect operators that will add, subtract, multiply, and divide.
5. Telling WordPerfect to calculate.
6. Turning Math off.

Let's go through each one of these, one step at a time, in the creation of a personal budget.

Locating the Cursor Using Tabs

You can use WordPerfect Math anywhere in a document, but the numbers have to be arranged in a column or columns.

Once you are sure of where you want your math activities to begin, then use the **Tab** feature (see Lesson 29) to set the columns. By doing this, you are preparing WordPerfect for the entry of information in columns, with each column defined by a tab stop. For our personal budget, we will place tab stops every half inch.

TIP

You must use tabs to separate columns, otherwise the Math feature will not work.

Defining Math Columns

All math operations begin with the **Alt+F7,3,2** key combination [Mouse Moves: **Tools, Math, Define**]. When you press this key combination, you will see the Math dialog box shown in Figure 13.1.

TIP

Use the Alt+F7,2 **key combination to begin the definition process.**

This screen is the main control center for WordPerfect Math, and it is here where you need to identify for each column:

▲ The column type
▲ How negative numbers will be displayed
▲ The number of digits to the right of the decimal

Our budget will have three columns, so we'll be defining Columns A, B, and C in the Math Definition screen.

The types of columns from which we can select are as follows:

▲ **Calculation** (enter **C**) columns are those that are used to calculate values across columns.

▼ *Figure 13.1.* *The Math Dialog Box*

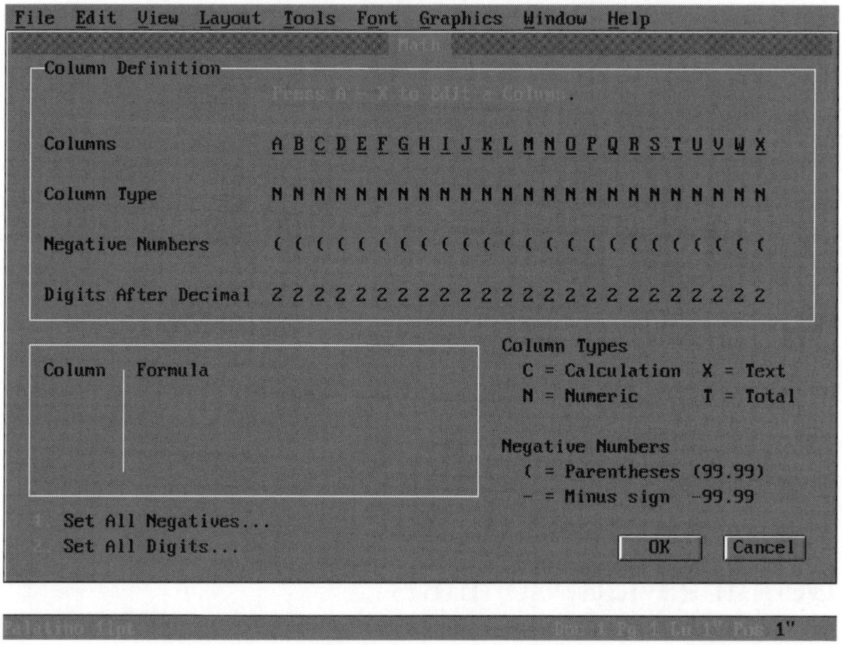

▲ **Text** (enter **X**) columns are those containing descriptions or labels.

▲ **Numeric** (enter **N**) columns are used to add numbers up and down columns. WordPerfect presets all columns to be numeric as you can see in Figure 13.1, where the value **N** is entered for each column as the type. Negative numbers can be expressed using parentheses such as (32.18) or with a minus sign such as –32.18.

This is the way that WordPerfect will show them on the screen after calculation has taken place, not the way you enter them in the table. The default, as you can see in Figure 13.1, is for parentheses. To enter a negative number, just enter it with a hyphen (such as -124).

You can indicate the number of digits to the right of the decimal point you want to use, sometimes called precision. The default is 2.

▲ **Total** (enter T) columns are used to display a total.

Our budget will be set up as follows, with columns A, B, and C being numeric. The text under Category (a column in our budget) is not considered a column by WordPerfect Math, since the Math feature does not consider the space between the left-hand margin and the first tab stop. So, although you might think that the text listed under Category in Figure 13.1 should be a column defined as text (X), it is not of concern to us in the definition of the columns.

On the Math Definition screen, you can also have up to four different calculation formulas. These formulas take information you provide as well as information from other columns and produce a new result. For example, if you wanted the value in column C to be the product of the values in columns *A* and *B*, then the entry on the Math Definition screen would look like:

```
Column          Formula
   C               A*B
```

WordPerfect will then automatically take the values in the first two columns (columns A and B) and place their product in the third (column C).

For our purposes, the Math Definition screen for the budget will appear exactly as the one you saw in Figure 13.1.

Your tables, like the budget example cited, may even begin to resemble programs you know as spreadsheet. Later on in this chapter when we talk about Math and Tables, you'll see how this new version of WordPerfect can do many of the powerful things that these spreadsheets (such as Lotus and Quattro and Excel) can do. It makes using WordPerfect even that much more useful. In fact, when we use math, we only use it with tables, because it is so much easier!

Operators

WordPerfect needs to know what you want to do with numbers, and you need special symbols to indicate the operations you want to perform. You probably already know from your basic math in high school that + represents add, − represents minus, * represents multiply, and / represents divide.

Use these, along with parentheses when necessary, to write formulas. For example, the formula **(A–B)/C** will first take the difference between *A* and *B* and divide that value by *C*. Remember, there's an order to the way operators work. When there are two or more operators, the order is always from left to right.

Defining a Column

OK. You've seen the Math dialog box. Let's go through the simple steps of defining a column if the default settings you see in Figure 13.1 don't fit your needs.

To change the definition of a column:

1. Select the column you want to redefine by entering the character from the keyboard or clicking with the mouse. When you do this, you will see the Define Math Column dialog box as shown in Figure 13.2.
2. Specify what type of column you want (Text, Total, etc.), how negative numbers should appear when WordPerfect finishes the on-screen calculation, and how many numbers you want to appear after the decimal.
3. Select **OK**. The column is now defined.

▼ *Figure 13.2.   The Define Math Column Dialog Box*

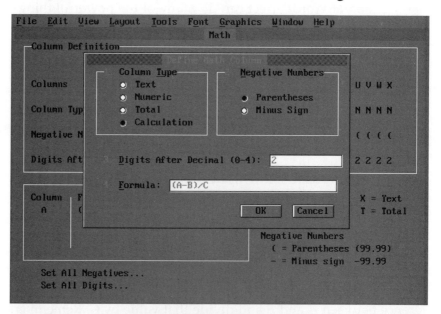

In Figure 13.2, you can see how we defined a formula that subtracts the value in column B from the value in column A and then divides by the value in column C. This is the formula that will be placed in column A, since that is the column we are redefining. The Define Math Column dialog box does not indicate what column is being defined.

**Lesson 37:
Math Basics**

Turning Math On

Now that the column definitions are complete, the Math function needs to be turned on using the **Alt+F7,3,1** key combination [Mouse Moves: Tools, Math, On]. WordPerfect inserts a [Math: On] reveal code and the word *Math* appears in the lower left-hand corner of the status line on your WordPerfect screen.

TIP

Turn Math on using the Alt+F7,1 **key combination.**

Enter the Information and Operators

The next step is to enter the text and numbers that you want to include. The space between the left margin and the first tab stop is not used by the Math feature, so you can enter labels in this area and not have to define it as a column. For each of the values under *Expenses*, a hyphen was entered to indicate that it is a negative value.

Also, enter any column headings you want before you turn Math on so they don't interfere in any way with calculations and such.

In Figure 13.3, you can see the information entered as three numeric columns along with the operators telling WordPerfect what to do. More about these in a moment.

Tabs were used to move from column to column, and the values that will be used as part of the calculation were entered. Now, some information about the special symbols called **functions**.

▼ *Figure 13.3.* **Budget Numbers Including Operators for Calculating Values**

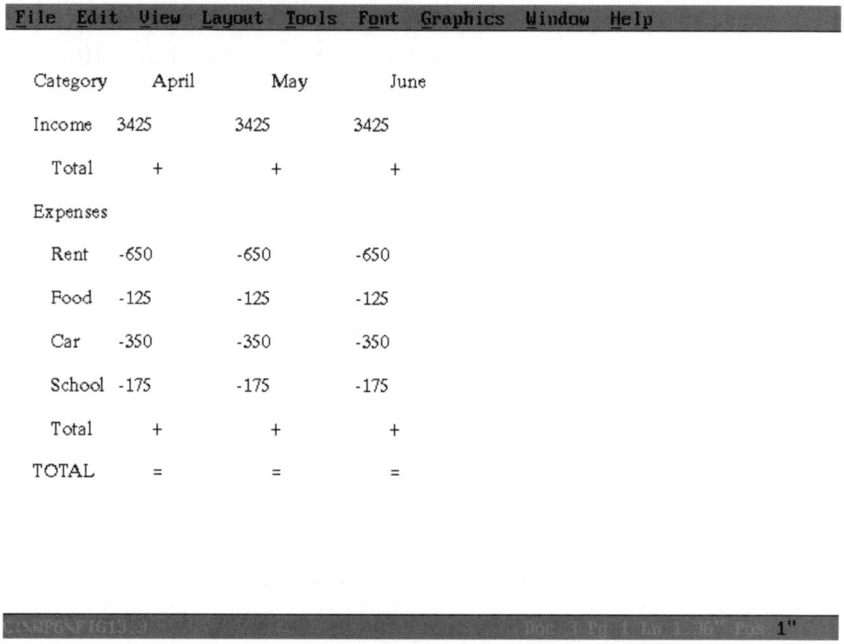

File	Edit	View	Layout	Tools	Font	Graphics	Window	Help

Category	April	May	June
Income	3425	3425	3425
Total	+	+	+
Expenses			
Rent	-650	-650	-650
Food	-125	-125	-125
Car	-350	-350	-350
School	-175	-175	-175
Total	+	+	+
TOTAL	=	=	=

The **+ function**, when placed in a column with Math on, will total all of the values that appear in the column above it. In other words, in the budget example you see in Figure 13.3, it provides a subtotal for income and expenses.

The **= function**, when placed in a column with Math on, will total all of the subtotals above it. In this case, it adds the subtotal for income (which is a positive number) to the subtotal for expenses (which is a negative number) and gives the difference.

The *** function**, when placed in a column with Math on, will give you a grand total of all totals above it.

Calculating

When you have entered all the values and all the functions, it's time to calculate the results. Use the **Alt+F7,3,3** key combination [Mouse Moves: **T**ools, **M**ath, **C**alculate] and WordPerfect will perform the math functions as they were defined and as you see in

Figure 13.4. You can see that though we entered negative numbers using hyphens (such as -175), WordPerfect uses parentheses (as defined in the Math dialog box) to express calculated negative numbers after the calculation has taken place such as (1,300.00)+.

On the actual WordPerfect screen, when math is performed, the functions (+, =, or *) remain visible. When the results are printed, however, the hard copy looks like any other WordPerfect document. You don't see any of the functions.

But, you can see how WordPerfect placed parentheses around the total for expenses because negative numbers were defined to appear with parentheses in the Math Definition screen shown in Figure 13.1. Remember, you could have defined negative numbers so they appear with a minus sign.

Turning Math Off

Your last step in the Math process is to turn Math off using the **Alt+F7,3,1** key combination [Mouse Moves: **T**ools, **M**ath, **O**ff].

▼ *Figure 13.4.   Final Values When WordPerfect Is Told to Perform a Calculation*

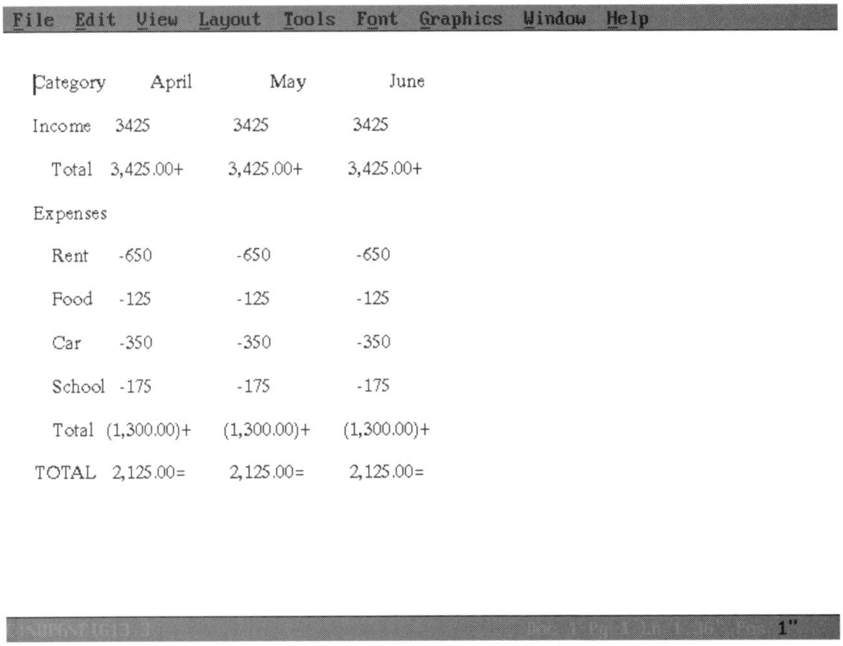

File	Edit	View	Layout	Tools	Font	Graphics	Window	Help

Category	April	May	June
Income	3425	3425	3425
Total	3,425.00+	3,425.00+	3,425.00+
Expenses			
Rent	-650	-650	-650
Food	-125	-125	-125
Car	-350	-350	-350
School	-175	-175	-175
Total	(1,300.00)+	(1,300.00)+	(1,300.00)+
TOTAL	2,125.00=	2,125.00=	2,125.00=

1"

TIP

The Alt+F7,3,1 **key combination turns Math off.**

Some Hints About Math with Columns

Using Math is helpful and fun, but keep the following in mind as you learn how to use this feature.

▲ Set the tabs in such a way that there is enough room for text labels in the first column.

▲ Be sure that you separate columns by only one tab space.

▲ All math columns are defined as Decimal tabs. That's why any values with decimal points, such as those you see in Figure 13.3, will align along the decimal point.

▲ Use your reveal codes! For example, the reveal code for the + function is [Do Subtot] and for the = function it is [Do Tot]. They really do tell you what's going on!

▲ Enter all your column headings before you turn Math on.

▲ You can change values at any time, but WordPerfect will not recalculate new totals until you tell it to do so by using the **Alt+F7,3,4** key combination [**Mouse Moves:** Select Layout, **Math, Calculate**].

▲ If there are only numeric values, you can skip the Math Definition step and go right to entering information (after you turn math on).

CHECK YOURSELF

1. Get your most recent department or food store receipt. Select three items and enter the name of the item, a tab, and the cost for each item. Now use WordPerfect Math to calculate the total cost of the five items.

2. In another column that you create, compute the total costs plus 10 percent for inflation purposes.

ANSWERS

1. Your finished screen could look something like this:

Milk	1.89
Bread	.68
Cheese	2.39
Total	4.96

2. The new total would be 5.46.

Lesson 38: Tables and Math

As we describe and use Math, you can see how handy a WordPerfect feature it is. But, there's an even handier, more powerful, and less cumbersome way to use WordPerfect Math. That's in conjunction with WordPerfect's Tables feature that we discussed in the last chapter.

You may remember that Math is one of the options on the Table Edit screen you see in Figure 13.5.

To use Math with a table:

1. Create the table.
2. Enter the Table Edit screen.
3. Place the cursor in the location you want to enter a Math function or a formula.
4. Select option 5 for Math.
5. Select the option you want to use (Calculate, Formula, etc.).
6. Exit the Table Edit screen.

The Math Options

In Figure 13.5, you can see the Table Edit window for a table was created that will be used to compute the costs of a job estimate.

The two options that we will deal with here are Calc and Formula (option 5).

Calc will perform the calculations you tell it through the use of various operators. For example, in Figure 13.6, the + operator will total the columns for B and C. As you will see, these operators are entered as formulas.

▼ **Figure 13.5.   In the Table Edit Window, Ready to Use Math**

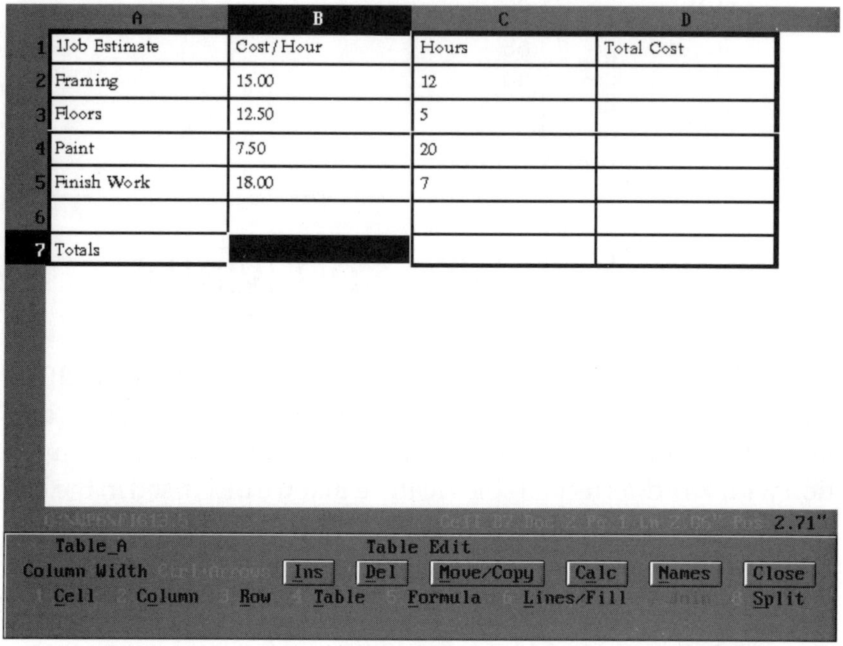

	A	B	C	D
1	1Job Estimate	Cost/Hour	Hours	Total Cost
2	Framing	15.00	12	
3	Floors	12.50	5	
4	Paint	7.50	20	
5	Finish Work	18.00	7	
6				
7	Totals			

```
                                                    2.71"
    Table_A                     Table Edit
 Column Width            Ins   Del   Move/Copy   Calc   Names   Close
   Cell    Column    Row    Table    Formula   Lines/Fill         Split
```

Formula (option 5) is one of the really exciting and time-saving features of WordPerfect.

Operators and Tables Math

Using operators in Tables and Math is not much different than using a formula. You enter in the cell of your choice, one of the operators we talked about earlier (such as + or =) and then have WordPerfect calculate the values. For example, if you wanted WordPerfect to sum all the values that appear in a table, enter the * function in the last cell in the column and select **Calc** in the Table Edit window. The calculation will take place.

Using a Formula

To use a formula in Tables and Math, you must first enter it into the cell where you want the results of the formula to appear. Here's

Lesson 38: Tables and Math

▼ ***Figure 13.6. Using an Operator in a Table to Perform Math***

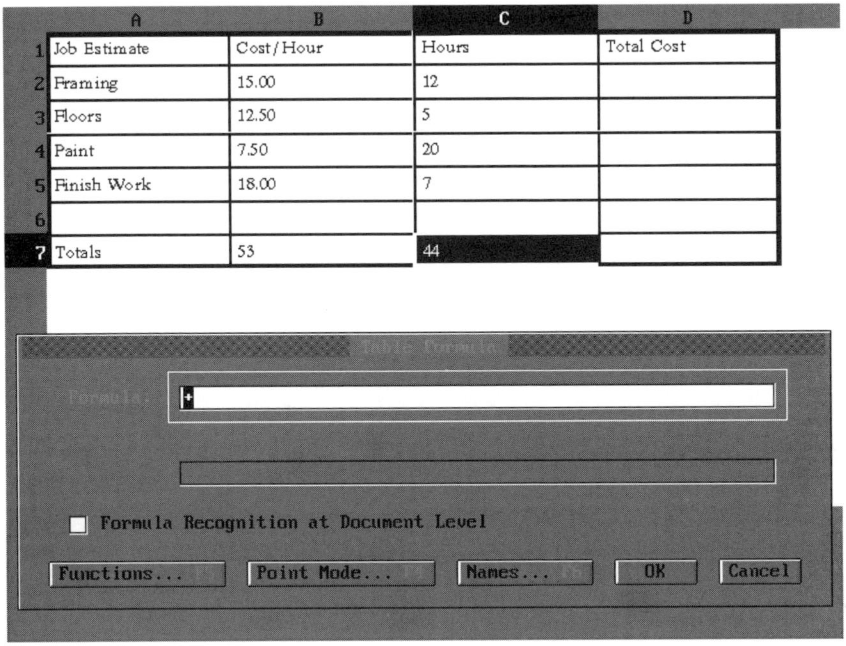

how we did it to compute the values that go in the column titled *Total Cost* as you see in the Table Edit window shown in Figure 13.7. When you enter this formula into cell *D2*, WordPerfect automatically computes the product which in this case is 180.00.

Notice how in the lower left-hand corner of Figure 13.7, on the status line, the formula is shown. WordPerfect always places an equals sign (=) at the beginning of the formula. You can't see the formula by examining the cell in which it appears in the Table Edit window. You have to look on the status line.

The total cost is the product of cost/hour times hours. In WordPerfect Math language, that turns out to be *B2*C2*, where *B2* represents the cell address for the cost/hour for framing and *C2* represents the hours. What goes in cell D2 is simply the product.

To create and use the formula:

1. Be sure you are in the Table Edit window.
2. Select **F**ormula (option 5). When you do this, you will see the Table Formula dialog box as you see in Figure 13.8.

▼ *Figure 13.7.   Using a Formula Placed in a Cell to Compute a New Value*

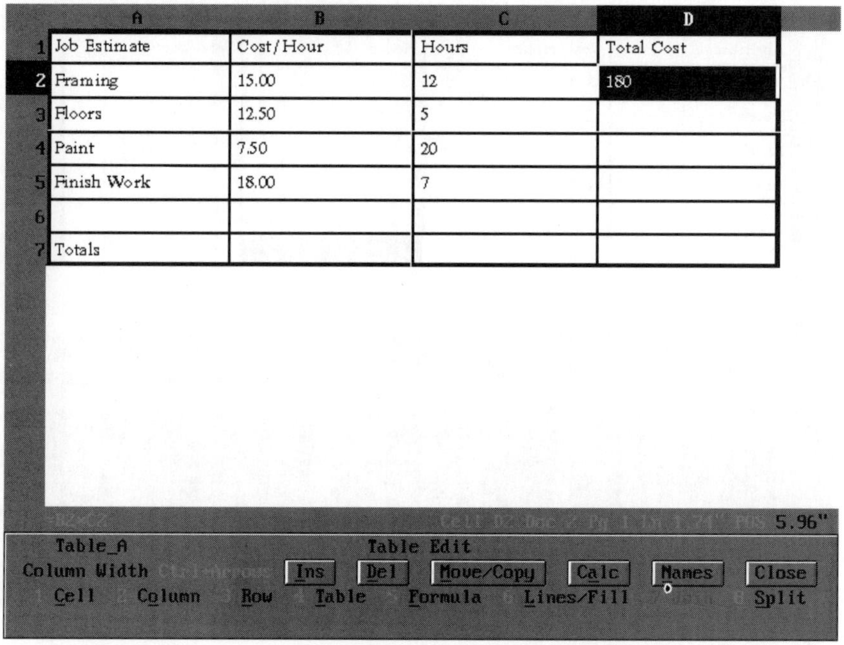

	A	B	C	D
1	Job Estimate	Cost/Hour	Hours	Total Cost
2	Framing	15.00	12	180
3	Floors	12.50	5	
4	Paint	7.50	20	
5	Finish Work	18.00	7	
6				
7	Totals			

```
                                                             5.96"
    Table_A                    Table Edit
Column Width              [Ins] [Del] [Move/Copy] [Calc] [Names] [Close]
   Cell    Column    Row    Table   Formula   Lines/Fill         Split
```

3.   Enter the formula you want to use. In Figure 13.8, you can see it's the B2*C2 formula to compute the product of the contents in cell B2 and Cell C2 and place it in cell D2.

4.   Select **OK** and the new value will be computed (as you can see in Figure 13.8, where the value 180 is in cell D2).

You can enter virtually any formula you want in a cell and refer to other cells for the values in the formula. Just remember that you must be in the Table Edit window.

Copying a Formula

Since we want to compute the total costs for all facets of this job, this same formula has to be used in *all* the cells in column *D*. We could enter a new formula for each cell, but that would be tedious. WordPerfect lets us take advantage of the fact that the formula is the same, except for different cell addresses. Where the formula in cell *D2* is *B2*C2*, the formula in cell *D3* is *B3*C3* and so on. WordPerfect remembers all of this.

Lesson 38: Tables and Math

▼ *Figure 13.8. The Table Formula Dialog Box*

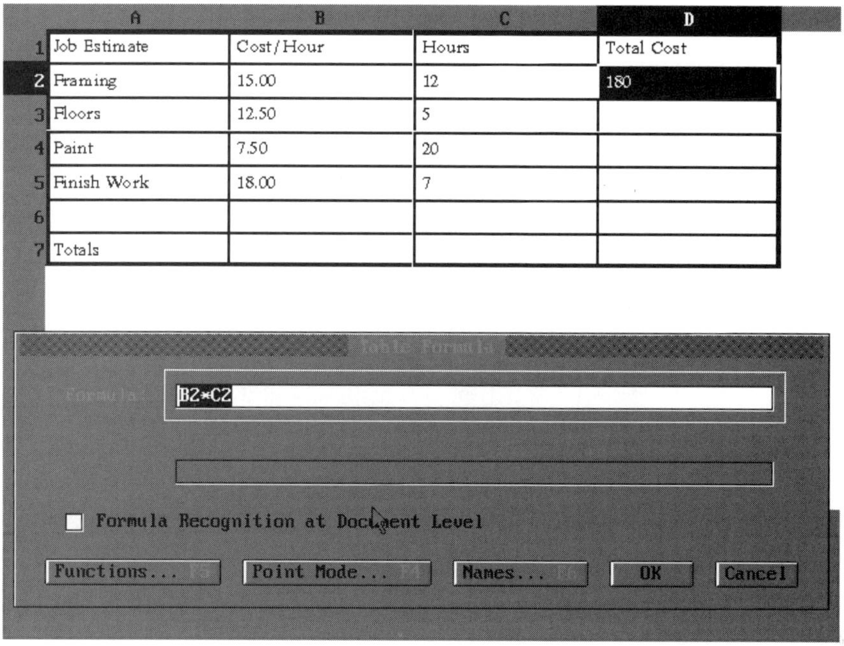

Formulas always maintain their relative references when copied, so there is no need to retype new cell addresses. What we need to do is take advantage of WordPerfect's Move/Copy feature found in the Table Edit dialog box.

To copy a formula:

1. Be sure that you are in the Table Edit window.
2. Place the cursor in a cell that has the formula you want to copy.
3. Select **M**ove/Copy. When you do this, you will see the Move dialog box shown in Figure 13.9.
4. Select Co**p**y to copy a cell to another location. You will then see the Copy Cell dialog box you see in Figure 13.10.
5. Select **D**own since we want to copy the formula down a column.
6. In the **How Many?** box in the Copy Cell dialog box, enter the number of times you want to copy the cell down. In this case, it is **3** times (see Figure 13.10), since there are three cells below the one containing the formula into which we want to copy the formula.
7. Select **OK**.

▼ *Figure 13.9.   The Move Dialog Box*

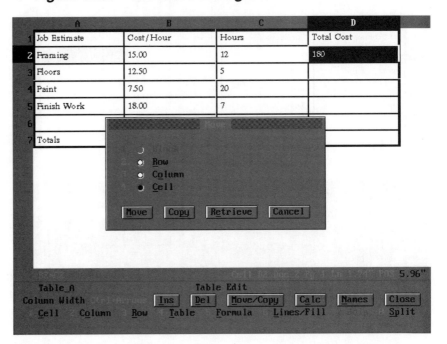

▼ *Figure 13.10.   The Copy Cell Dialog Box*

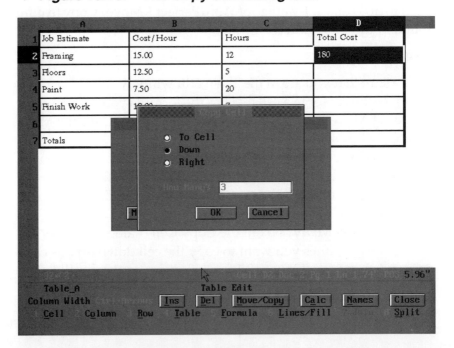

WordPerfect does the rest. As you can see in Figure 13.11, the formula is copied down the specified number of times. The formula will be copied and the values inserted.

We finished off the table by entering a new formula in cell B7 that would sum the values in cells B2, B3, B4, and B5. The formula looked like this:

B2+B3+B4+B5

You can see in Figure 13.12, how the formula was then copied to the right (see the Copy Cell dialog box in Figure 13.10) as you can see by examining the left side of the status line where the formula *D2+D3+D4+D5* is apparent.

Formulas can be as complex as you would like and can reference any cell in a table. One important thing to remember about formulas is that you should make sure that you have the correct cell references. For example, if you reference the cell in which the cursor is located in a formula, it will use the value in that cell to compute the result.

One very useful and interesting application of WordPerfect Tables Math is to do the traditional "What If . . . " that's usually left

Lesson 38: Tables and Math

▼ **Figure 13.11.** *Copying a Formula Down a Column*

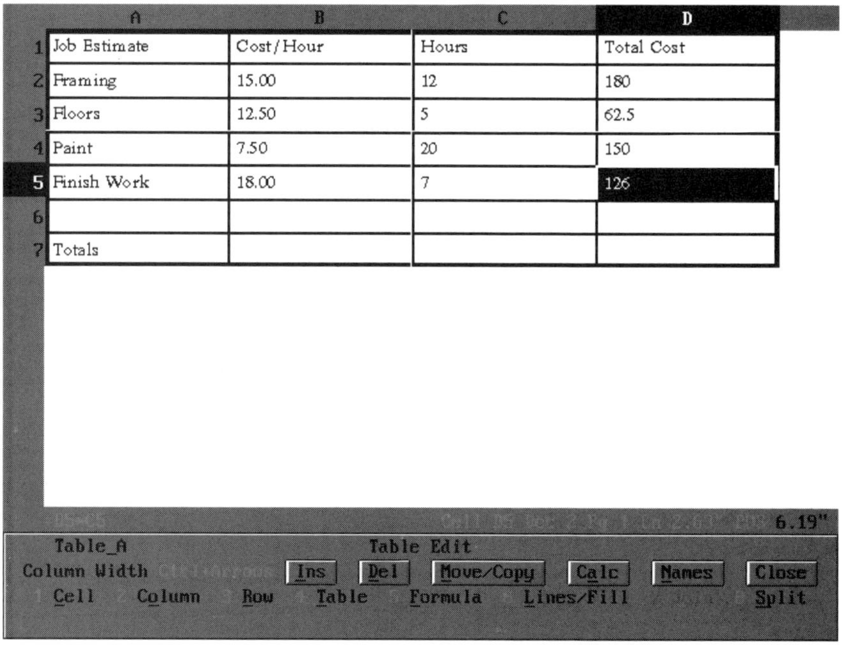

▼ *Figure 13.12.* *Copying a Formula to the Right*

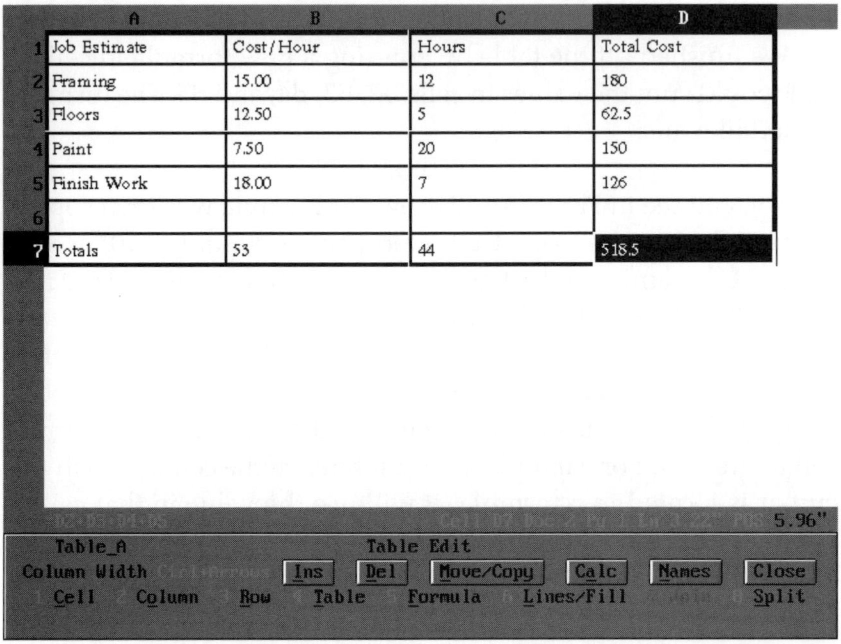

	A	B	C	D
1	Job Estimate	Cost/Hour	Hours	Total Cost
2	Framing	15.00	12	180
3	Floors	12.50	5	62.5
4	Paint	7.50	20	150
5	Finish Work	18.00	7	126
6				
7	Totals	53	44	518.5

```
                                                                    5.96"
      Table_A                        Table Edit
   Column Width          Ins   Del    Move/Copy   Calc   Names    Close
     Cell    Column   Row   Table   Formula   Lines/Fill         Split
```

to spreadsheets. Here, you keep one or two values constant and create a formula that shows the effects of varying one value on a set of others.

In Figure 13.13, you can see a table that computes the simple interest on an investment for various interest rates. Here's how the values in the cells were computed and what formulas were used. We also used the Column option in the Table Edit window to change the format of the values to currency. The last thing we did was make format changes. Remember, first substance, then style.

To compute simple interest:

1. The column labels were entered and the *5000* value was entered in cell *A2* and then copied down the rest of the column.
2. The value *.10* was entered in cell *B2*, then a formula (*B2+.10*) was written in cell *B3* that added .10 to the contents of cell *C2*. This formula was then copied down the column so that each result was the addition of the previous cell's value plus .10.
3. In *C2*, the formula *A2+(A2*B2)* was entered. This adds 10 percent of the investment to the investment and prints the result.

Lesson 38: Tables and Math

▼ ***Figure 13.13. Computing Values Using a Formula***

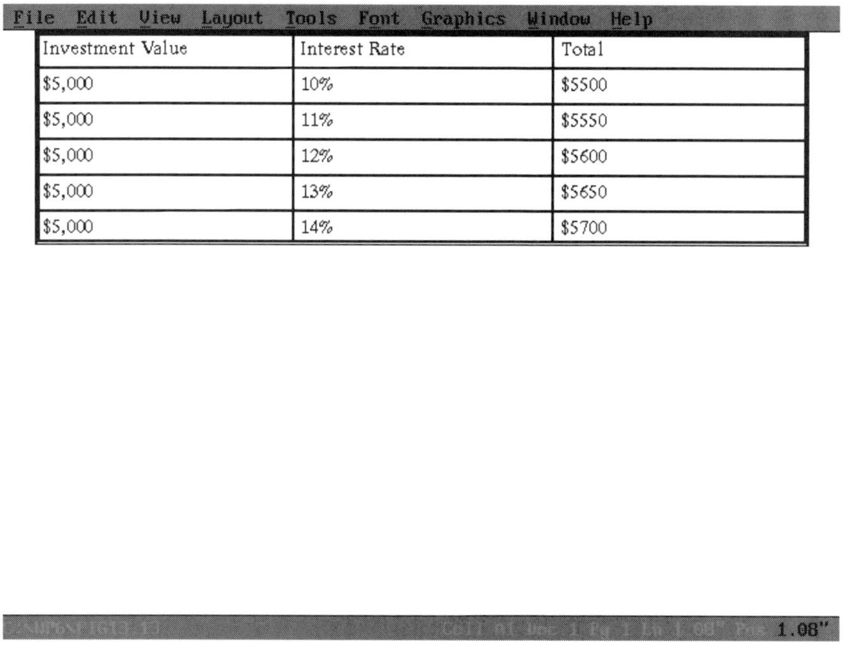

File Edit View Layout Tools Font Graphics Window Help
1.08"

Investment Value	Interest Rate	Total
$5,000	10%	$5500
$5,000	11%	$5550
$5,000	12%	$5600
$5,000	13%	$5650
$5,000	14%	$5700

CHECK YOURSELF

1. Create a four-column table that lists your expense category, what you spent last week, what you plan on spending this week, and the difference.
2. Add a fifth column to the table and compute a percentage (use a formula) of the increase or decrease from last week to this week.

ANSWERS

1. Your table could look like this:

Rent	325	325	0
Food	26	23	3
Gas	12	6	6

2. Your table could look like this:

Rent	325	325	0	0
Food	26	23	3	.115
Gas	12	6	6	.50

Remember, WordPerfect does all the figuring for you.

Lesson 39: Using Functions in Tables

Here's the best part of Tables and Math WordPerfect functions. A **function** is a predefined formula. So, instead of creating a formula such as B2+B3+B4+B5, you can simply sum the values in all those cells using the **SUM** function. WordPerfect has almost 100 of these functions. As with a formula, the function is placed in a cell and it carries out a particular operation. Functions operate on a range of numbers that you define using the cell addresses.

What can some of these functions do? Here's just a sample of ten popular ones.

▲ The **AVE** function averages a range of numbers.
▲ The **COUNT** function counts the number of values in a list.
 · ▲ The **CURRENCY** function takes a value and automatically formats it in the currency format.
▲ The **DATE** function automatically enters the date in a cell.
▲ The **FACT** function computes the factorial of a value.
▲ The **FV** function computes the future value of a number.
▲ The **LOWER** function converts characters to lowercase.
▲ The **PMT** function calculates the amount of a payment.
▲ The **RANDOM** function generates a random number.
▲ The **SQRT** function computes the square root of a number.
▲ The **SUM** function computes the sum of a list of numbers.

Here's a simple example of how functions work.

Let's say you want to know what the future value of your investment program will be at various interest rates. You have $1,000 in the bank, and plan on investing $50 per month for 20 years.

To use the PMT function:

1. Create a table as you see in Figure 13.14.
2. Go into the Table Edit screen.
3. Place the cursor in cell **E2**.
4. Select Formula (option 5).
5. Press **F5** for functions. When you do this, you will see the list of functions that WordPerfect makes available.

▼ **Figure 13.14.** **Starting to Use a Function**

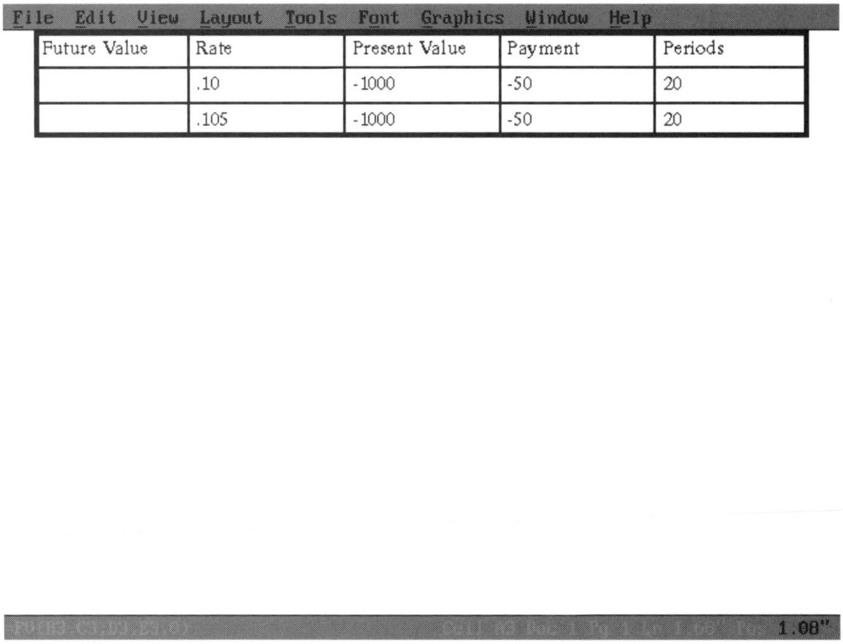

File Edit View Layout Tools Font Graphics Window Help

Future Value	Rate	Present Value	Payment	Periods
	.10	-1000	-50	20
	.105	-1000	-50	20

1.08"

6. Use the down arrow key to find the **FV** function as you see in Figure 13.15.

TIP

When searching in a list, you can also enter the first few characters of the function and WordPerfect will take you there or as close as possible.

7. Select **FV(rate%, PV, payment, periods [,type])**.
8. Enter the cell addresses that represent the values that need to go into the function as you see in Figure 13.16.
9. Select **OK** and the future value of $1,000 invested at 10% with additions of $50 every month for 20 years is $9,591, a tidy little sum as you see in Figure 13.17 (after some new formatting). You can see we also copied the function into cell *A3* to find out what the future value would be at 1/2% higher interest rate.

▼ *Figure 13.15.* **Finding the FV Function**

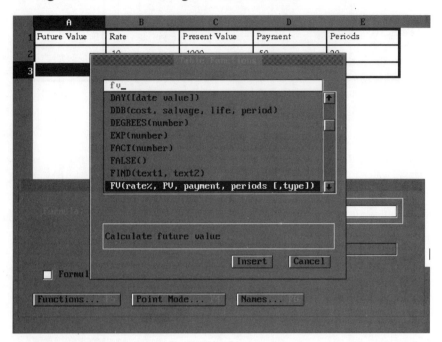

	A	B	C	D	E
1	Future Value	Rate	Present Value	Payment	Periods
2		10	1000	50	20
3					

fv_

DAY([date value])
DDB(cost, salvage, life, period)
DEGREES(number)
EXP(number)
FACT(number)
FALSE()
FIND(text1, text2)
FV(rate%, PV, payment, periods [,type])

Calculate future value

[Insert] [Cancel]

☐ Formul

[Functions...] [Point Mode...] [Names...]

▼ *Figure 13.16.* **Entering Cell Addresses in a Function**

	A	B	C	D	E
1	Future Value	Rate	Present Value	Payment	Periods
2		.10	-1000	-50	20
3		.105	-1000	-50	20

Formula: FV(b2,c2,d2,e2)

Example: FV(rate%, PV, payment, periods [,type])

☐ Formula Recognition at Document Level

[OK] [Cancel]

▼ *Figure 13.17.* *The Results of the PV Function*

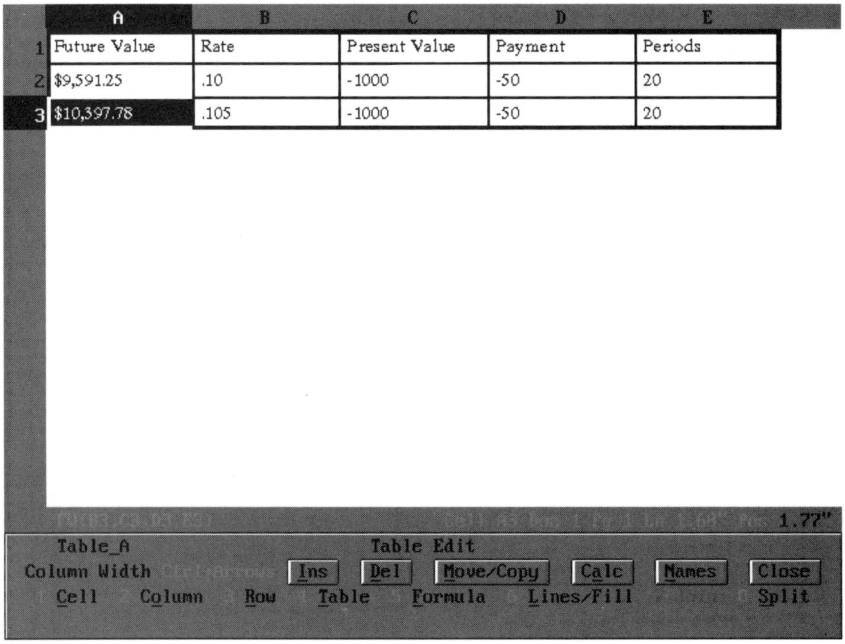

	A	B	C	D	E
1	Future Value	Rate	Present Value	Payment	Periods
2	$9,591.25	.10	-1000	-50	20
3	$10,397.78	.105	-1000	-50	20

```
                                                              1.77"
   Table_A                  Table Edit
Column Width              Ins  Del  Move/Copy  Calc  Names  Close
   Cell    Column   Row   Table   Formula   Lines/Fill        Split
```

TIP

If you mess up in entering a function, you can easily edit it by placing the cursor in the cell and selecting Formula in the Table Edit window.

CHECK YOURSELF

▲ Create a table with 2 columns and 5 rows. In column *B* use the **SQRT** function to compute the square roots of each number in column *A*. In cell *A11*, use the **SUM** function to sum all of the values in column *A*.

If you use numbers and you use WordPerfect, then you will be using WordPerfect Math. Once you combine the Math feature with WordPerfect Tables, you have a one-two combination that is unbeatable for arranging numerical information exactly as you would like. The Tables and Math features both need columns for various operations. In the next chapter we'll learn more about columns, the different kinds there are, and how they work.

PRACTICE WHAT YOU'VE LEARNED

1. What is the advantage of using Tables for Math versus using Math alone?
2. What is the difference between the * and the + symbol in WordPerfect Math and when should each be used?
3. When is the only time that WordPerfect can recalculate new totals?
4. If you only have numeric values in your table, what steps can you skip in the use of WordPerfect Math?

ANSWERS

1. With tables, you can align values in columns and rows for a much neater appearance and easier entry.
2. The * symbol gives you the grand total of all the values (or subtotals) above it. The + symbol totals the values in the column above it.
3. When you tell it to use the **Alt+F7,3,4** key combination.
4. The math definition step.

WordPerfect Columns

There are so many reasons why columns are an important feature to have available in any word processor. The most obvious is when you want to write something that will appear in newspaper format. With all the newsletters being written these days, to say nothing about the buzz words and desktop publishing, you'll surely see how the Columns feature adds to your arsenal of powerful tools. In this chapter you will learn how to:

▲ Distinguish between newspaper and parallel style columns

▲ Define columns

▲ Enter text into newspaper and parallel style columns

▲ Edit newspaper and parallel style columns

▲ Edit column definitions

Important Keys
Alt+F7

Important Terms
column definition
columns
newspaper style columns
parallel style columns
Text Column Definition dialog box
Text Columns dialog box

Lesson 40: Creating WordPerfect Columns

WordPerfect offers two types of columns: **newspaper style**, where text ends at the bottom of the page and continues at the top of the next column, and **parallel style**, where columns are adjacent to each other but are independent of one another. Figure 14.1 shows you a comparison of the two styles. On the left are the newspaper columns that snake from the bottom of one column to the top of the next. On the right are parallel (or side-by-side) columns, where the related entries are presented parallel to one another.

Column Basics

There are four basic steps involved in creating columns:

1. Place the cursor in the location where you want the columns to begin.
2. Define the type of columns you want to use. When you do this, you automatically turn columns on.
3. Enter the text you want to appear as columns.
4. Turn the **Column** feature off.

TIP

You can also enter text and then go back and transform that into columns. You just skip step 3 above.

▼ *Figure 14.1.* *Two Types of WordPerfect Columns*

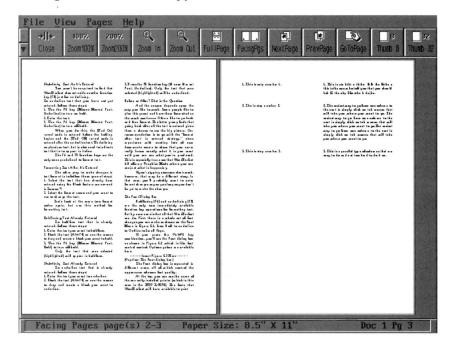

Defining Columns

To begin the **column definition** operation, you use the **Alt+F7,1,3** key combination [**Mouse Moves:** Select **L**ayout, **C**olumns], which produces the Text Column Definition dialog box you see in Figure 14.2. Whether you are defining newspaper or parallel style columns, you then need to make five decisions about how you want your columns to be defined.

TIP

Use the Alt+F7,1 **key combination to define columns.**

TIP

Don't forget to use the Column option on the Ribbon to quickly set columns.

▼ *Figure 14.2.* *The Text Columns Dialog Box*

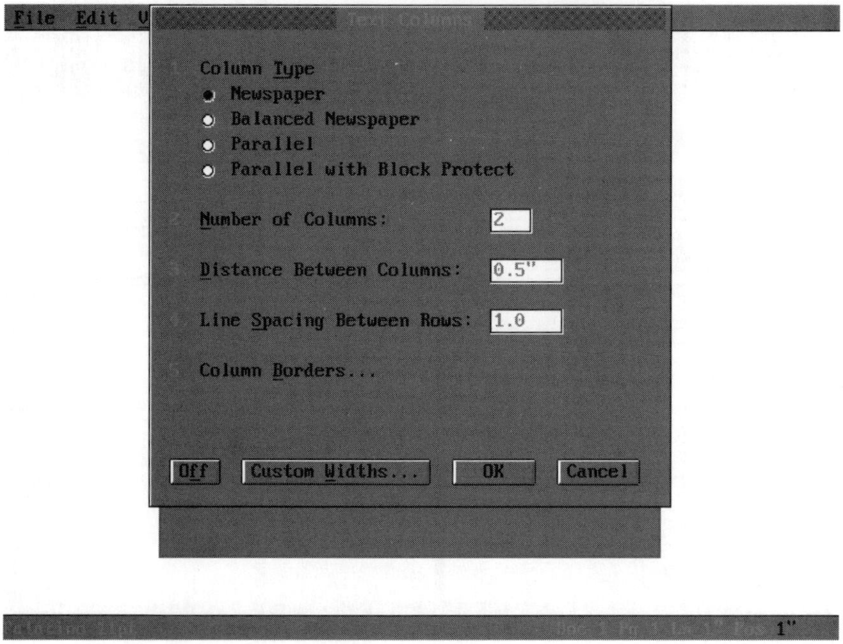

First, you have to decide whether you are going to format the columns as newspaper or parallel style columns. As you can see, the default (it's already selected) is for newspaper style columns. To change to parallel style columns, just select Column **T**ype (option 1) and then select **P**arallel (option 3).

Besides newspaper and parallel style, you can select **Balanced Newspaper**, where WordPerfect will ensure that columns are the same length, and **Parallel with Block Protect**, where Wordperfect ensures that blocks of parallel columns text will stay together on one page.

Second, you need to indicate the number of columns you want to have. The default is 2 and you can have up to 24.

Third, you need to indicate the amount of space that you want between columns (the default is one-half inch). If you do not enter a value here, WordPerfect will calculate the proper spacing given the margins that have been set and the number of columns you want to use.

Fourth, you can set the line spacing between rows or lines of text.

Finally, you can select Column **B**orders, and define the type of line you want to appear around columns—often a nice touch, as you see in Figure 14.3. By the way, the columns you see in Figure 14.3 are balanced and of equal length.

You can define columns anyplace in a document. The text will not be affected, however, until you turn the Column feature on.

Lesson 40: Creating WordPerfect Columns

Deleting Columns

This is simple. You can delete a column by deleting the [Col Def] code that appears once it is defined.

Creating Newspaper Style Columns

Since WordPerfect defaults fit perfectly in the generation of newspaper columns, you only need the following keystrokes to define newspaper columns: **Alt+F7,1,1** [Mouse Moves: **L**ayout, **C**olumns].

▼ *Figure 14.3.* *Balancing Column Length*

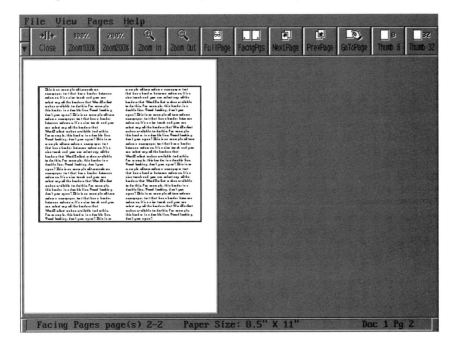

These keystrokes select:
The Column/Tables dialog box
The Columns option
The default of two columns
One-half inch between columns (and sets the columns)
One space between rows
No column borders

TIP

Use the Alt+F7,1,Enter **key combination to create newspaper style columns.**

Entering Newspaper Style Text

There are two ways to format text as a newspaper style column. The first way is to simply enter the text after you define the columns and then select **Columns** as we discussed earlier. As you enter text and it reaches the bottom of the page, it will snake to the top of the next column and format as a newspaper style column.

The second way is to enter the text before you define the column, then go back to the beginning of the text, and define the columns. Some people find this way easier, since they can then edit away and worry only about content before becoming concerned about format. If you choose to enter text first and then format, be sure that you have only straight text and no tables or other columns in the text that you intend to turn into columns. If you are not careful you will create a mess that will be difficult to undo.

Once you are finished creating columns, be sure of select Off with the **Alt+F7,1,Off** key combination [**Mouse Moves:** Layout, Columns, Off]. Make sure that the cursor is located after the text you want to appear as columns.

TIP

Once you turn a type of column on, you cannot create another type of column until that first column definition is turned off.

Creating Parallel Columns

Lesson 40: Creating WordPerfect Columns

Defining parallel columns is much the same process with a few more keystrokes. Use the **Alt+F7,1,1,3** key combination [**Mouse Moves:** **L**ayout, **C**olumns, **T**ype, **P**arallel]. The only difference between defining newspaper and parallel style columns is that with parallel style columns, you have to select **Type** in the Text Columns dialog box and then select **P**arallel.

Parallel columns (of the type that you see in Figure 14.4) are absolutely stunning columns, especially for instructional purposes where, for example, you can list steps on the left and explain them on the right. To make these columns even more attractive, we centered column heads (Stop, Title, Description) and fully justified the text.

Entering Parallel Style Text

Entering text into parallel columns is not as straightforward as entering text in newspaper style columns. Although it's not difficult,

▼ ***Figure 14.4. An Example of Parallel Columns***

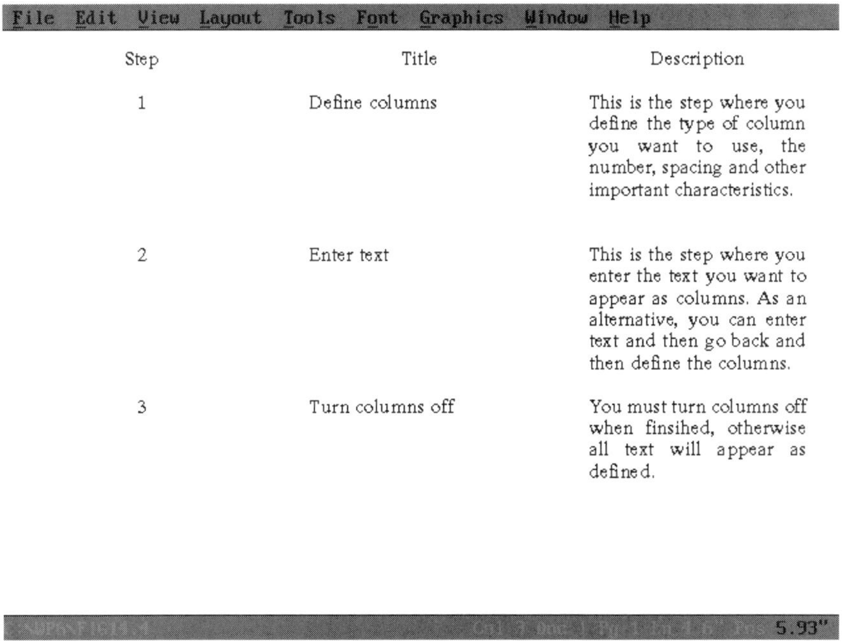
File Edit View Layout Tools Font Graphics Window Help

Step	Title	Description
1	Define columns	This is the step where you define the type of column you want to use, the number, spacing and other important characteristics.
2	Enter text	This is the step where you enter the text you want to appear as columns. As an alternative, you can enter text and then go back and then define the columns.
3	Turn columns off	You must turn columns off when finsihed, otherwise all text will appear as defined.

5.93"

there is one important thing you need to remember. To switch from one column to the next, use the **Ctrl+Enter** key combination. This key combination will switch from one column to the other. Or, you can, of course, just use the mouse to place the cursor in the next column.

TIP

You can use a table (without lines) to appear as parallel style columns. There will be no difference in appearance.

To create the parallel columns you see in Figure 14.4:

1. Press **Alt+F7,1,1,3** [**Mouse Moves: L**ayout, **C**olumns, Column Type, **P**arallel].
2. Select **N**umber of Columns.
3. Enter **3**.
4. Select **OK**. The three parallel columns will appear with one-half inch space between them.
5. Use the **Shift+F6** key combination to center the text in column 1.
6. Enter the text **Step**.
7. Press the **Ctrl+Enter** key combination to move to column 2.
8. Use the **Shift+F6** key combination to center the text in column 2.
9. Enter the text **Title**.
10. Press the **Ctrl+Enter** key combination to move to column 3.
11. Use the **Shift+F6** key combination to center the text in column 3.
12. Enter the text **Description**.
13. Press the **Ctrl+Enter** key combination to move back to column 1 and then continue centering and entering text until your screen looks like the one shown in Figure 14.4.

TIP

The Ctrl+Enter **key combination is the critical keystroke combination to go from one column to the next and then back again.**

Unlike newspaper style columns, there's no easy way to enter text and then go back and define it as a parallel style column.

Once you are finished entering the text that you want to appear as parallel style columns, turn the Column feature off.

TIP

If you want to adjust the space between columns, select Custom Widths from the Text Columns dialog box and edit the width as needed.

CHECK YOURSELF

1. Retrieve a page of text from any WordPerfect file that you have created. Format the text into three newspaper style columns. Print out a copy of the page.
2. Create four columns of parallel style text (call them *col 1*, *col 2*, etc.) and make five entries into each of the columns (enter *1*, *2*, *3* through *5*).

ANSWERS

1. You can set almost as many columns as you want on a page (up to 24), but keep in mind that you may have to decrease the font size to make lots of columns work and fit together.
2. Remember that parallel columns are quite different from newspaper style columns and are used for different reasons as well.

Lesson 41: Editing Columns

Now that you've learned how to create newspaper and parallel style columns, it's time to turn our attention to how to edit them.

Editing Newspaper Style Columns

You can use all the regular keystrokes to move text around within any newspaper column and make whatever edits as are necessary.

For example, the **Ctrl+Right Arrow** key combination will move you to the beginning of the next word to the right. You can only move from word to word within one column. And, the **Up** and **Down Arrow** keys will move you line by line through one column.

But what if you need to go to another column and do some editing? Easy. Here's a summary of how to get from column to column within a document that is formatted as newspaper style columns.

TIP

WordPerfect always shows you what column you are in on the status line.

To Move From	Key Combination
Column to column	Ctrl+Home, Right or Left Arrow key
First or last column on a page	Ctrl+Home, Home, Left or Right Arrow key
Top or bottom of the current column	Ctrl+Home, Up or Down Arrow key

TIP

If you place the cursor on the last word in a column at the bottom of a page and then use the Ctrl+Right Arrow **key combination, the cursor will automatically move to the next column.**

You can also move to any newspaper style column in a document by clicking the mouse pointer on that column.

Editing Parallel Style Columns

You edit parallel style columns in exactly the same way as you edit newspaper style columns, and you can, of course, move to any parallel style column in a document by clicking the mouse pointer on that column.

Editing the Column Definition

You might have completed all the tasks for defining columns and entering text, and you may even like the way things look, but . . . something just doesn't look right. Perhaps you want to add another column, but not go through the trouble of redefining everything.

For example, let's say you have names, addresses, and product information that appears as two newspaper style columns such as those you see in Figure 14.5, but you find that you have enough room on the page to use three instead of two columns.

To change the column definition:

1. Turn reveal codes on [Alt+F3].
2. Go to the position in the document where you defined the columns. Look for the [Col Def] reveal code.
3. Place the cursor on the [Column Def] reveal code.
4. Press the **Alt+F7,1** key combination [**Mouse Moves:** Layout, Columns].

▼ **Figure 14.5. A Two-Column Layout**

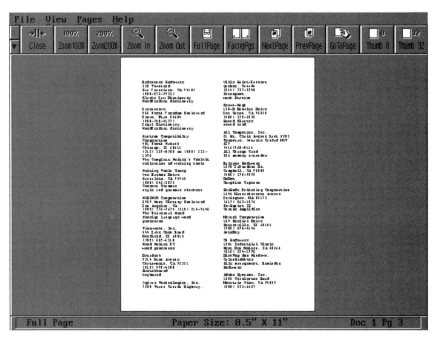

5. Edit the Text Columns dialog box as you see fit.
6. Select **OK** and the new column definition will take effect.

You can see the result in Figure 14.6. There are now three columns of names and addresses. We cut down the amount of space we used by one-third.

CHECK YOURSELF

▲ In the last check you created three newspaper style columns. Now go back and edit the Text Columns dialog box so that you have two newspaper columns that are one-half inch apart.

ANSWER

▲ To change the definition of a column you need not redefine columns or turn them off. Just go to the reveal codes and follow the instructions in this lesson.

▼ **Figure 14.6. A Three Column Layout**

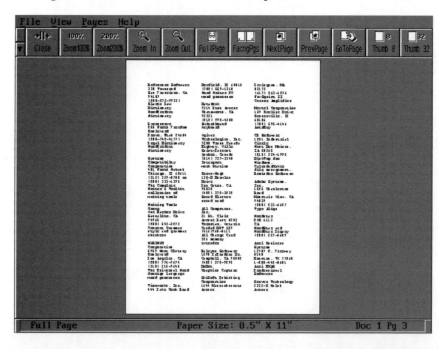

Columns are cool. There's no other way to arrange text in a neat and clean format with so few keystrokes and so little effort. It's only another way that WordPerfect provides for the arrangement of text to fit your needs. Similarly, sorting information in numerical and alphabetical order is also a WordPerfect specialty, as you will see in Chapter 15.

Lesson 41: Editing Columns

PRACTICE WHAT YOU'VE LEARNED

1. What are the exact keystrokes you would enter to create a set of two parallel columns?
2. What is the primary difference between newspaper and parallel style applications?
3. How do parallel style columns differ from tables text, and when would you use one rather than the other?
4. How can you use parallel and newspaper style columns in the same document?

ANSWERS

1. **Alt+F7, Enter**
2. Newspaper style columns snake from the bottom of one to the top of another as you commonly see in newspapers. Parallel columns appear as corresponding entries on a page and are related to one another.
3. They are basically not much different. Tables are easier to use and can only be used if you want lines around entries in the tables or columns.
4. By turning the columns definition off and entering a new definition.

Sorting with WordPerfect

If you have ever had to alphabetize a long list of names or items, or place in numerical order a group of numbered entries, you know how tedious a job that can be. WordPerfect's Sort feature takes care of all this for you and sorts lists, lines, whole paragraphs, and even table entries in either ascending or descending order. You'll learn how to perform these types of sorts in this chapter. In this chapter you'll learn how to:

▲ **Use WordPerfect Sort**

▲ **Sort a simple list**

▲ **Sort by line or paragraph**

▲ **Sort blocks of text**

▲ **Sort on more than one field**

▲ **Sort within a table**

▲ **Use the sort feature to select and then sort records**

Important Keys	*Important Terms*
Ctrl+F9	Edit Sort Key dialog box
	Edit Sort key dialog box
	field
	Merge/Sort dialog box
	record
	select
	sort
	Sort dialog box
	Sort (Source and Destination) dialog box
	type
	word

Lesson 42: Sorting Basics

The sorting process begins once you have identified the list or group of entries you want to sort and press the **Ctrl+F9** key combination [**Mouse Moves: T**ools, Sort]. Let's look closely at the basic steps that are involved in any sort.

How WordPerfect Sorts

WordPerfect will automatically sort on the first character that it encounters in any list, unless you tell it otherwise.

To initiate the sorting process:

1. Press the **Ctrl+F9** key combination [**Mouse Moves: T**ools, Sort].
2. Select Sort (option 2).
3. Press **Enter** to sort the document on the screen or enter the name of the file you want to sort.
4. Identify the criteria you want to use for the sorting.
5. Select **P**erform Action in the Sort dialog box.

A Simple Sort

Let's go through these steps and a simple sorting of a list of ten items as shown below. Enter this list for practice on a clean document screen.

nails
hammer
screws
lumber screening
glue
shingles
tar paper
wrench
pry bar
wire

Lesson 42:
Sorting Basics

We'll assume that is the only information on your screen. It doesn't matter where the cursor is located as long as the document you want to sort is on the screen.

To sort this list of ten items:

1. Press the **Ctrl+F9** key combination [**Mouse Moves:** **T**ools, Sort] and you'll see the Merge/Sort dialog box shown in Figure 15.1.
2. Select Sort (option 2) and you will see the Sort (Source and Destination) dialog box shown in Figure 15.2 asking you for

▼ *Figure 15.1.   The Merge/Sort Dialog Box*

▼ *Figure 15.2.* **The Sort Source and Destination Dialog Box**

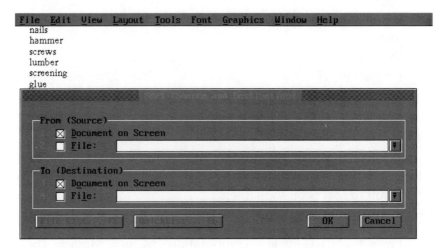

the name of the file you want to sort. As you can see, WordPerfect assumes that the file you want to sort is the one currently active.

TIP

Most of the time, you will just press the Enter key when WordPerfect asks you for the name of the input and output files, since you will be sorting what's on the screen.

Once you indicate the name of the input and output files (or just press **Enter** twice), WordPerfect will show you the Sort screen you see in Figure 15.3.

3. Select **P**erform Action and WordPerfect will complete the sort.

You can see the results of the sort right here.

glue
hammer
lumber

nails
pry bar
screening
screws
shingles
tar paper
wrench

WordPerfect sorted each of the lines in ascending order. Let's look more closely at the Sort dialog box, since it's here that you control all of WordPerfect's sort options.

TIP

Always save whatever you are working on before you sort. Just in case you make a mistake, you can always recall the original document.

▼ *Figure 15.3. The File to Be Sorted*

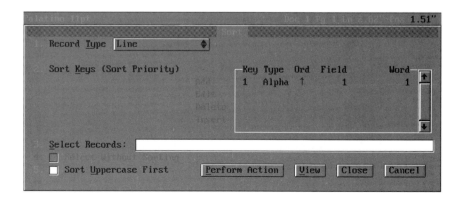

TIP

Watch your WordPerfect window when sorting is going on. WordPerfect lets you know exactly how many records are being sorted and when the sort is complete.

The Sort Dialog Box

In Figure 15.3 you see WordPerfect's Sort dialog box. On the top part of the window is some or all (depending on how big it is) of the document you are working with.

In the lower part of the window, is the sort information and options you can work with. In Figure 15.3 you can see that the **type** of sort is by Line and the order of the sort is ascending ↑ order. But there is much more to the sorting process than that.

In the Sort dialog box (to the right), you can see that the default is for WordPerfect to sort by alphanumeric characters (Alpha under **Type**), on Field 1 and Word 1. Let's take a closer look at these options. Since sorting can be very complex, we will only cover the most important options.

The Sort Options

Record **T**ype (option 1) allows you to sort by line, paragraph, or on a merged file.

Sort **K**eys (option 2) allows you to define the elements of a file on which you want to sort as well as the order. For example, a sample sort (like you saw earlier in this lesson) sorts on the first character. A more complex sort might sort on the last name or zip code.

Perform Action begins the sorting process.

View provides you with a tool for scrolling through the document that is in the upper half of the sort screen. It allows you to examine the context within which something appears before you perform any type of action. To return to the lower half of the sort screen, press the **F7** function key or the **Esc** key.

WordPerfect defines a line as text that is separated by a hard return (or a press of the **Enter** key). So, for a simple list of items such as the one you saw earlier, each item is listed on one line. If the list were double spaced, there would be a space between each entry, but only one hard return separating each line. As you know, WordPerfect's default is to sort by line.

TIP

Once you sort by paragraph, the next time you see the Sort screen, the type of sort will still be Paragraph. If you want to sort lines, you will have to reset the type. Remember to save before you sort!

Here are three paragraphs that do not appear in the correct order and here's how to sort them by paragraph:

Second, tell WordPerfect what you are sorting.

First, understand the difference between a line and a paragraph.

Third, perform the sort.

To sort the preceding three paragraphs:

1. Press the **Ctrl+F9,2** key combination [**Mouse Moves: T**ools, **S**ort] to begin the sort process.
2. Press **Enter** once.
3. Select Record **T**ype (option 1).
4. Select **P**aragraph. WordPerfect is so smart that it recognizes the entries in the window are paragraphs and defaults to that option.
5. Select **P**erform Action.

The paragraphs will be sorted as you see here.

First, understand the difference between a line and a paragraph.

Second, tell WordPerfect what you are sorting.

Third, perform the sort.

You already know that WordPerfect will, by default, sort on the first character on the first line, and that's all it will do (unless you tell it otherwise). It will not see or sort on the second word in a line or paragraph. So sorting the paragraphs

This is number 1.
This is number 3.
This is number 2.

will not result in a sort by the entire line (such that number 1, number 2, and number 3 are in order), but only the first character of the first word of each line.

Sorting Blocks

There is no reason why you have to sort all of the lines or paragraphs in a particular document to sort just some of the information. One thing you can do is copy the material you want to sort, paste it into a blank window, sort it, and then copy it back into the original document. That's a lot of work for so simple a task. Instead, why not just create a block and sort that?

TIP

Sorting a block of information comes in very handy when you have column headings that you don't want included in the sort.

To sort only part of a document:

1. Use the **Alt+F4** key combination or mouse and block the material you want to sort.
2. Use the **Ctrl+F9** key combination [**Mouse Moves: T**ools, Sort] to start the sort.

    Now continue with the steps we described earlier in this chapter. You will have all the options available just as if you were sorting an entire document, but WordPerfect will not ask you to name an input or an output file, since there aren't any. You go directly to the Sort dialog box.
3. Press **Enter** to perform the sort.

Sorting in Tables

WordPerfect can sort the rows in tables just as it can sort any other set of information.

For example, here's a simple table with two columns and three rows:

Bowman	Howard
Rose	Bill
Green	Michael

▼ *Figure 15.4.* *Sorting Lines in a Table*

Bowman	Howard
Rose	Bill
Green	Michael

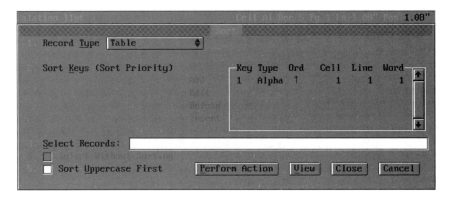

To sort the rows in a table:

1. Place the cursor in any cell in the table.
2. Use the **Ctrl+F9,2** key combination [**Mouse Moves:** Select **T**ools, **S**ort]. WordPerfect will skip the input, output prompts again, and get you right to the options, as you can see in Figure 15.4, WordPerfect already knows it is a table that is being sorted.
3. Select **P**erform Action.

Sorting on More than One Field

Now that you know how to do simple sorts, let's move on and address the situation where you need to sort on more than one element in a line or a paragraph or you want to select specific records to sort on.

Using the Sort Keys

WordPerfect is born sorting on the first word, but you need to change that. Why? What if you have a list of customers, such as:

Mike Ott
Pat Mont
Larry Brad
Harold Yar
Debbie Altus
Bob Hazlik
Dennis Rose

and you want to sort by last name? What good is a sorting tool if you have to first reenter all the information last name first? Instead, you can select a key to sort on the last name (see Figure 15.5).

Before we go further, let's look at a few definitions:

A *key* is something that you define for sorting purposes. It might be a name, a date, or a number. For example, you can select to sort on last name, date of birth, ZIP code, or phone number. You can sort on up to nine different keys.

Type refers to whether you want the information to be considered as alphanumeric (alpha) or numeric (numeric). Alphanumeric text can be characters or numbers, such as *124 Wilson Avenue*. Numeric text is only numbers where dollar signs ($), commas, and periods are ignored.

▼ *Figure 15.5.* **Names Sorted by Last Name**

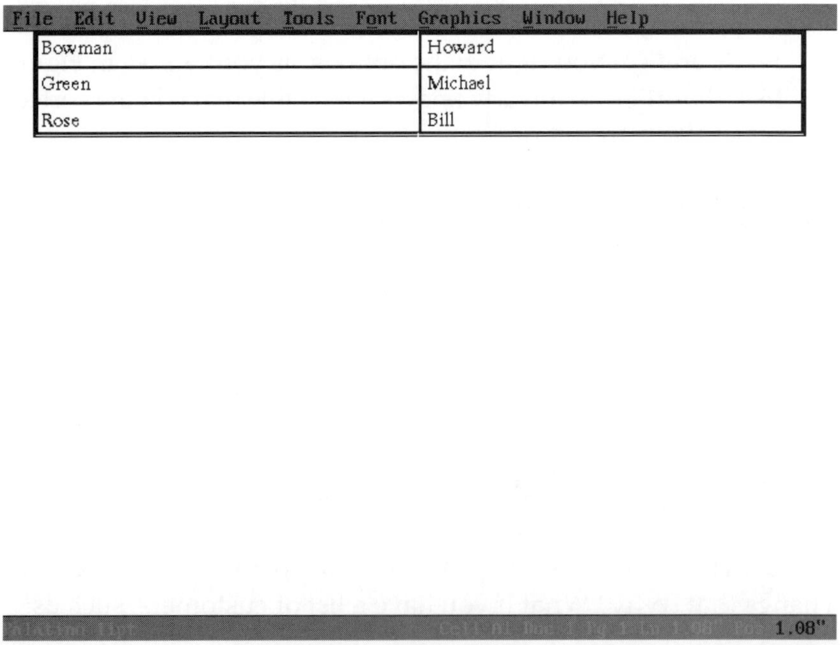

File Edit View Layout Tools Font Graphics Window Help	
Bowman	Howard
Green	Michael
Rose	Bill

Field refers to text that is separated by tabs. If you enter a line of text without any tabs, there is only one field in that record.

Word is the individual word (separated by spaces) that you will be sorting on. To sort using keys, you must indicate the field and the word. In the first and last name example, there is one field (with two words), and we are sorting on the second of those.

To use the sort keys option to sort on the last name:

1. Use the **Ctrl+F9,2** key combination [**Mouse Moves:** **T**ools, Sort] to begin the sort operation.
2. Press **Enter** and you'll see the Sort dialog box.
   The important elements on the screen now are the **Key**, **Type, Field**, and **Word** indicators.
3. Select Sort **K**eys (option 2).
4. Select Edit (option 2) and you will see the Edit Sort Key dialog box shown in Figure 15.6.
5. The only element in the Edit Sort key dialog box that needs to be changed is **W**ord (option 6). Select that and change the 1 to a 2, since we are interested in sorting on the second word. You can see this in Figure 15.7.

TIP

Remember, fields are separated by tabs and words by spaces within fields.

Let's look at a sorting when there are two fields in each record. We'll take the same information as above and add phone numbers (using a tab to separate name from telephone number) and then sort only by phone number.

Here's the information before the sort:

Mike Ott	856–7980
Phil Montgomery	456–7089
Larry Brady	365–1067
Harold Yarger	415–6697
Debbie Altus	232–8837
Bob Hazlik	335–3558
Debbie Faurox	212–2212
Dennis Rosen	228–8878

▼ *Figure 15.6.* *The Edit Sort Key Dialog Box*

Mike Ott
Phil Montgomery
Larry Brady
Harold Yarger
Debbie Altus
Debbie Faurox
Bob Hazlik
Dennis Rosen

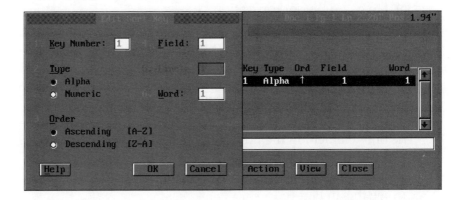

▼ *Figure 15.7.* *Changing the Word Number in a Sort*

Debbie Altus
Larry Brady
Debbie Faurox
Bob Hazlik
Phil Montgomery
Mike Ott
Dennis Rosen
Harold Yarger

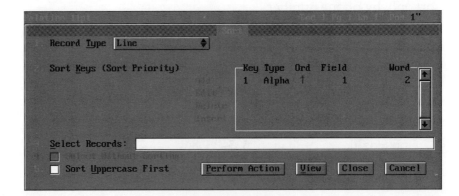

TIP

It doesn't matter where the tabs are set, as long as the Tab **key is pressed to separate fields from one another.**

The Sort screen and the completed sort is shown in Figure 15.8. As you can see in Figure 15.8, the names are now sorted by phone number and not by last name.

Now, let's get even more fancy and add the gender (*M* for male or *F* for female as a new field), and we will sort using two keys: first by gender and then by last name. The Sort screen you see in Figure 15.9 shows how we are first sorting on Field 3, Word 1 (gender), and then Field 1, Word 2 (last name) and the results. All males and females are grouped together, and within that grouping, sorted by last name. To add a second sort key, select **A**dd (option 1) from the Edit Sort key dialog box and provide the necessary information.

▼ *Figure 15.8. Sorting by the Second Field in a Key*

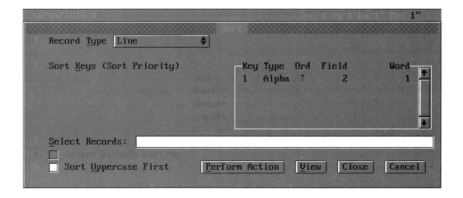

▼ *Figure 15.9.* *Sorting with Three Fields*

```
Debbie Altus   232-8837      F
Debbie Faurox          212-2212   F
Larry Brady   365-1067       M
Bob Hazlik    335-3558       M
Phil Montgomery      456-7089    M
Mike Ott      856-7980       M
Dennis Rosen  228-8878       M
Harold Yarger          415-6697   M
```

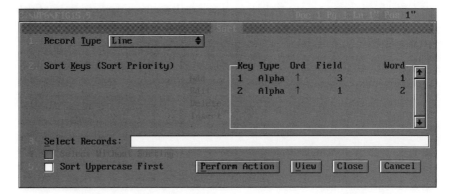

Selecting Records

You can define keys, but you can also define which records you want to select before the sort, using the Select Records (option 3) in the Sort dialog box. For example, in the set of records we have been working with, let's select only females and then sort by last name.

When you select records, you have to provide WordPerfect with the defining criteria for the selection. In this case, we will be defining *key1=F* as you can see in Figure 15.10. Once this file is sorted, only those records with an *F* in Field 3 were selected and then sorted according to last name (key #2).

In this example, we used the equals sign (=) to indicate that the key had to be equal to *F* for the record to be selected. As you can see in Figure 15.10, there are other selection parameters in the Sort dialog box as well. Here's what they mean, how they can be used, and how they can be combined.

▼ *Figure 15.10.* *Defining Keys for Selection*

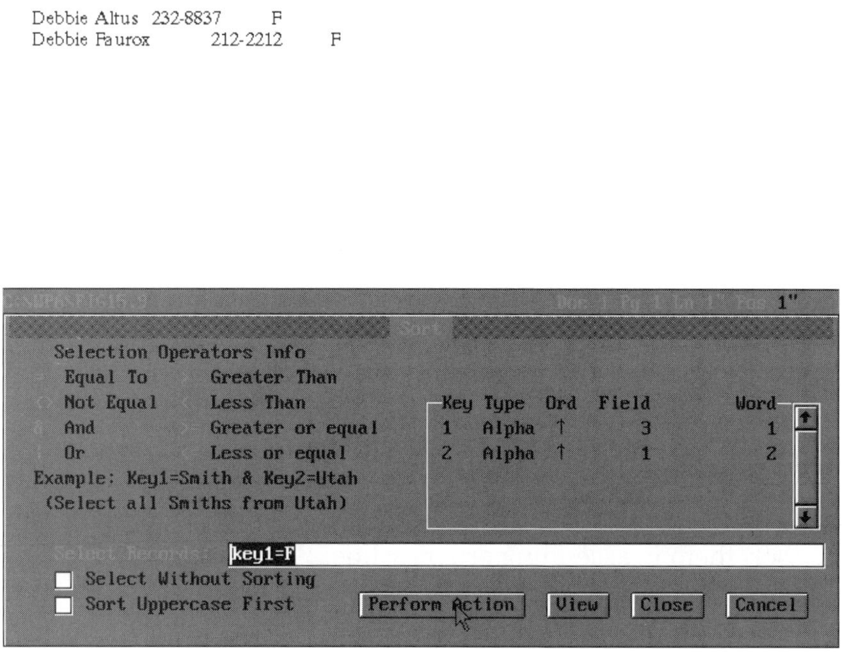

```
Debbie Altus  232-8837     F
Debbie Faurox       212-2212     F
```

Operator	Function	Example
= +	Selects records meeting either condition	key=1Bob+key 2=M selects all males or anyone named Bob
*	Selects records meeting both conditions	key 1=M*key 2=Bob selects all males named Bob
=	Selects records containing exactly the same information	key 1=Bob selects only those records with Bob
<<>>	Selects records that don't match the information	key 1<<>>bob selects all those records except those with Bob
>>	Selects records that have information greater than	key2>>3453 selects those records with a zip code greater than 3453
<<	Selects records that have information less than	key2<<3453 selects those records with a zip code less than 3453

Operator	Function	Example
>>=	Selects records that have information greater than or equal to	key 4>>=25 selects those records where people are 25 years or older
<<=	Selects records that have information less than or equal to	key4<<=25 selects records where people are 25 years or younger

A frequent use for the sort feature is to sort names and addresses by zip code or whatever for the preparation of personalized form letters, sometimes called **Merge**. They're on the same menu for good reason, and that's what you'll learn next.

CHECK YOURSELF

1. Enter the following list of words as separate documents and sort them in ascending order by line:

   size
   doctor
   place
   type
   wife
   fun
   house
   tree
   dog
   car

2. Enter the following text as separate paragraphs and sort them in descending order by paragraph.

   Julie works outside of the house at the university.
   Richard works outside of the house as an architect.
   Nicky is a sweet little boy who loves to drive Rich and Julie crazy and play house with Alexandra.
   Alexandra is Nicky's sister.

ANSWERS

1. car
   doctor
   dog

> fun
> house
> place
> size
> tree
> type
> wife

2. Alexandra is Nicky's sister.
   Julie works outside of the house at the university.
   Nicky is a sweet little boy who loves to drive Rich and Julie
   crazy and play house with Alexandra.
   Richard works outside of the house as an architect.

Sorting puts things in the order we want so that we can easily go through a list and find the information that we need. Take a list of names and addresses. Once sorted, it's a snap to edit the list. Using the Merge feature discussed in the next chapter, it's even easier to take the name and addresses and use them to create customized letters. This is just one example of the hundreds of ways to save time using Merge.

PRACTICE WHAT YOU'VE LEARNED

1. How does WordPerfect sort work?
2. Sort the following list and notice how WordPerfect handles symbols, capital letters and diacriticals:
   United States of America
   æ
   cookies
   45.887
   locomotive
   ç
   future
   1,234.45
   321
3. When might you want to sort a list of names in ascending order versus descending order?
4. Generate a list of records with three different fields, with fields one and two having two words, and field three having three words. Now sort on the second word.

5. Enter the names and addresses of five friends. Select only those whose last names begin with the letters *S* through *Z* and sort on their first name.

ANSWERS

1. WordPerfect sorts on the first character that it encounters unless you indicate otherwise.
2. 1,234.45
   321
   45.887
   æ
   ç
   cookies
   future
   locomotive
   United States of America
3. When you want the later alphabetical entries to be considered first.

Customizing Letters and Documents

In this chapter, you'll see how WordPerfect allows you to take information created in one document and merge or combine it with information that was created in another document. For example, imagine taking a list of ten friends, creating a general letter, and with a few keystrokes, generating ten letters with each friend's name and address, or any other personalized information, inserted. In this chapter you'll learn how to:

- ▲ Use WordPerfect merge
- ▲ Create a form file
- ▲ Create a data file
- ▲ Merge files
- ▲ Use special merge codes

Important Keys	***Important Terms***
Ctrl+F9	boilerplate
F9	data file
Shift+F9	form file
	merge
	Merge Codes (Form File) dialog box.
	Merge Codes dialog box
	Merge Codes (Text Data File) dialog box
	Merge Codes dialog box
	merged document
	Parameter Entry dialog box
	Run Merge dialog box

Lesson 43: Merging Documents

When you merge data, you don't have to just be using names, addresses, and a form letter. You can merge products to be ordered into order forms, lists of responsibilities for different people, scheduling matters, and more. Since the form letter is the most frequent use of the merge feature, we'll use that as an example.

How Merge Works

There are four steps in the creation of a merged document:

1. Defining the type of document to be used in the merge
2. Creating a form file
3. Creating a data file
4. Merging the form and the data files

A **form file** contains text and instructions, into which information from a data file is inserted to produce the merged document. For example, a form file might begin with a letter that instructs people when their interviews are scheduled. For each letter, however, the name, address, greeting, and place and time of the interview are variable and not included in the form file. Figure 16.1 shows you what such a letter might look like. We haven't entered WordPerfect's special codes yet, but you can see where information will go. It's shown in brackets.

▼ *Figure 16.1. A Form File Showing Where WordPerfect's Special Codes Will Be Placed*

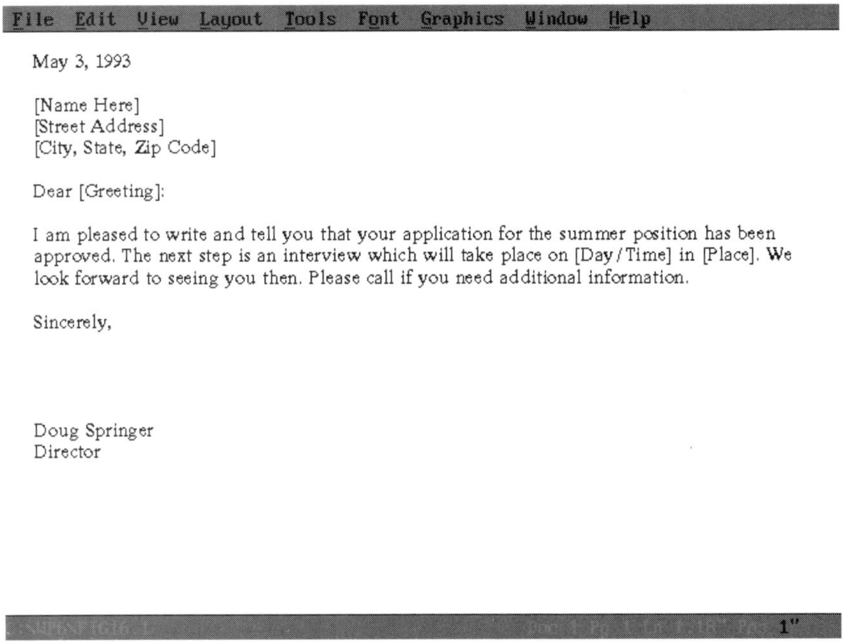

Lesson 43:
Merging
Documents

File   Edit   View   Layout   Tools   Font   Graphics   Window   Help

May 3, 1993

[Name Here]
[Street Address]
[City, State, Zip Code]

Dear [Greeting]:

I am pleased to write and tell you that your application for the summer position has been approved. The next step is an interview which will take place on [Day/Time] in [Place]. We look forward to seeing you then. Please call if you need additional information.

Sincerely,

Doug Springer
Director

1"

The **data file** contains the information that will be merged with the form file to produce the merged document. Information in data files are often called *records*, since they are related pieces of information. For example, Figure 16.2 shows you the information that can be used as a data file with the letter you saw in Figure 16.1. In Figure 16.2, there are three records, each one containing six individual pieces of information that will be merged with the letter you saw in Figure 16.1.

The **merged document** will contain the results of combining the form and data files.

Creating the Form File

A form file contains special codes that indicate where information from the data document will be placed. You use the **Shift+F9** key combination [**Mouse Moves: T**ools, Me**r**ge, **D**efine] to begin the process. When you do this, you will see the Merge Codes dialog box you see in Figure 16.3.

▼ Figure 16.2. A WordPerfect Data File

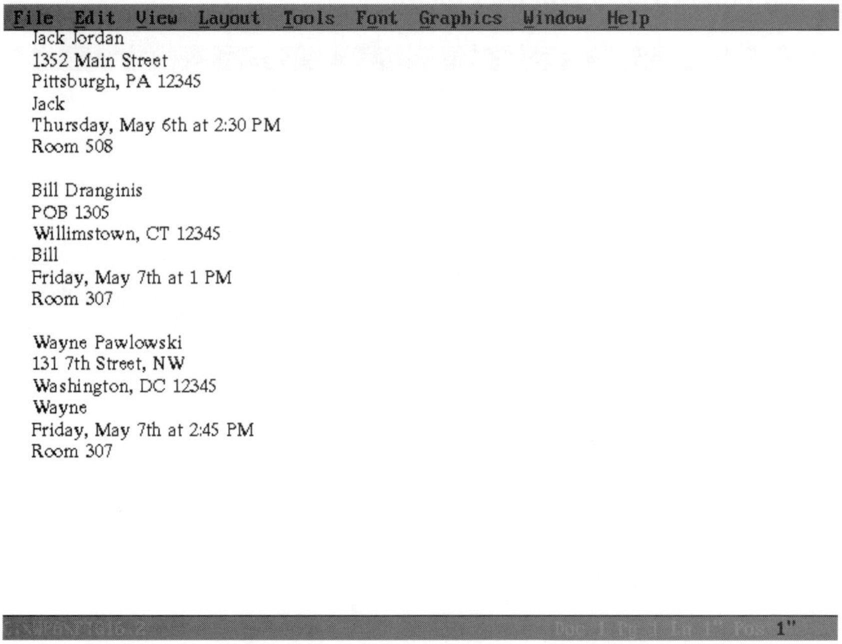

File Edit View Layout Tools Font Graphics Window Help
Jack Jordan
1352 Main Street
Pittsburgh, PA 12345
Jack
Thursday, May 6th at 2:30 PM
Room 508
Bill Dranginis
POB 1305
Willimstown, CT 12345
Bill
Friday, May 7th at 1 PM
Room 307
Wayne Pawlowski
131 7th Street, NW
Washington, DC 12345
Wayne
Friday, May 7th at 2:45 PM
Room 307

▼ Figure 16.3. The Merge Codes Dialog Box

File Edit View Layout Tools Font Graphics Window Help
Merge Codes
Select the type of merge document you are creating.
This will determine the merge codes to be shown.
Form
This type of document contains the form for
the merge (such as a letter or mailing label).
Data [Text]
Data [Table]
This type of document contains the data for the
merge (such as a list of mailing addresses).
This list can be in a normal document or a table.
OK
Cancel

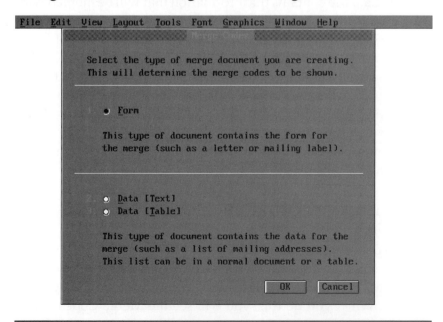

In the Merge Codes dialog box shown in Figure 16.3, you can see that we will first create a form file. Keep in mind that we will need entries for the name and address information, one for the greeting, one for the date and time of the interview, and one for the location of the interview. This means we have to specify fields for each one of these entries.

Lesson 43:
Merging
Documents

To create a form document, based on Figure 16.1:

1. Go to a blank WordPerfect screen.
2. Press **Shift+F9** [**Mouse Moves:** Select **T**ools, **M**erge]. Select **F**orm (option 1). You will then see the Merge Codes (Form File) dialog box.
3. Select **F**ield (option 1). You will then see the Parameter Entry dialog box (see Figure 16.4) asking for a name for the field and as you can see, this first field is specified as 1.
4. Select **OK**. As you can see in Figure 16.5, the field number 1 is entered as the first field in the form file.

▼ *Figure 16.4.   Entering a Field Number in the Parameter Entry Dialog Box*

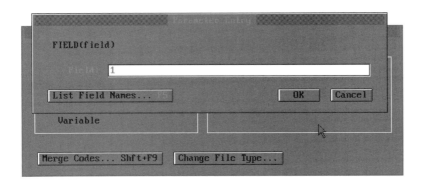

▼ *Figure 16.5.   Entering Fields in the Actual Form File*

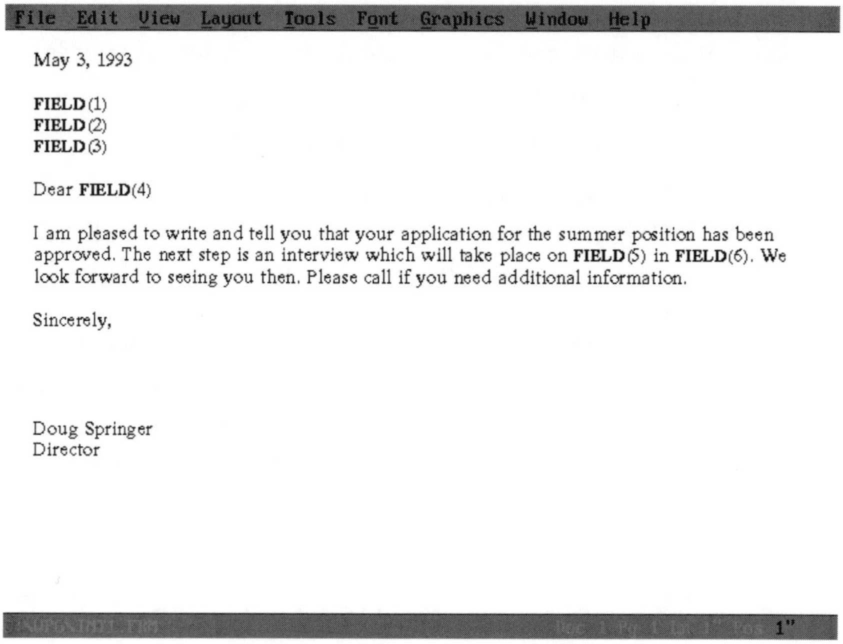

File Edit View Layout Tools Font Graphics Window Help

May 3, 1993

FIELD(1)
FIELD(2)
FIELD(3)

Dear **FIELD**(4)

I am pleased to write and tell you that your application for the summer position has been approved. The next step is an interview which will take place on **FIELD**(5) in **FIELD**(6). We look forward to seeing you then. Please call if you need additional information.

Sincerely,

Doug Springer
Director

INT.FRM   Doc 2 Pg 1 Ln 1" Pos 1"

5. Press **Enter**. You should be on the second line of the form document. Now repeat steps 2 through 5 until the WordPerfect document looks like the one shown in Figure 16.5. Remember that you have to also enter text as you type.

6. Save the form document as a file. Use a name you will remember. For example, the name *int.frm* would tell you that it's the form file for the interview.

Creating the Data File

Your data file will contain all of the information that will be merged into the form file. Each record in a data file usually contains as much information as needed to complete the fields in the form file.

The data file that we create here is based on the information you see in Figure 16.2.

To create a data file:

1. Enter the first piece of information from the first record. In our example (see Figure 16.2), it is Jack Jordan.
2. Press **Shift+F9** [Mouse Moves: **T**ools, **M**erge, **D**efine], and you will once again see the Merge Codes dialog box you saw in Figure 16.3.
3. Select **D**ata (option 2) and you will see the Merge Codes (Text Data File) dialog box as shown in Figure 16.6. Press **1**. A code will be entered after the entry you see in Figure 16.6.
4. Repeat steps 2 and 3 until all the information is entered for the first record and your WordPerfect document looks like the one you see in Figure 16.7. Now that all the fields have been entered, it's time to end the record by entering an ENDRECORD code.
5. Move to the next line in the data file by pressing **Enter**.
6. Use **Shift+F9, 2** [**Mouse Moves:** Merge, Define, End Record] to insert an ENDRECORD code.

▼ *Figure 16.6.   The Merge Codes Dialog Box*

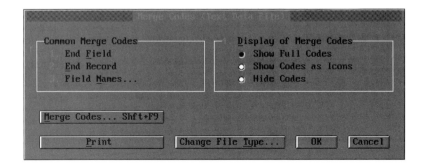

▼ *Figure 16.7.* *Ending a Record*

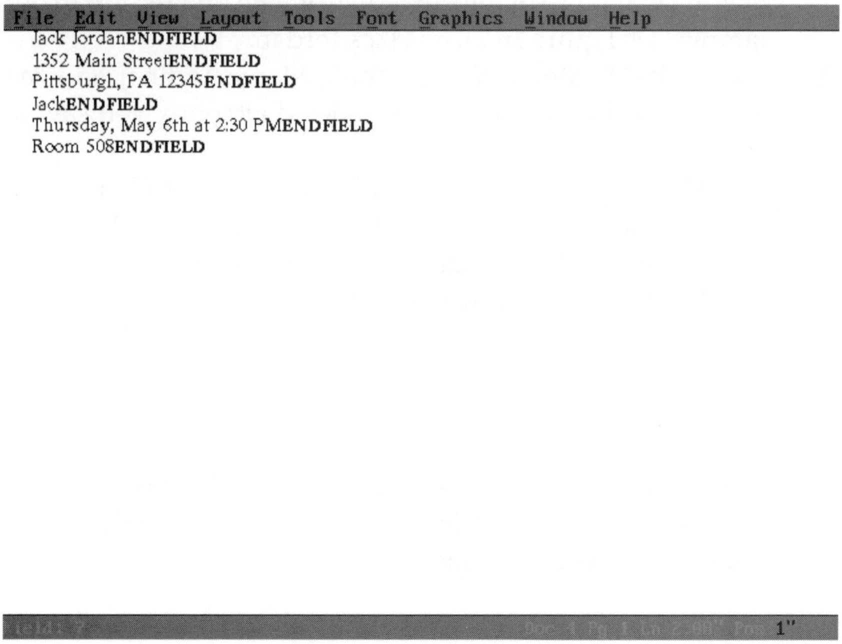

File Edit View Layout Tools Font Graphics Window Help
Jack JordanENDFIELD
1352 Main StreetENDFIELD
Pittsburgh, PA 12345ENDFIELD
JackENDFIELD
Thursday, May 6th at 2:30 PMENDFIELD
Room 508ENDFIELD

---

7. Now enter the rest of the information you see in Figure 16.2 remembering that there is an ENDFIELD code at the end of each line, and an ENDRECORD code at the end of each record.
8. Save the file. We use the name *int.dta* and the final window is shown in Figure 16.8.

The ENDRECORD code indicates that this record is finished and WordPerfect is ready to look for Field 1 from the next record. Why the page break? WordPerfect assumes that the major purpose for using the Merge feature is to create letters and that each letter begins on a new page. The page break ensures this.

If you are going to use more than one form and data file, be sure you use names that mean something. Imagine naming a form file *form*. How will you ever know the name of the appropriate data file?

Merging the Form and Data Files

OK, now the magic begins.

▼ *Figure 16.8.* *The Completed Data Form with All the*
Important Codes Entered

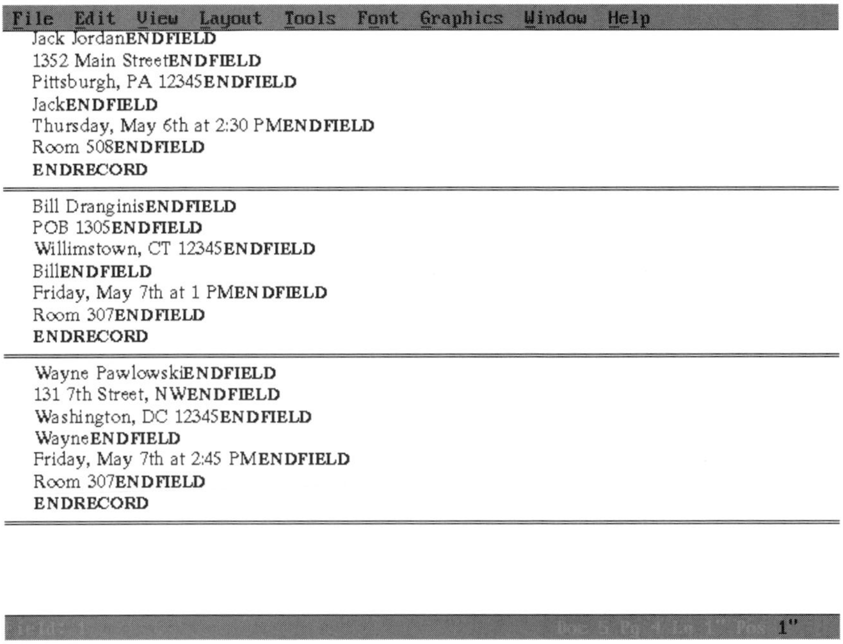

```
File  Edit  View  Layout  Tools  Font  Graphics  Window  Help
Jack JordanENDFIELD
1352 Main StreetENDFIELD
Pittsburgh, PA 12345ENDFIELD
JackENDFIELD
Thursday, May 6th at 2:30 PMENDFIELD
Room 508ENDFIELD
ENDRECORD

Bill DranginisENDFIELD
POB 1305ENDFIELD
Willimstown, CT 12345ENDFIELD
BillENDFIELD
Friday, May 7th at 1 PMENDFIELD
Room 307ENDFIELD
ENDRECORD

Wayne PawlowskiENDFIELD
131 7th Street, NWENDFIELD
Washington, DC 12345ENDFIELD
WayneENDFIELD
Friday, May 7th at 2:45 PMENDFIELD
Room 307ENDFIELD
ENDRECORD
```

To merge the two files:

1. Be sure you are in a clear WordPerfect screen.
2. Use the **Ctrl+F9,1** key combination [**Mouse Moves: T**ools, **M**erge, **R**un] and you will see the Run Merge dialog box as shown in Figure 16.9.
3. Supply the name of the form file. In this example, it is *int.frm*.
4. When WordPerfect asks you for the name of the data file, supply it and press **Enter**.
5. Select **Merge**.

WordPerfect will be busy for a moment and then, wonders of wonders, it's done. You can see the first of the three merged letters in Figure 16.10. The new file that is created (containing all the merged letters) is just that—a new one without a name. If you want to save the merged document, you must give it a name and save it as you would any new file.

▼ *Figure 16.9.   The Run Merge Dialog Box*

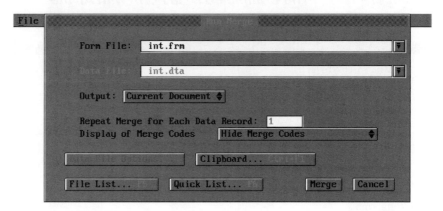

▼ *Figure 16.10.   The Newly Created File*

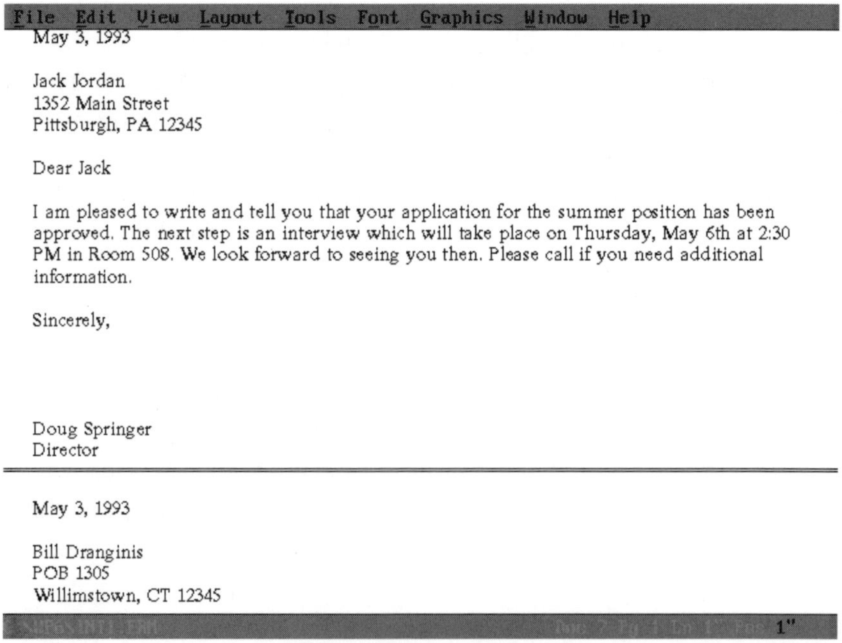

May 3, 1993

Jack Jordan
1352 Main Street
Pittsburgh, PA 12345

Dear Jack

I am pleased to write and tell you that your application for the summer position has been approved. The next step is an interview which will take place on Thursday, May 6th at 2:30 PM in Room 508. We look forward to seeing you then. Please call if you need additional information.

Sincerely,

Doug Springer
Director

May 3, 1993

Bill Dranginis
POB 1305
Willimstown, CT 12345

Using Form and Data Files More Than Once

You can use information in form and data files over again as the need arises.

A form file can also be called a template (or a **boilerplate**), and you can use it with several different data files. For example, you might have other applicants that need to be interviewed. Just save the letter for later use, or just create a new form file and only use three fields from the data file.

You could also use the same data file information to print envelopes. Since you only need the first three fields for envelopes, create a data file that looks like the one in Figure 16.2 and merge it to print envelopes with only the first three fields from the data file that contains mailing address information. See your printer manual for adjustments you may have to make.

CHECK YOURSELF

1. Create a form file that invites three friends to a party. Use the following for the form file, with the asterisks representing where the fields should appear.
    Dear *:
        Finally we're finished with finals. Please join us on * at * for an end of semester fling.
    Best,

    Joan and Frank
2. What are three other applications for using the Merge feature that are not customized form letters?

ANSWERS

1. Use names for form and data fields that reflect the content of the file, rather than *form* or *data*.
2. One example is creating a form file that is a contract and using the data file to fill in the particulars, such as specific terms of agreement, the name of the various people involved, and so forth.

▼ *Figure 16.11.* *Using a Data File with a New Form File to Prepare Envelopes*

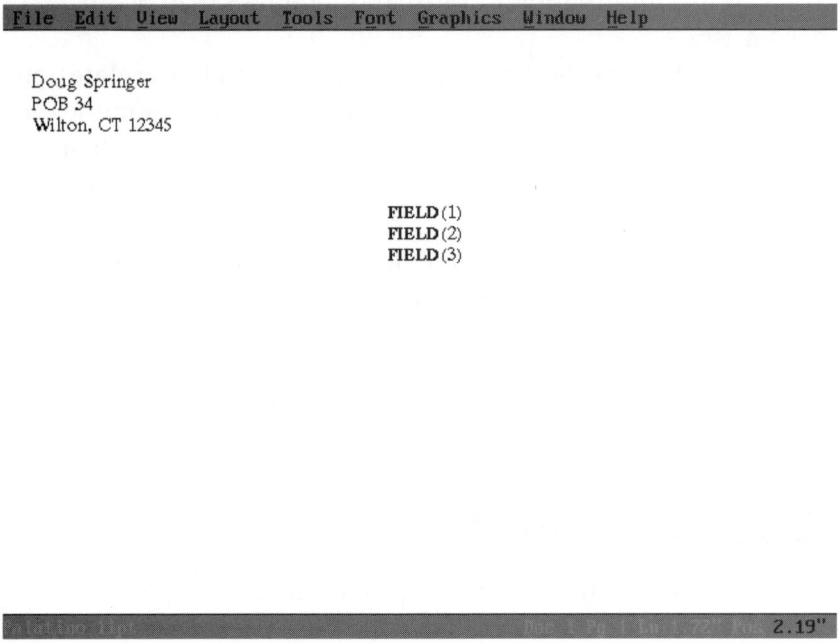

File Edit View Layout Tools Font Graphics Window Help

Doug Springer
POB 34
Wilton, CT 12345

FIELD (1)
FIELD (2)
FIELD (3)

2.19"

Lesson 44: Using Special Merge Codes

WordPerfect doesn't just give you simple codes that can be used in the merge operation. There's a whole set of others that make the Merge feature very powerful. In this lesson we'll explore some codes that illustrate that power.

Inserting the Date

Customized letters, and especially when the form file might be used more than once, may contain a date that changes depending on when the letter is written. For example, in the form file you see in Figure 16.1, you could place the DATE Merge code at the top of the letter. Each time any letter with that code in the form file is printed, the current date will be printed as well.

Inserting the DATE code opens a whole new set of options.

TIP

If you run into trouble and it seems like your merge is caught in an endless loop and won't end, use the Shift+F9,1 **key combination to quit the merge.**

To insert the date merge code:

1. Place the cursor in the location in the form file where you want the DATE code entered.
2. Use the **Shift+F9,M** key combination [**Mouse Moves:** Select **T**ools, **M**erge, **D**efine, **M**erge Codes] to see the other Merge code options available shown in Figure 16.12.
3. Highlight the **DATE** code and press **Enter**. The DATE Merge code will be inserted into the form file.

Pausing for Keyboard Entries

Imagine a form document where you don't need a data document but have WordPerfect pause for you to enter whatever special points you want in the document!

▼ *Figure 16.12.   Highlighting the Date Merge Code*

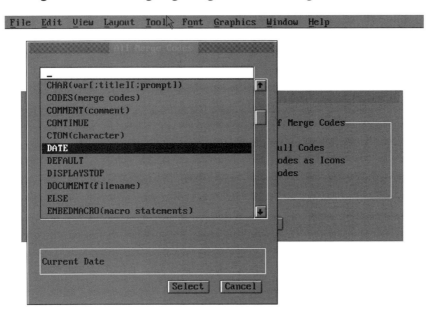

To do this, use the **Shift+F9,M** key combination [**Mouse Moves:** Select Tools, Merge, Define, Merge Codes] and select the **KEYBOARD** Merge code, telling WordPerfect that it should stop when it reaches this code and wait for you to input some information from the keyboard.

For example, in Figure 16.13 you can see a set of Merge codes will pause and allow you to enter name and address information at the beginning of a document (notice the date is inserted as well).

Using the keyboard option means you could sit down at your keyboard, recall the file with the KEYBOARD codes inserted, and go to work entering what you want.

To use the KEYBOARD option:

1. Create a form document and insert the KEYBOARD code (and any other Merge codes) where you want WordPerfect to pause for input.
2. Save the file as a form file.

▼ *Figure 16.13.   Using Merge Codes to Pause for Input from the Keyboard*

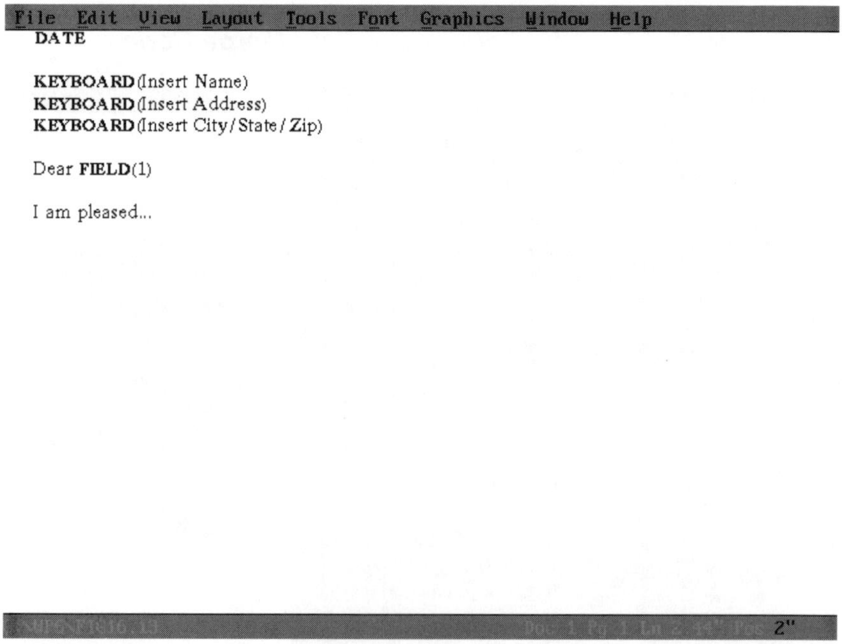

File Edit View Layout Tools Font Graphics Window Help

DATE

KEYBOARD(Insert Name)
KEYBOARD(Insert Address)
KEYBOARD(Insert City/State/Zip)

Dear FIELD(1)

I am pleased...

3. Use the **Ctrl+F9,1** keyboard combination to begin the Merge process.
4. Enter the name of the form file and press **Enter**.
5. Select **Merge**. There is no data file.

WordPerfect will go to the first KEYBOARD code and wait for your input, and as you see in Figure 16.14, prompt you on the status line. Once you enter what you want, press the **F9** function key and WordPerfect will go to the second KEYBOARD code. When you have entered all the information in response to the presence of KEYBOARD codes, press the **F9** function key again. WordPerfect will continue to prompt you until it goes through all of the codes.

CHECK YOURSELF

1. Use the special Merge codes and create a form document that asks the user to record the responses to five questions about his or her favorite foods.

▼ **Figure 16.14.**   *Waiting for Input from the Keyboard*

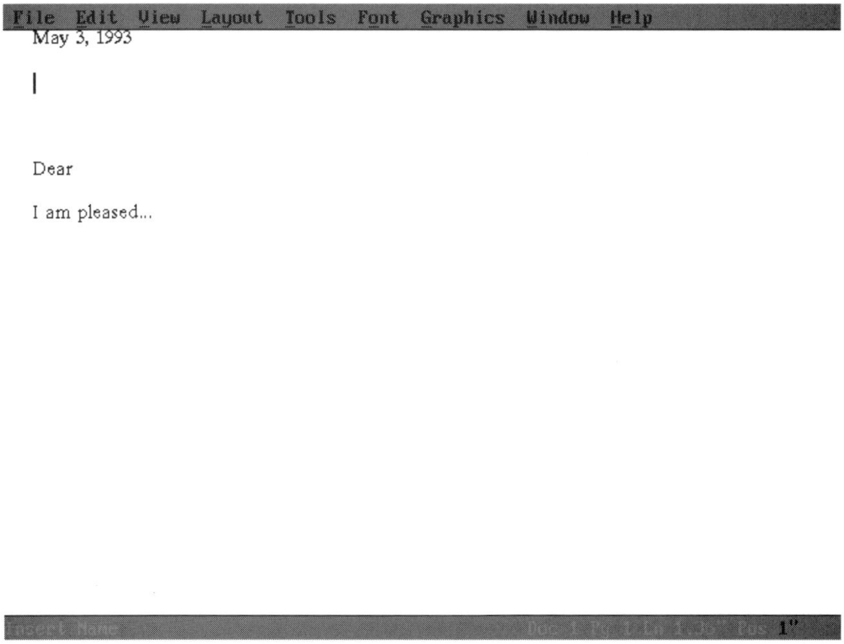

File   Edit   View   Layout   Tools   Font   Graphics   Window   Help

May 3, 1993

Dear

I am pleased...

1"

2. Under what circumstance would the DATE code not give the current date?

ANSWERS

1. The prompt is a great way to create a form that can be completed at the user's convenience.
2. When the system date has not been set or is set incorrectly.

It's tough to find an easier WordPerfect feature to use than Merge. It automates your word processing system and can save you tons of time and effort in getting complex documents out quickly. But whatever you produce, you will most likely have to print. We touched on printing earlier, but in the next chapter we'll go into greater detail and show you how to control many of your printer's functions.

PRACTICE WHAT YOU'VE LEARNED

1. What would happen if you had more fields in your data file than you provided room for in your form file? What would happen if the reverse were the case?
2. How would you correct the situation where you just produced 100 merged letters and you find that you spelled the name of the city incorrectly in 50 of them?
3. Provide an example of where the same data document might be used with different form documents.
4. Provide an example of where the same form document might be used with different data documents.
5. Why does WordPerfect insert a page break (HPg) after each record, and why would you not want to delete them?

ANSWERS

1. Nothing, since WordPerfect only uses those fields that are specified in the form file. More fields from a data record would be merged with the form document than you specified.

2. You can either correct the spelling of the city and then merge again, or use a global search and replace to correct the error.
3. The same list of customers might be used for billing as well as for advertising purposes.
4. The same form document, welcoming new customers, can be used whenever a new customer is added to the data file.
5. It assumes that each record is a separate document, such as a letter or a label, and is to be printed on a separate page.

Printing with WordPerfect

One of the great first moments using WordPerfect is when you print out your first hard copy of any document you have created. It's at that moment you realize that you really know what you're doing. And while printing is a relatively straightforward process (using the **Shift+F7** key combination), WordPerfect offers many other options you can take advantage of. In this chapter you'll learn how to:

- ▲ Select and add a printer
- ▲ Use WordPerfect's print options
- ▲ Create special characters using the Compose feature
- ▲ Use WordPerfect's various control functions

Important Keys	*Important Terms*
Shift+F7	character code
	character
	compose
	Control Printer dialog box
	diacriticals
	digraphs
	Print dialog box
	The Select Printer dialog box
	WordPerfect Compose dialog box
	WordPerfect Characters dialog box

Lesson 45: Selecting a Printer

WordPerfect will automatically default to a standard printer. Even though this is fine for producing a hard copy of your document, it does not allow you to take advantage of all the other features that your printer might offer. It's for that reason that you need to select the particular printer you intend to use with WordPerfect so that WordPerfect can take advantage of its capabilities.

To select a printer:

1. Use **Shift+F7 [Mouse Moves:** Select File, **P**rint] to begin the printer selection process. By the way, this is the same key combination you use for all print operations as shown in Figure 17.1. This is the Print dialog box.
2. Select option **S** (for Select Printer). When you do this, you will see the Select Printer screen as shown in Figure 17.2. Here, you can already see that the NEC Silentwriter LC-890 and the Panasonic KX-P4455 printers have been installed. When you do this for the first time, no printers will be listed.

   If you have several printers already listed, then you just highlight the one you want to use and press **Enter**. The highlighted printer will become the active one.

▼ *Figure 17.1. The Print Dialog Box*

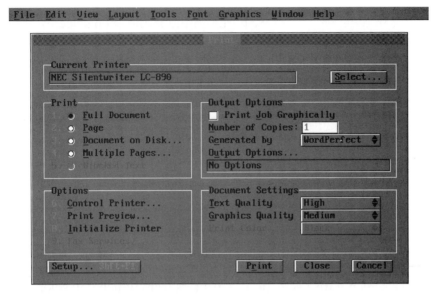

▼ *Figure 17.2. The Select Printer Dialog Box*

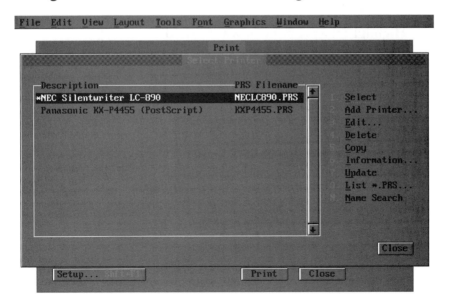

Deleting a Printer

You can delete a printer by highlighting it and then selecting option 4, **D**elete. This deletes or erases the addition of that printer, and you will not be able to use that printer until you once again add it to the list of printers on the Select Printer screen.

If you do delete a printer, and you want to add it back to the selection menu, you may have to insert some of the other WordPerfect printer disks to locate the driver.

Adding a Printer

If you have not yet selected any printers, you will have to add a printer using the second option on the Select Printer screen. When you select option 2, **A**dditional Printers, WordPerfect will show you a screen with a selection of printers from which you select the one you want to add.

For example, in Figure 17.3, you can see a listing of printers that was copied when you initially installed WordPerfect.

To add an additional printer:

1. Highlight the printer you want to add.
2. Press **Enter**. WordPerfect will take it from there and make sure that all the important printer files for that printer are available to WordPerfect.

You can add as many printers as you would like to the Select Printer screen that you saw in Figure 17.2. In our example, the NEC laser printer is used for final production of documents, and the Panasonic dot matrix is used for drafts of documents. Switching from one to the other is very easy and takes very little time.

CHECK YOURSELF

▲ Add a new printer to the list of printers from which you can select. Now delete it. Note the changes that take place on the Select Printer screen when you add a new printer and what happens when you delete it.

▼ *Figure 17.3.* *Adding a Printer*

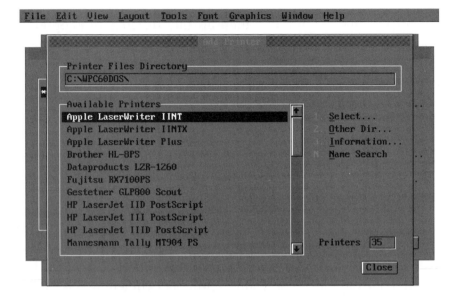

ANSWER

▲ The new printer will appear on the Select Printer screen. To change printers, just highlight the one you want to use.

Lesson 46: Controlling Your Printer

Once you have selected the printer that you want to use, you can control the activity of your printer in many different ways. We need to turn to the options available on the Print screen (see Figure 17.1) to explore what they are and how they work.

Main Printer Options

As you can see in Figure 17.1, there are nine different print options that you access through the **Shift+F7** key combination [**Mouse Moves:** Select File, Print].

Full Document (option 1) will print a copy of the active document (the one you have on screen). The **Shift+F7,1** key combination [**Mouse Moves:** Select File, Print,1] is the most common printing operation.

Page (option 2) will print the page on which the cursor is located. If you want to print a particular page, move the cursor to the page and then use **Shift+F7,2** [**Mouse Moves:** Select File, Print,2].

Document on Disk (option 3) will print a document that has been saved to a disk. When you select this option, WordPerfect will ask you to provide a name for the document. Don't forget to indicate the drive in which the disk containing the document is located. For example, if you want to print a document that is saved on a disk placed in disk drive A, the WordPerfect prompt and your response might look like this:

```
Document Name: a:final.rpt
```

Control Printer offers a bunch of other options that we'll get to in a moment.

Multiple Pages (option 4) provides you with a **Page(s):** prompt, requesting that you provide the pages you want to print. For example, if you want to print pages 4 through 10, then you would enter **4-10**. If you want to print pages 4 through the end of the document, you would enter **4-**.

Blocked Text (option 5) will print text that has been blocked.

Control Printer (option 6) provides you with extensive information about the document that is being printed and allows you to control much of what happens. You can see the Control Printer dialog box in Figure 17.4.

First, the Control Printer dialog box provides extensive information about the printer activity. At the top of the dialog box, you can see how the job number, the status of the job, and even the page (of how many) is being printed. You can even keep up with the percentage of a job being processed.

In the second half of the Control Printer dialog box, you can see how jobs are listed in the order in which you directed WordPerfect

▼ *Figure 17.4. The Control Printer Dialog Box*

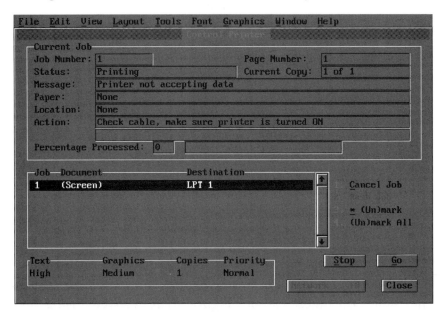

to print them. For example, in Figure 17.4, there is only one job being printed with the destination to the parallel port #1 (which is connected to the printer).

To the right of the job list box are four different options, all of which can affect jobs that are waiting to be printed. Here's what you can do with each of these.

TIP

Once a job has started being printed, you cannot cancel or rush it.

Cancel Job (option 1) cancels the job that is highlighted. If you want to cancel more than one print job, use the * key to mark each one, then select **C**ancel. If you want to unmark those jobs that were selected to be canceled, use **Unmark** (option 4).

Rush Job (option 2) allows you to move a single file up to the top of the print list so that it takes precedence over others in being printed. This is the option you want to select when you need to rush a job that is scheduled behind other jobs.

Mark(*) and Unmark and Mark and (Un)mark All (options 3 and 4) allow you to mark and unmark more than one file to be canceled or rushed. For example, if you had five jobs waiting to be printed and you wanted jobs 4 and 5 to be printed first, you can mark them, select **Rush Job** (option 2) and WordPerfect will move up these jobs so their printing is a priority. Let's return to the Print/Fax dialog box (Figure 17.1).

Print Preview (option 7) provides you with a variety of views of the document on which you are working. This is the choice when you want to see how things are formatted and how the document will appear when printed. The nicest thing about this feature, of course, is that you don't have to print (what might be a very long and cumbersome document) before you need to.

For example, in Figure 17.5, you can see a full-page view of the WordPerfect Printer Test document. You can see along the top of the View Document screen that you have several options available for viewing a document in this mode. In Figure 17.6, you can see the same document as in Figure 17.5, viewed using the Zoom200%. You can move around the View Document screen using the **PgUp** and **PgDn** and the **Cursor Arrow** keys. This option takes advantage of WordPerfect's graphic capabilities. If your computer or monitor cannot do graphics, then you will not be able to use this feature.

Want to see what your printer can do? Recall the file named *printer.tst* from the WordPerfect directory and print it. You'll see what WordPerfect printing features your printer is capable of producing.

Initialize Printer (option 8) is an advanced printer function that is used to add new fonts to your printer. This option is also used when you need to reset your printer to ground zero. For example, you might have sent a huge graphic to your printer and you're afraid that it's all tied up. Reinitializing it can clear its memory.

Finally, Fax Services (option 9) allows you to fax using Word-Perfect.

Other Printer Options

There are four other options on the Print screen (Figure 17.1) we need to be concerned with.

▼ *Figure 17.5.* **One View of a Document**

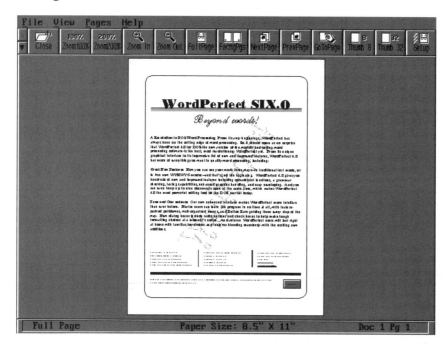

▼ *Figure 17.6.* **Another View of the Same Document**

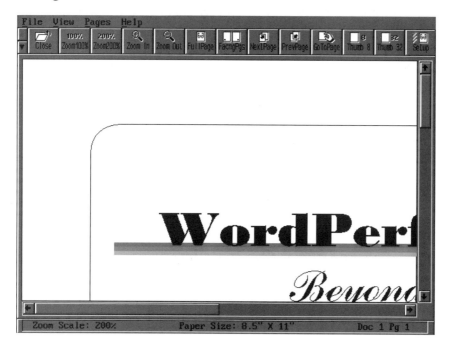

You have already seen how the Select Printer option is used to select the printer that you want to use. The active printer is always listed next to the Select Printer option.

Number of Copies sets the number of copies of the document, or a portion of the document, that will be printed. This value does not reset itself each time you print, so if you change it to, let's say five, and then want to print only one copy of something else, you have to go back into the Print screen and adjust the setting.

Generated by is used to determine if you want WordPerfect or your printer to generate the copies you want to print. If WordPerfect does the work, then it will generate and print as many copies as you want with each copy collated (all the pages in order). If you have your printer do the job, it will generate only one copy and then print the number of copies of each page that you indicate. The copies are not collated. The one advantage to this method is that having the printer do the work saves time since WordPerfect is freed up that much earlier in the printing process so you can continue your WordPerfect work.

The same thing is true for **T**ext Quality as for Graphics quality. Set the level of resolution you want. There is less of a difference in the effect that Text quality settings have for laser printers, but it is dramatic for dot-matrix printers.

Graphics Quality allows you to select from Draft, Medium, and High quality. The higher the quality, the better the finished product will look, but the more time it will take to produce. Both for laser and (especially) dot-matrix printers, differences in these settings can make a dramatic difference in your output.

Printing Different Characters

There are two very cool ways to generate hundreds of different characters to use in your WordPerfect documents such as ↕, ®, and £. You can do this through the Compose feature or through the Font menu and work with WP Characters. In both cases, you need to remember that what you can print is limited by the capability of your printer.

TIP

If WordPerfect cannot produce a character, you'll see a ■ on your monitor screen and nothing will print.

Composing Characters

One way to create special characters in a document is through the use of the **Compose** option, which allows you to print thousands of different characters (if your printer can do it!).

To compose a character:

1. Turn to Appendix A in your WordPerfect manual, titled "WordPerfect Character Sets."
2. Find the symbol you want.
3. Press the **Ctrl+a** key combination and you will see the WordPerfect Compose dialog box as shown in Figure 17.7.

▼ ***Figure 17.7. Creating New Characters in the Compose Dialog Box***

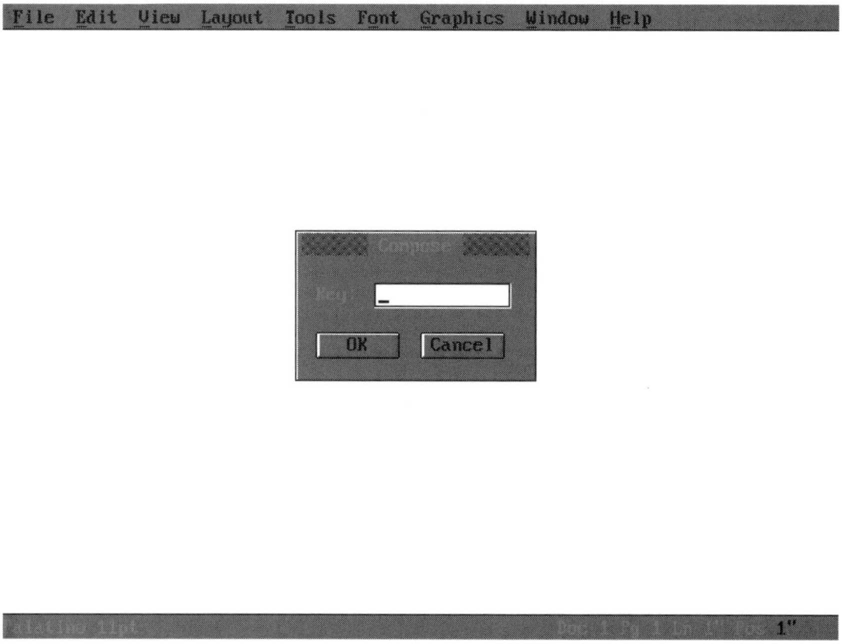

File Edit View Layout Tools Font Graphics Window Help
Compose
OK
Cancel
1"

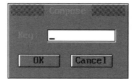

4. Enter a two-number code with the numbers separated by a comma. The first number represents the **character set** and the second number represents the character. For example, to create a star, you would enter the following keystrokes

Ctrl+a,6,184, Enter

and you would see ★ in the document.

The character may appear on your monitor screen as a small, white rectangle, but if you check the View Document screen, you'll see if your printer can reproduce it. Here are some other keystrokes and the characters they produce. By the way, these can be a lot of fun. Don't forget, you learned how you can set the size of the font in Lesson 24.

You can combine what you learned with the Compose feature to produce characters that can be used as graphics, such as ®.

Character Set	Character	Result
5	0	♡
1	80	Ø
5	51	✔
6	52	ℜ

Fun, right?

Want to see what your printer can do with these character sets? Retrieve the file named *charmap.tst* (for character map test) and print it. Those your printer can handle will appear on hard copy. Keep in mind that different fonts produce different characters. You might want to test *charmap.tst* with different base fonts.

Using WordPerfect Characters

Here's the best addition to version 6.0 as far as printing and creating special characters. Some of you who know something about WordPerfect for Windows will find this feature familiar, easy to use, and very useful.

To use WordPerfect characters:

▲ Press the **Alt+O,W** key combination [Mouse Moves: Font, **WP** Characters]. When you do this, you will see the WordPerfect Characters dialog box shown in Figure 17.8.

▼ *Figure 17.8.   The WordPerfect Characters Dialog Box*

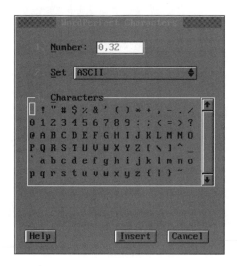

In this dialog box you can see:

▲ the Number that represents the character set number and character number (in this example it is 0,32),
▲ the character set (in this example it is ASCII), and
▲ the characters that are available in this character set.

To insert a character into a document:

▲ double-click on that character with the mouse, or
▲ use the cursor arrow keys to highlight the character you want to insert and then press the **Enter** key, or
▲ click on the Insert key once you have made your selection.

To change character sets, you can either enter a new code in the **Number:** text box, or click on the ▲ or ▼ in the **Set** text box. As you can see in Figure 17.9, there is quite a selection of different sets of characters from which you can select. For example, in Figure 17.9, you can see the Multinational set. Just click or select any one of these.

▼ *Figure 17.9.* *The Different Sets of Characters That Are Available*

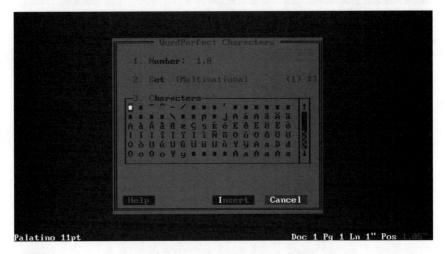

TIP

If you don't see the character you need in a character set, remember that this is only a partial view of what's available. Drag the scroll bar to see everything.

Creating Digraphs and Diacriticals

Last cool printing/font feature. **Digraphs**, such as Æ, and **diacriticals**, such as ç, are special characters that are used in foreign languages and scientific work.

To create a digraph or a diacritical:

1. Press the **Ctrl+a** key combination.
2. Enter the two characters you want combined either as a diacritical or as a digraph, such as Æ, ç, or é.

CHECK YOURSELF

Retrieve a document that you have already created and save it to disk. Do the following:

1. Clear your WordPerfect screen and print that document from the disk.
2. Change the quality of the text to Draft (or High), print it again and compare the two.
3. Print three copies of the document through your printer, not through WordPerfect.

So, now you can control many of the most important printing functions. But, though you can't print two documents at once, WordPerfect has the tools for working on more than one at the same time. That's what the next chapter is all about.

PRACTICE WHAT YOU'VE LEARNED

1. What are the exact keystrokes you would have to use to print a page of a particular document?
2. There are at least two ways to print a set of pages from a document. Name and describe two.
3. The View Document option allows for various views of a document. When might you use each of these views?
4. How can you tell if your printer can print every character that WordPerfect is potentially capable of printing?

ANSWERS

1. Shift+F7,2.
2. First, you can block and then print the pages you want to print. Second, you use option 4 on the list Files (F5) screen and print the range of pages you want.
3. The general value of the View Document screen is to be able to see how documents will appear before they are printed. The larger image (200 percent) is ideal for checking intricate graphics and the placement of items on the page. The Full Page option gives you an exact picture of

how a page will appear when printed. Facing pages works very well for those people designing books and other materials where page numbering and placement of images and text need to be very precise.

4. Print the *char.map* file that came as part of your WordPerfect package and you'll see what the current font can do with your printer.

Multiple
Documents

It seems that every time we come to a new chapter, we rave about yet another WordPerfect feature that is new to version 6.0. Don't look now, but it's the same once again.

The more you use WordPerfect, the more likely it is that you will be dealing with several different documents at the same time. For example, you might be creating merged letters and want to work with the form and data documents simultaneously. The skills that are involved in being able to work with multiple documents are valuable ones. In this chapter you'll learn how to:

▲ **Create multiple WordPerfect documents**

▲ **Switch from document to document**

▲ **Share information between documents**

▲ **Append information to a file**

Important Keys	*Important Terms*
F3	Append dialog box
Shift+F3	cascade
	split screen
	Switch to Document dialog box
	tile
	windows

Lesson 47: Creating Multiple Windows

WordPerfect allows you to have anywhere from two to nine documents active at the same time and makes switching from one to the other as simple as a few keystrokes. You can display different documents in different windows, or even display the same document in different windows.

Making Several Documents Active

Each time you open a document into its own window [Mouse Moves: **File, O**pen] or create a new document [Mouse Moves: **File, New**], WordPerfect creates a new place for that document in a new window. For example, if you selected New from the File menu nine times in a row, then WordPerfect would open nine different document screens, and the right side of the status line at the bottom of the last WordPerfect window would look like this.

```
Doc 9 Pg 1 Ln 1" Pos 1"
```

Switching Between Documents

There's a very simple way to switch between documents. That's through the use of the **F3** function key [Mouse Moves: **W**indow, **S**witch to]. When you do this, you will see the Switch to Document dialog box you see in Figure 18.1. As you can see in Figure 18.1, five different documents are open.

▼ *Figure 18.1.* *The Switch to Document Dialog Box*

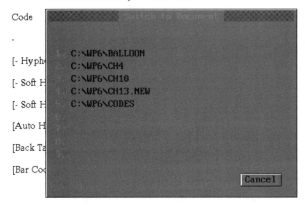

To switch between open documents:

1. Be sure that the Switch to Document window is showing (as you see in Figure 18.1).
2. Click on the document you want to make active or press the corresponding key. For example, if we wanted to open the document titled *CH13.NEW*, we could either click on it using the mouse or just press the corresponding number, which is 4 in this case and WordPerfect takes you right there!

Switching Between Documents (Only Faster!)

There's another way to switch that's even faster. Just use the **Home** key plus the number of the document that represents the window you want to become active.

For example, if we wanted to make document #4 active, we could just use the **Home,4** key combination and we'd be there in a flash.

If you use the Home,document # key combination and such a document does not exist, WordPerfect will take you to a clean screen with that document number. For example, in Figure 18.2, you can see how we used the Home,8 key combination. Since it's a new document, WordPerfect considers it to be Untitled.

TIP

Although up to nine documents can be open, only one can be active.

Switching Between Two Documents

Regardless of how many documents are open, the **Shift+F3** [Mouse Moves: **W**indows, **S**witch] key combination will switch between the currently active document and the most previous document that you have worked with.

▼ *Figure 18.2.* **Switching to a New Document Using the Home, Document Number Key Combination**

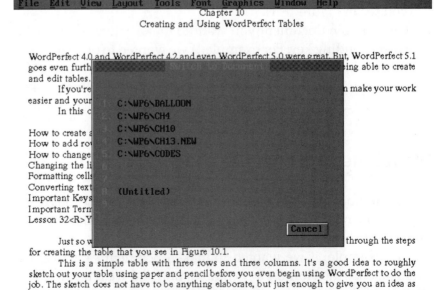

For example, let's say you were working in document #2 and then used the **F3** function key to switch to document #5, and then switched once again to document #1. If you used the **Shift+F3** key combination, you would find yourself in document #5, since that is the most previous document that was active.

The **Shift+F3** key combination acts like a toggle switch where you can switch from the currently active document to the most recently active document (regardless of the number) and back again very easily.

Lesson 47: Creating Multiple Windows

Viewing Documents Simultaneously

So it's great to be able to have more than one document available at the same time, but what about being able to see them simultaneously on the same screen? Easy. Let's use the five documents that were used in Figure 18.1 and go through the hows of viewing multiple documents on the same screen.

There are two ways to view multiple documents on the same screen. Both of these are available on the Windows menu you see in Figure 18.3.

The first one of these, **Tile**, creates a view where the contents of all the windows can be seen simultaneously as you can see in Figure 18.4. Here, each of the five open documents can be seen, reduced in size so that all the windows can fit. Notice how two of the windows take more room on the screen. When the number of active files is even, each window gets an equal amount. When the number is odd, windows will always be different sizes. You can tell that CH10 is the active window (although there are five that are open) since it has the darkened title bar.

TIP

When windows are tiled, the active window is the one that has a dark title bar.

What can you do now? Several things.

First, you can click on any window to select it and make it active. Try that now. You can use the **Shift+F3** key combination to switch between multiple open windows if you are a keyboard user.

▼ *Figure 18.3. The Options for Working with Multiple Documents*

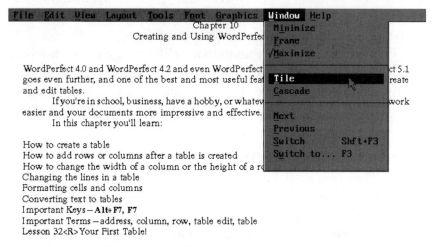

Second, you can actually work in the window once it is active. Just place the cursor where you want in the document and begin typing. In fact, you can perform any WordPerfect function in a window, whether one or nine are opened at the same time. But the windows are too small, you say, and the characters even smaller? That's the trade-off for seeing several at once. But, there's no reason why you can't work conveniently between two as you see in Figure 18.5.

The second way of viewing windows is through the use of the **Cascade** option on the **Window** menu. Rather than showing all the open documents, Cascade places them in the order in which they were originally opened as shown in Figure 18.6.

To make any one of these documents active, either click on it using the mouse (and it will come to the front of the stack) or use the **Shift+F3** key combination, which allows you to cycle through the open windows.

▼ *Figure 18.4.* **Using the Tile Option**

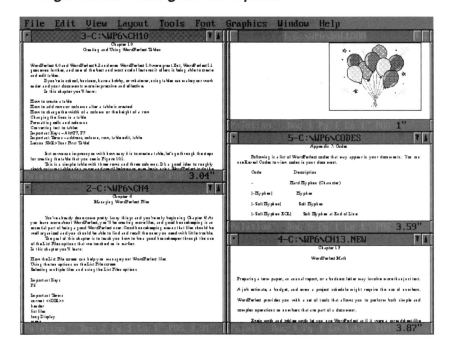

▼ *Figure 18.5.* **Working with Two Documents**

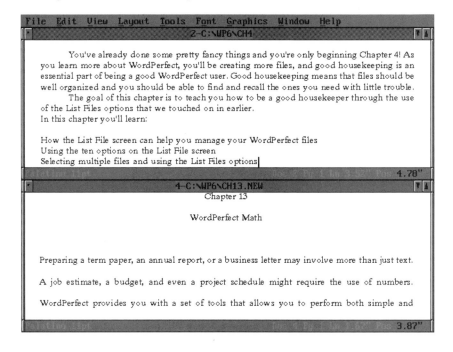

▼ *Figure 18.6.* *Using the Cascade Option*

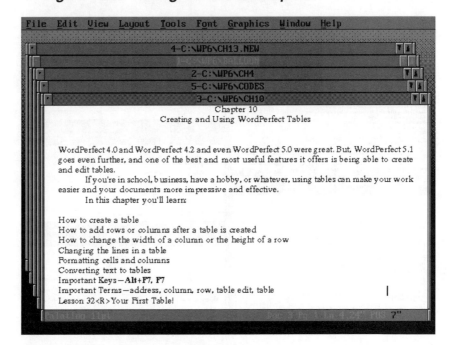

CHECK YOURSELF

1. Create three different documents and call them doc1, doc2, and doc3. Open them all on the screen at the same time. How is the fastest way to get from doc1 to doc3?
2. What are some of the advantages of being able to view multiple documents at the same time?

ANSWERS

1. Use the Home plus the document number key combination.
2. You can see the information you might need to complete a document, cut and paste between documents, and generally be more in command of the way your already created files are used.

Lesson 48: Working with Windows

There are lots of other things you can do with multiple windows on the screen such as changing their size and their location. Here's how to do each.

Changing Window Size

You saw in Figure 18.4 that five windows being open simultaneously requires that each one be pretty small and relatively difficult to work in. You can easily change the size of a window (or even close one), but first you need to select the Frame option on the Window menu. This option provides you with the icons that you will need to maximize, minimize, and close windows.

To maximize the size of a window:

1. Click on the ▲ in the window, or
2. Select Maximize from the Window menu.

When you do either of these, the open window will fill to take up the entire monitor screen and will become the active document.

To minimize the size of a window:

1. Click on the ▼ in the window, or
2. Select Minimize from the Window menu.

When you do either of these, the open window will shrink to take as little space as possible on the monitor screen as you see in Figure 18.7.

The other way to change the size of a window is by placing the mouse pointer on the lower or right edge of a window and dragging the edge until the window is the size you want it to be.

To change the width of the window, drag on the right edge. To change the height of the window, drag on the bottom edge. To change both dimensions of the window at once, drag in the upper or lower right-hand corner by the small rectangle next to the right of the POS indicator.

▼ *Figure 18.7. Minimizing a Window*

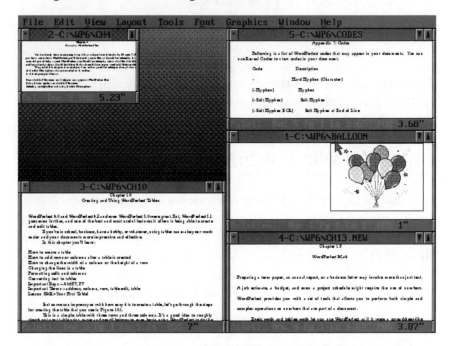

In Figures 18.8 (see the dotted frame?) and 18.9 you can see a window that was being dragged to increase its size and the result when the mouse button was released.

TIP

Want to go back to the Tile or Cascade after you change the size of a window? Just select either one.

Moving a Window

You may want to rearrange the location of open windows on the desktop. This is an easy task, and especially so if the various windows are relatively small.

To move a window to a new location, simply place the mouse pointer on the title bar and then drag the window to the new location. In Figures 18.10 and 18.11 you can see the before and after for moving the active window (CODES) to the center of the screen.

▼ *Figure 18.8.* *Changing the Size of a Window*

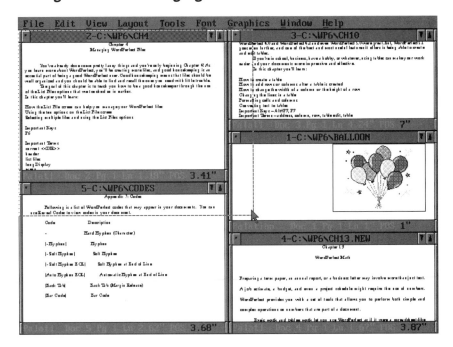

▼ *Figure 18.9.* *The Enlarged Window*

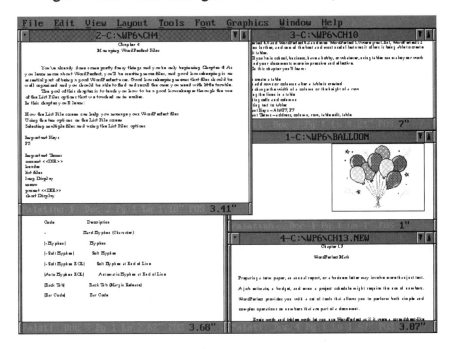

▼ *Figure 18.10.　Moving a Window*

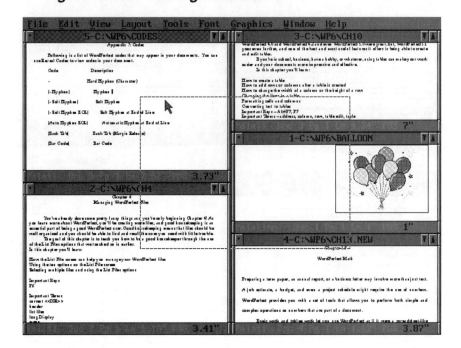

▼ *Figure 18.11.　The Repositioned Window*

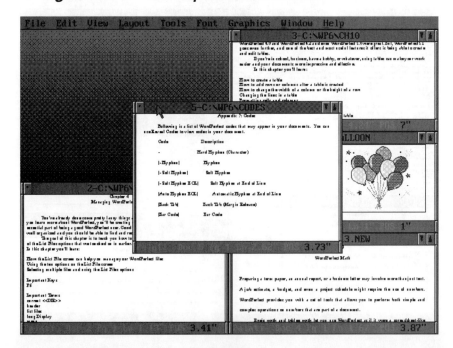

Notice that when you move a window, an empty space appears on the screen.

Closing a Window

There's another way to close a window besides selecting Close on the File menu. You can close any window by clicking on the Close button in a window. That's the small dot in the upper left-hand corner that you see in every open window shown in Figure 18.7.

Just a click on that dot (sorry, no keyboard users allowed here!) and you'll see the familiar WordPerfect message asking whether you want to save the modified file before closing it.

TIP

The ▲ (maximize), ▼ (minimize), and • (close) icons do not appear in a window when it is maximized.

TIP

After maximizing a window, to return to a tiled or cascaded arrangement, select Frame from the Window menu.

When you do close a window however, it leaves a nice empty space as you see in Figure 18.7. WordPerfect does not know to fill in that area. But, if you select Tile or Cascade from the **Window** menu, then the remaining opened windows will fill the entire monitor screen.

CHECK YOURSELF

1. Why would you want to change the size of a window?
2. What are the two ways to close a window?

ANSWERS

1. You might have closed another window and want to expand the size of the window where you do most of your

work and keep others small, where you can easily cut and paste from them to the main window you are working on.

2. You can select Close on the File menu or click on the • icon in the window.

Lesson 49: Cutting, Copying, and Pasting Between Documents

You can paste between documents when they are both immediately available (or visible) just as you would with any other two documents. For example, let's say that you are working on a paper that needs to incorporate material from another document. You could:

1. save the first document,
2. open the second,
3. block and copy the material you need,
4. close the second document,
5. open the first document,
6. locate the cursor in the correct position, and (finally)
7. paste the material from the second document into the first (whew!).

Or you could:

1. open all the documents you need on the same screen,
2. block and copy the material from the second document,
3. place the cursor in the correct location in the new document, and
4. paste the material from the first document into the second.

It would seem that the second strategy makes much more sense since it saves you so many keystrokes and you can see what you are doing all the time.

This cut or copy and paste operation uses skills you already know. In Lesson 14 you learned about cutting and copying and pasting text. In this lesson you learned about using multiple documents. Combining these skills means you can block text in one window, cut or copy it, move to another window, and then paste it. Fast and simple.

Lesson 49:
Cutting,
Copying,
and Pasting
Between
Documents

Closing Windows and Exiting WordPerfect

Well, now that you have all those documents open in their own windows, how do you close up after a busy work session? You can do it the same way you did with only one document open. Each window has to be closed one at a time and that process begins by selecting the **C**lose option from the File menu or using the **F7** function key. WordPerfect will ask you if you want to save the file (if any modifications were made). Once you close that active file, you'll see the next window containing an active file and you will then have to close that.

The faster way is to use the **Home,F7** key combination [Mouse Moves: File menu, E**x**it WP], which will show you a list of all the open windows. You can then select which ones you want to save (just click on the file name) and then exit all the windows at once. This is a terrific feature, since who wants to even think of having to close nine windows(!).

Appending Blocks of Text

Our last multiple document skill has to do with copying a block of text and instead of pasting it into another file directly, having Word-Perfect automatically append it to another file that we identify.

For example, lets say you have a file named notes, and whenever something strikes you as important to remember, you just enter it and then have WordPerfect automatically append it to the notes file. Here's how to append a block of text to a file.

To append a block of text to a file:

1. Create the file to which you want to append text. You need to have a filename to which you want text appended to.

2. Block the text you want to append to the existing file.The text should contain only the information you want to append to another file.
3. Select **A**ppend from the **E**dit menu.
4. Select To File. When you do this, WordPerfect will show you the Append dialog box.
5. Provide the name of the file to which you want to append text.
6. Press **Enter**.

The appended text will always appear at the end of the file. If you want it placed in another location, you will have to go to the file and then move it from there. Here's an example of how you might want to use the append block feature.

Let's say that you have a detailed manuscript that has headings and subheadings.

To create a table of contents:

1. Create a file and name it *toc* (for table of contents).
2. Go back to the original document and move the cursor to the first heading or subheading you want contained in the table of contents.
3. Block the text you want to append.
4. Select **A**ppend from the **E**dit menu.
5. Select To File.
6. Enter the name of the file to which you want the text appended (in this case it would be *toc*).
5. Press **Enter**.

As you go through the file, the headings will be added at the end of the table of contents. If it is not in the correct place, it is simple enough to move.

CHECK YOURSELF

▲ Create a list of items and save it as a file called list. Now, create another list and block the first two items on the new list and use the Append feature to add the list of two to the list of ten items without retrieving the original list.

ANSWER

▲ Being able to switch screens and work on multiple documents can be a real time-saver. Just be careful not to save the wrong version of a document, if you are working on more than one version of the same document.

Enough of this useful stuff! Let's move on to something that's enormously useful and also lots of fun—graphics. Graphics are becoming the cornerstone for word processors that go beyond simply manipulating words. You'll see how WordPerfect can manipulate graphics as well!

Lesson 49: Cutting, Copying, and Pasting Between Documents

PRACTICE WHAT YOU'VE LEARNED

1. Open any three documents that you have already created. Select **T**ile from the **W**indow menu.
   a. How are they arranged?
   b. What happens when you close one?
   c. What happens if you select **T**ile from the **W**indow menu?
2. Why do you need to create a file before you can append a block of text to that file?

ANSWERS

1. a. One file window occupies one-half of the screen and the other two windows each occupy one-fourth.
   b. The space is no longer occupied for that file.
   c. The remaining open files take up the available space.
2. Because WordPerfect will not know where to append the blocked text.

Great Graphics

WordPerfect brings you a superb set of tools to include and edit graphics in all your documents. Graphics like this trophy (you deserve it for doing so well this far) are easy to place, easy to edit, and easy to caption.

In this chapter you'll learn how to:

▲ **Insert a graphic in a document**

▲ **Use the various graphic definition options**

▲ **Edit WordPerfect graphics**

▲ **Use WordPerfect lines**

▲ **Use text boxes**

▲ **Rotate text**

▲ **Create and edit an equation**

Important Keys	*Important Terms*
Alt+F9	Create Graphics Line dialog box
Shift+F7	Edit graphics Box Border/Fill dialog box
	Edit All dialog box
	equation
	Fill Styles dialog box
	Graphics dialog box
	Retrieve Image File dialog box
	rotate
	scale
	Select Box To Edit dialog box

Lesson 50: Working with Graphics

Graphics include a large category of everything from a simple line to a complex figure. As the good witch Glinda said to Dorothy about how to get to Oz, it's best to start at the beginning. That's what we'll do here with an example of inserting a figure into a document.

Adding a Figure to a Document

Graphic images that are compatible with WordPerfect must have been created within a particular format. For example, all graphic images created within a WordPerfect format have a .WPG extension (for WordPerfect graphic) such as flag.wpg, duck.wpg, or globe.wpg.

TIP

Not all graphics files are compatible with WordPerfect. Check your WordPerfect manual or the source of the graphic to see if it will work.

Lesson 50: Working with Graphics

To add a figure to a document:

1. Place the cursor in the location where you want the graphic to appear.
2. Use the **Alt+F9,R** key combination [**Mouse Moves:** Select **G**raphics, **R**etrieve Image] to begin using WordPerfect graphics. The key combination produces the Graphics dialog box you see in Figure 19.1. The mouse moves produces the Retrieve Image File dialog box you see in Figure 19.2.
3. Enter the name of the file.
4. Select **OK** and WordPerfect will insert the selected graphic in the location of the cursor. For example, in Figure 19.3, you can see how we inserted the graphic named *trophy.wpg*.

TIP

If you don't include the .wpg extension, WordPerfect will not know what to find and insert into the document.

▼ *Figure 19.1. The Graphics Dialog Box*

File Edit View Layout Tools Font Graphics Window Help
Graphics Boxes
Create...
Numbering...
Styles...
Graphics Lines
Create...
Styles...
Borders
Paragraph...
Page...
Column...
Styles...
Fill Styles...
Retrieve Image...
Close

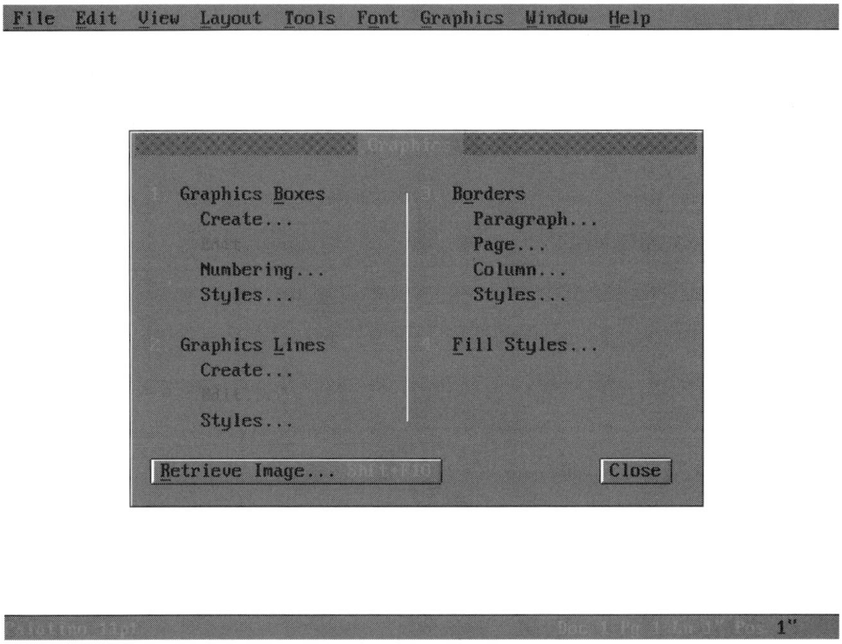

▼ *Figure 19.2.* *The Retrieve Image File Dialog Box*

▼ *Figure 19.3.* *Inserting a Graphic*

That's how easy it was and exactly how we got the trophy graphic to appear at the beginning of this lesson (except that we centered it and also provided a caption). If you are in the Text mode, such a figure does not actually appear on the WordPerfect screen, but instead a label such as BOX 1 or BOX 2 (depending on the number of the graphic) appears. You can see the actual graphic in the View Document mode or if you print out a hard copy of the document or if you are working in the Graphics or Page mode, as you can see in Figure 19.3 (Graphics mode).

Lesson 50:
Working with
Graphics

The Figure Edit Dialog Box Options

Once a figure is retrieved into a document, then the fun begins. As you can see in Figure 19.4, WordPerfect offers lots of options for editing the appearance, location and more of a graphic. In Figure 19.4, you can see that there are different options for working with a figure. Here's a brief description of how each one can be used.

▼ **Figure 19.4.** **The Edit Graphics Box Dialog Box**

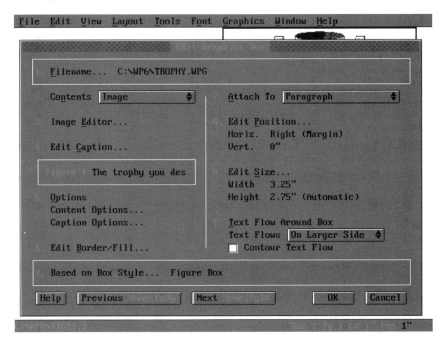

Filename (option 1) is used to enter the name of the file you want to edit. Since many of the figures that you use will be provided by third parties (companies other than WordPerfect), your entry here could look something like this:

```
b:football.wpg
```

if the figure is located on the disk in the B drive.

The Contents option (option 2) provides you with a menu that allows you to indicate what type of content you want to place in the graphics box that you are creating. For example, it might be images, text, or equations.

The Image Editor (option 3) takes you to a new window where you can change almost every facet of the graphic. We'll talk more about this important option later in this chapter.

Create Caption (option 4) allows you to create and add a caption to a graphic. Once you make this selection, you will be shown a special screen where you can enter text that will be automatically placed under the graphic, as you saw in the Trophy graphic at the beginning of this lesson. The caption that you assign will appear underneath the option (as you see in Figure 19.4).

Options (option 5) allows you to control the placement of material within a graphics box. Caption Options allows you to place the option anywhere around the graphic you created or retrieved.

TIP

WordPerfect creates a box into which it will place text, a graphic image, or an equation.

Edit Border/Fill allows you to edit the line that surrounds the graphic making up the graphic box line. The default single border is shown in Figure 19.1, but as with any line, you can select a single line, double line, dashed line, or any of the lines we discussed in Lesson 36.

Attach To (option 7) determines whether the figure will remain with the paragraph closest to it (should you reformat and change locations of the text, etc.) or whether it will remain in a fixed position on the page.

Edit **P**osition allows you to change the vertical and horizontal position of the image. If you're a mouser, you can also just drag the graphic to any position on the screen you might like.

Edit **S**ize lets you adjust the size of the image. When you adjust height or width, WordPerfect will automatically adjust the other dimension to keep things in proportion, unless you tell it otherwise and you want to set both independently of one another.

Text Flow Around Box is one of those options that work incredibly great. As you can see in Figure 19.5 (the Print Preview), WordPerfect can be directed to flow text around an object making for a particularly attractive page. If you check the Contour Text Flow check box in the Edit Graphics dialog box, WordPerfect will flow the text around the image as you see in Figure 19.5. If you don't select the Contour option, then the original graphic box (even if lines are removed as they were for Figure 19.5) will remain and a bunch of white will appear as you see in Figure 19.6. Quite a difference in the way things look.

Lesson 50: Working with Graphics

▼ *Figure 19.5.   Flowing Text Around a Graphic Box*

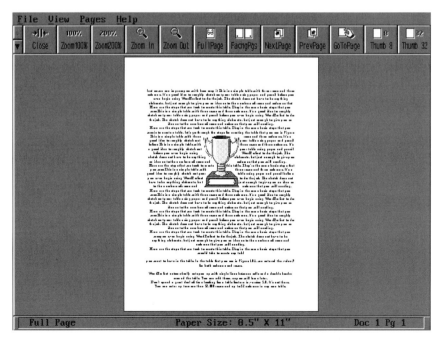

▼ *Figure 19.6.* **Text and a Graphic Box**

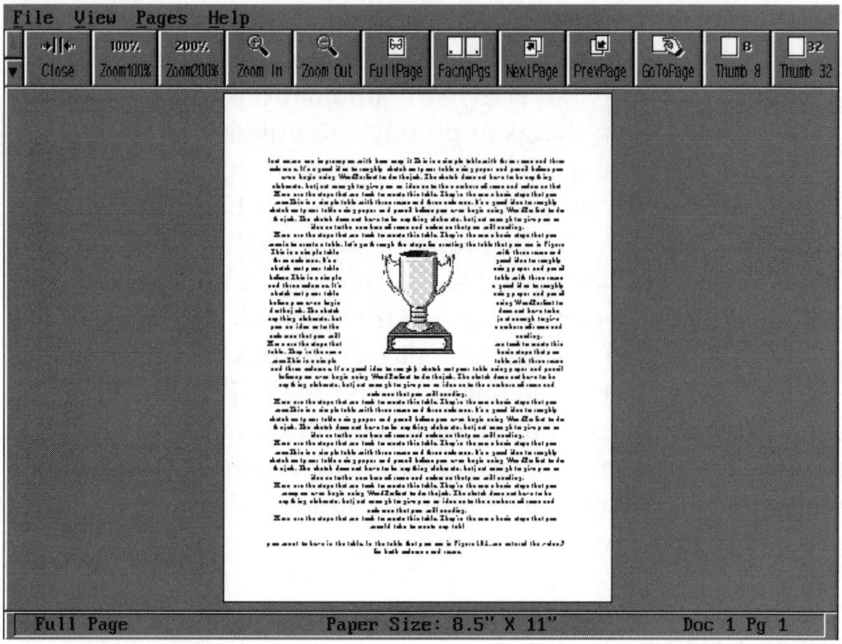

Editing a Figure

Once you have created a graphic, you can customize the image itself to fit your document's needs. And the selection of things you can do is outstanding—including moving the graphic, scaling it, rotating it, and even inverting black and white.

The options you see in Figure 19.4 deal with the placement, size, captions and other facets of the graphic in the document. What we are dealing with here is the actual graphic itself.

To edit figures (as you would any graphic):

1. Use the **Alt+F9,1,2** key combination [**Mouse Moves:** Select **G**raphics, Graphics **B**oxes, **E**dit] to begin the figure edit. When you do this, you will see the Select Box To Edit dialog box as shown in Figure 19.7.
2. Select Edit Graphics Box.

▼ *Figure 19.7.* *The Select Box To Edit Dialog Box*

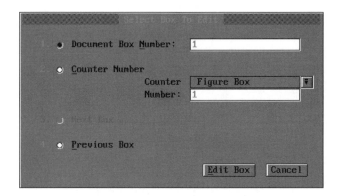

3. Select Image **E**ditor (option 3) and you will see the Image Editor window as shown in Figure 19.8. This is where it all happens!

As you can see, there's a convenient button bar across the top of the window that allows you to perform a variety of editing tasks. But for our purposes, the really important options are all available through the **E**dit All button in the lower right-hand corner of the Image Edit window. When you click that, you see the Edit All dialog box shown in Figure 19.9.

Let's examine these and show you examples of the effect the various options have on an image.

Attributes changes the orientation of a figure and through these options you can flip the graphic horizontally or vertically, invert the colors and more. For example, in Figure 19.10, the image was flipped vertically and the colors inverted. All this was done by selecting the Flip **V**ertical and **I**nvert Color options and then selecting **OK**.

▼ *Figure 19.8.* *The Image Editor Window*

▼ *Figure 19.9.* *The Edit All Dialog Box*

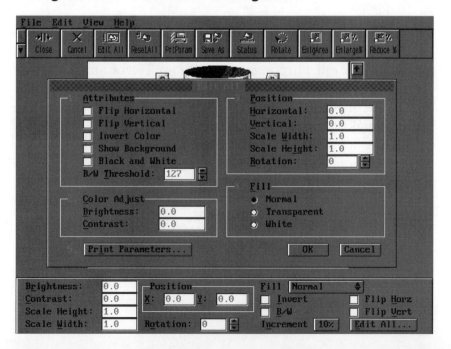

▼ *Figure 19.10.* *Flipping an Image and Inverting Colors*

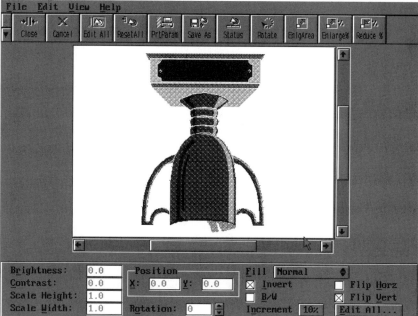

TIP

When you edit an image, you will see the edited version in the Image Editor window before any change in the actual graphic takes place in the document.

Color Adjust allows you to adjust both the brightness and the contrast, useful tools if you are dealing with colors that differ widely in their intensity. This option helps balance aspects of a color presentation.

Position provides you with options to set the exact position of a graphic in a document, work scale and rotate the image. For example, in Figure 19.11, the scale of the image has been reduced by one half (1.0 is equal to full size) and rotated 45°.

TIP

Images can be rotated up to 359° by either entering the exact value in the Rotation text box or clicking on the ▲ and ▼ icons.

▼ *Figure 19.11.   Scaling and Rotating an Image*

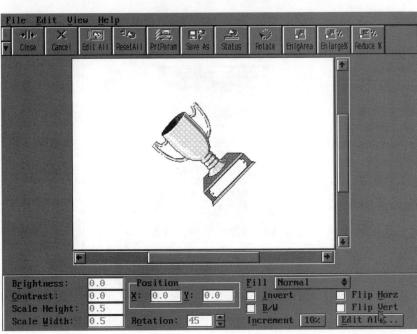

You can also scale images in width or height greater than the value of 1 to get fat and short (Scale Width) or thin and tall (Scale Height).

Those are some of the easiest way to edit an image but we should not ignore some of the options on the button bar you see in Figure 19.8 in the Image Editor window.

TIP

Sorry keyboarders, the button bar is accessible only through use of a mouse. Keyboarders should use the Edit menu, which has many of the same options available.

The **Close** button closes the Image Editor window.

The **Cancel** button cancels whatever changes that you made and returns you to the Edit Image dialog box.

The **Edit All** button reveals the Edit All dialog box shown in Figure 19.9.

The **ResetAll** button resets whatever edits you might have made to the initial image's attributes. ResetAll does not return you to the Edit graphics dialog box as does Cancel.

The **PrtParam** button provides you with a set of controls over how images will appear when printed.

The **Save As** button, like with any other WordPerfect document, will save an image under a new name.

The **Status** button provides you with a full monitor screen of how the image will appear given the changes and edits that have already taken place. All of the options at the bottom of the Image Editor window will no longer be present.

TIP

To see the Image Editor options at the bottom of the screen use the Status button as a toggle switch.

The **Rotate** button allows you to rotate an image by dragging on the perpendicular lines you see in Figure 19.12. Place the mouse pointer on either of the lines and drag in a rotating motion as you see in Figure 19.12. As you rotate the image, the Rotation value at the bottom of the Image Editor Window changes. In this example, the Rotate button on the Button Bar was used to rotate the image 45°.

The **EnlgArea** button allows you to focus in on a particular area of the image and enlarge it. When you select this option, the mouse pointer turns into a magnifying glass; you drag the magnifying glass cursor and form a box over the area you want to enlarge.

Clicking on the **EnlLarge%** will increase the size of the image by 10% for each click (as indicated in the Increment box shown at the bottom of the Image Editor window). For example, if you change the increment to 25% (it only comes in 1%, 5%, 10%, and 25%), one click will increase the scale of the image from 1.0 to 1.25 as you can see in Figure 19.13.

You can reduce the size of an image the same way by selecting the **Reduce%** button on the button bar.

▼ *Figure 19.12.* **Rotating an Image**

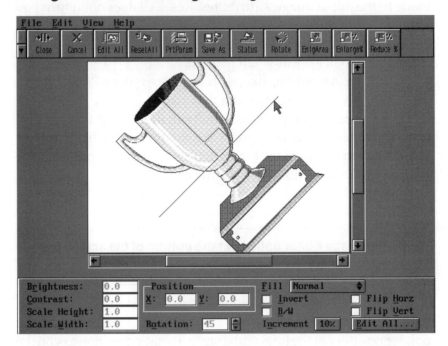

▼ *Figure 19.13.* **Changing the Size of the Image**

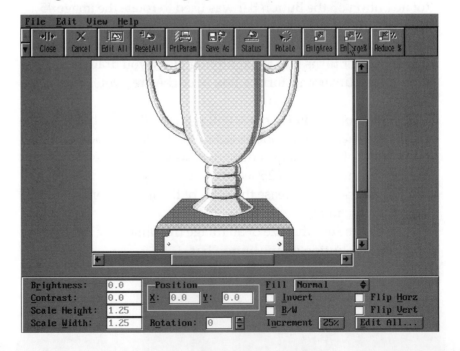

Placing Text in Boxes

You just saw how you can place an image in a graphics box. You can also place text in a box as well. A text box is useful for everything from a table you want to highlight in a report to the title page of the report. How about a sidebar? (That's what journalists call a story within a story; you often see it in magazine articles.) All are possible using text boxes.

Remember, a text box is just like any other graphic, once placed in your document. A box is a box.

To create a text box:

1. Use the **Alt+F9**,C key combination [**Mouse Moves:** Select Graphics, Graphics **B**oxes, **C**reate] to get to the Create Graphics dialog box you saw in Figure 19.1.
2. Select Text from the Contents option (option 2).
3. Select Create Text (option 3) and you will see a separate window as shown in Figure 19.14 with text entered. Note that all WordPerfect menus are active, so you can change fonts, styles, and so on as needed.
4. When you are finished entering text, press the **F7** key.
5. Select **OK** in the Create Graphics box and you will be returned to the document with the text box inserted in the document.

TIP

Want to edit a text box? Just double-click on it with the mouse or select the Edit option from the Graphics menu.

Everything that is done in the creation of a text box is very similar to any WordPerfect graphic as far as position, word wrap, captions, and so forth.

TIP

Figure or text or any other kind of boxes are basically the same—all are graphics boxes, and you have available the same number and type of options for customizing them.

▼ *Figure 19.14.* **Creating a Text Box**

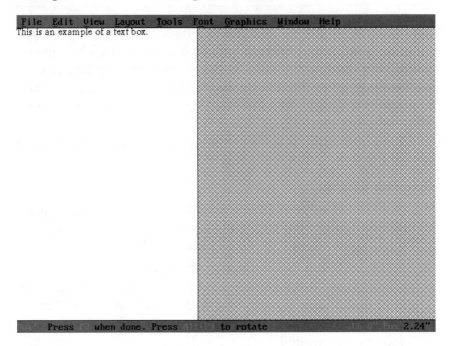

Using Text Box Options

Let's take a look at how some of the options in the Edit Graphics Box dialog box affect the appearance of text boxes.

For example, in Figure 19.15 you can see two text boxes showing you how different borders can look. The box on the left has a shadow added to it and the one on the right has a solid line. The Edit Border/Fill feature (option 6) in the Edit Image window (see Figure 19.4) was used to accomplish both.

When you are editing a text box and inserting the text you want to appear, you can format it in any way you choose. In Figure 19.15 the type size was changed for both boxes, and the fonts were changed as well. Also, the size of the boxes were changed through the use of the Edit **S**ize option (option 9) in the Edit Graphics dialog box or through simply dragging on the border you want to change.

You can easily use text boxes for borders around entire pages, to create fancy posters, or even to prepare the camera-ready copy you want for a book cover.

▼ **Figure 19.15.** *Creating Different Types of Borders Around Text Boxes*

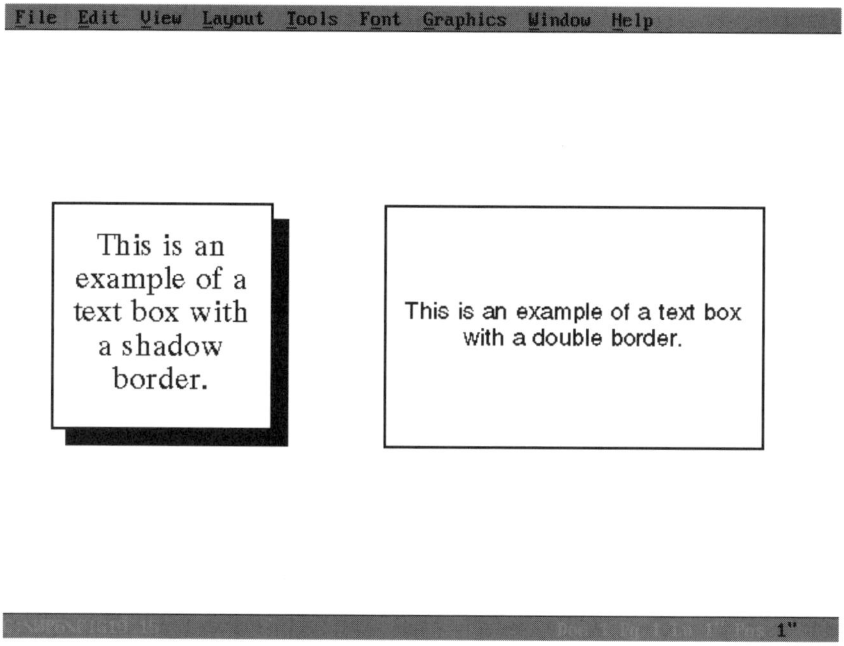

File Edit View Layout Tools Font Graphics Window Help

This is an
example of a
text box with
a shadow
border.

This is an example of a text box
with a double border.

1"

Shading Text Boxes

One other nice addition to changing the appearance of text in boxes is to shade them as you can see right here.

This box is shaded 30%.

To shade a text box:

1. First create a graphics box, using the **Alt+F9** key combination.
2. Enter the text.
3. Select Edit **B**order/Fill (option 6) on the Create Graphics Box.
4. Select **F**ill (option 7).
5. Select **Fill Style** (option 1) in the Edit Graphics Box Border/Fill dialog box.
6. Then select **30% Shaded Fill** from the Fill Styles dialog box.

It might sound like a lot of steps, but it's really pretty simple and becomes second nature after you do it once or twice.

TIP

When creating a text box, create the text first and then cut and paste it into the box. If you get the text perfect before placing it in the box, you can avoid editing to fit the box.

Rotating Text

When you combine scaling, text boxes, and rotating text, you can get some very interesting effects such as what you see in Figure 19.16. This is a great technique for adding pizazz to newsletters, stationery, and so on.

You rotate text using the **Alt+F9** key combination after you enter it into the text box (see Figure 19.14) and before you press the **F7** key to exit from the screen.

After we created the text *The WordPerfect Adviso*r, we rotated it 90° (using the Alt+F9 key combination) in the text box and then selected Rotate Box **C**ontents (option 5) in the Graphics dialog box you saw in Figure 19.9. Then we selected the 90° option and the text was rotated after we exited using the F7 function key.

TIP

You'll never see text in a text box rotated while it is being created. You have to get back to the document where the text box is placed before you can see it rotated.

Working with Lines

You've just seen how easy it is to work with graphics boxes (such as images and text). Adding and working with horizontal and vertical lines is even easier.

To add a line to a document:

1. Place the cursor in the location where you want the line to appear.

Lesson 50: Working with Graphics

▼ ***Figure 19.16. Rotating Text***

The WordPerfect Advisor

Your Guide To Creative Documents

July 20, 1993

Mr. John Lee
476 Indiana Street
Davenport, IO 12345

Dear John:

We are pleased to accept your bid for the article that you proposed. We look forward to your formal letter of acceptance.

Sincerely,

I.M. Wright

POB 1456   Wilson, MT 12345   (914) 867-5767

2. Use the **Alt+F9,2** key combination [**Mouse Moves: G**raphics, Graphics Lines, **C**reate] to begin creating a WordPerfect line. When you do this, you will see the Create Graphics Line dialog box as shown in Figure 19.17.
3. Select the type of line you want to use (horizontal or vertical) using the Line **O**rientation feature in the Create Graphics Line dialog box.
4. Indicate the horizontal and vertical positions, the thickness, and the style.

You can set the horizontal position of the line on the page through the **H**orizontal Position option. For example, you can have the line begin at the left-hand margin, be centered, or run across the entire page.

You can set the vertical position of the line as well, either at the position of the cursor or some other location you indicate. The default line is for a horizontal line running the full width or height of the page.

The line that you see in the stationery heading (shown below) underneath the name of the company is centered, has the baseline

▼ *Figure 19.17. The Create Graphics Line Dialog Box*

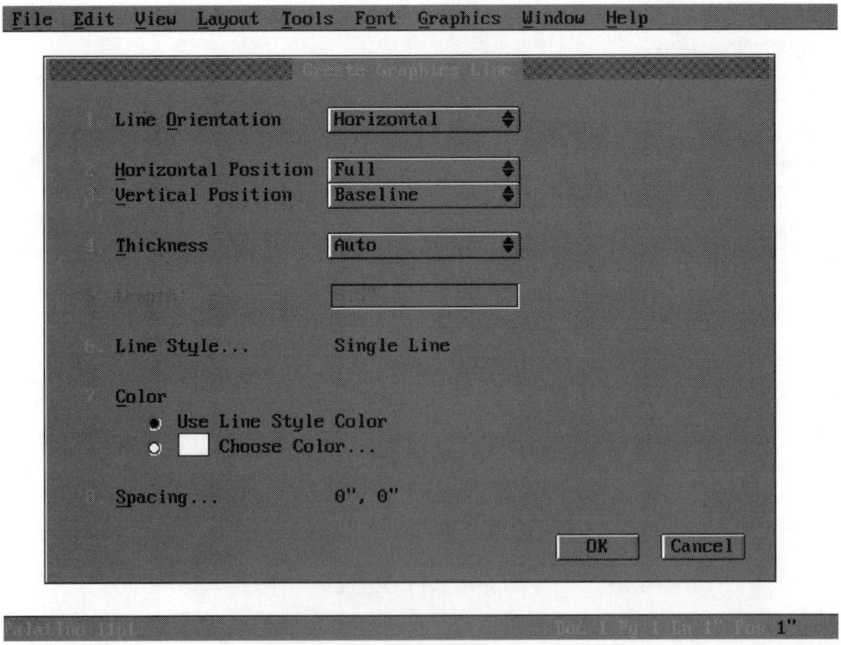

as the vertical position, runs across the entire page, is .125 inches wide, and is 20 percent shaded.

Delphi Associates   3340 Williams Tower, Sante Fe, NM 23133

Editing a Line

To edit a line once it has been created:

1. Use the **Alt+F9,2,2** key combination [Mouse Moves: **G**raphics, Graphics Lines, Edit] to see the Select Graphics Line to Edit dialog box.
2. Enter the number of the graphics line you want to edit.
3. Make the adjustments you want in the Edit Graphics Line dialog box. The graphics line you see above is 50% shaded and centered. The text was entered before the line was drawn.

TIP

To delete a line, locate the cursor to the right of the reveal code and backspace.

CHECK YOURSELF

1. Here's a good exercise. Using only the line option (5) on the graphics menu, draw a square or a rectangle!
2. Create two different text boxes that have different borders and different degrees of shading within them.
3. WordPerfect comes with 30 images. Create a graphic and retrieve the image named *banner.wpg*.

ANSWERS

1. Use both the vertical and horizontal line options and the **Alt+F9,5** key combination, drawing the lines and connecting them as you go.

2. Remember that you have to design the border of the text box and shading before you go in and enter text.
3. You can use any image that has the .wpg extension, as well as several others that are listed in your manual.

Lesson 51: Creating Equations

All you scientific and math types, listen up! Don't ever worry about taking those equations you create and physically pasting (really) into a document. Version 6.0 of WordPerfect has a terrific set of tools for creating and editing equations.

Creating an Equation

Equations are WordPerfect graphics just like boxes and lines and are treated in much the same way. Here are the steps we used to create the simple equation for the length of the hypotenuse of a right triangle that you see here.

$$C = \sqrt{A^2 + B^2}$$

To create an equation, we start in the same way as with any graphic, but in the Create Graphics Box dialog box select **E**quation in the **C**ontents (option 2) box.

To create an equation:

1. Use the **Alt+F9**,1,**C** key combination [**Mouse Moves:** Select **G**raphics, Graphics **B**oxes, **C**reate] to get to the Create Graphics Box dialog box you saw in Figure 19.1.
2. Select **E**quation from the **C**ontents box (option 2).
3. Select C**r**eate Equation (option 3). When you do this, you will see the Equation window as shown in Figure 19.18.

   The Equation Definition window consists of an area where you enter the text of the equation (the Type Equation Text area) and an area above it where what you type will appear in equation format.

▼ *Figure 19.18.* *The Equation Definition Window*

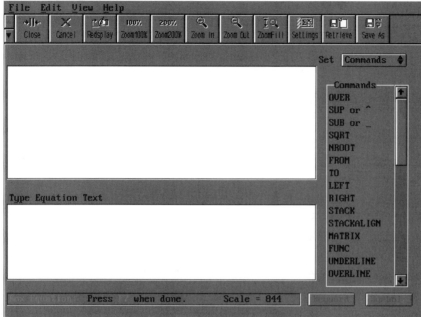

4. Enter the following in the editing window:

   C=sqrt{A^2+B^2}

   A little translation of symbols.
   ▲ The ^ sign is used for superscripting the character that follows it.
   ▲ The **sqrt** is a function that tells WordPerfect to insert a radical or square root sign.
   ▲ The { and } are brackets that tell WordPerfect to include certain operators, but not to act as parentheses such as in the mathematical expression (A-B)/2 which would subtract B from A, before dividing by C.

TIP

Editing an equation is like editing any graphics box. Just tell WordPerfect which one you want to edit, make the changes and push F7 **and you're back in your document.**

To see what the equation will actually look like, click in the **View Equation** area of the Equation Definition window (the upper part of the screen). You can see the result of your effort at entering the above equation in Figure 19.19. Congratulations, you've created your first equation.

TIP

To redisplay what you enter in the Type Equation text area you need to click in the View Equation area or use the Ctrl+F3 **key combination, or click on the** Redisplay **button on the button bar or (whew!) use the** Tab **key.**

Once you press the **F7** key to exit the Equation Window, the equation you created will be inserted in the document as indicated in the Edit Graphics box for that particular graphic. As with other graphics boxes, you can change everything from the location in the document to the type of border that surrounds it.

▼ *Figure 19.19. Creating Your First Equation*

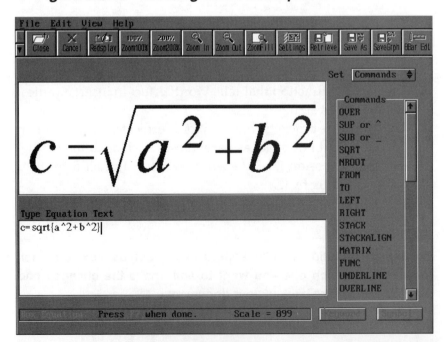

The Equation Window Commands

To the right of the Type Equation Text and View Equation areas are a series of commands you can use to create equations. These can be selected by highlighting them or clicking with the mouse pointer. When selected, they are entered into any equation that you are creating in the Type Equation text area. For example

$$A \ OVER \ B$$

would look like this:

$$\frac{A}{B}$$

You can enter this either by typing the word *over* or by highlighting the word in the list of commands and then pressing **Enter** or just clicking on it. WordPerfect will automatically enter it into the equation.

Here are some other common commands in equations that you might find useful.

Here's what you type to get the formula for a standard score:

$$z\text{~}score=\{X-overline \ X\} \ over \ sigma$$

which looks like this

$$z \ score \ = \frac{X-\overline{X}}{\sigma}$$

Here, the z score is equal to X with a line over it subtracted from X, all divided by the Greek letter sigma. The ~ enters a space and the overline command places a line over the character that follows it in the equation.

$$Mean=\{sum \ X \ sub \ i\} \ over \ n$$

$$Mean \ = \frac{\sum X_i}{n}$$

Here, the Mean is equal to the sum of X with an i subscript divided by n.

$$S=P*(1+i)^n$$

Here, value of investment is equal to P times the quantity 1+i raised to the n power. This equation computes compound interest, where S is the value of an investment, P is the principal, i is the interest rate and n the number of periods P has been at interest.

Finally, here's how to compute the values of an annuity. We constructed it like this

```
A=R[{{ (1+i) sup n-1} over {i(1+i) sup n}}]
```

and it looks like this

$$A=R[\ \frac{(1+i)^n-1}{i(1+i)^n}\ ]$$

Equations can be as simple or as complicated as you wish to make them and this tool is incredibly powerful for illustrating the relationship between variables.

CHECK YOURSELF

1. Use the equation feature and write an equation that computes the value of a equal to b times c divided by d.
2. How do you change the location of an equation on the screen?
3. How can you place a border around an equation?

ANSWERS

1. The finished equation should look like this:

$$a=b(\frac{c}{d})$$

2. Use the **Alt+F9,1,2** (equation number you want to edit) key combination and enter new position coordinates.
3. By placing the equation in a text or figure box that has nothing entered into it.

Often, the difference between a good and a great document is how well graphics are integrated into the content. WordPerfect graphics tools are easy to use and powerful. It takes a bit of practice to know-how to use all of the different options, but it is well worth your efforts.

PRACTICE WHAT YOU'VE LEARNED

1. Retrieve any of the graphics in your WordPerfect directory. Now change the border in the graphics box to None and rotate the image 90 degrees.
2. What does the extension .wpg stand for and why is it important?
3. List the exact set of steps you would use to rotate a graphic 45 degrees. What about rotating it 46 degrees? What's different about the way you would do the rotation?
4. Create a text box and shade it 50%. Now enter the following message, This Is A Text Box, and see if you can rotate the text.
5. What would you enter in the Type Equation text section of the Equation Editor to create the following equation?

$$d = \frac{(C-CL)}{L}$$

ANSWERS

1. There are hundreds of combinations of things you can do to change the appearance of an image. Borders and rotation are only two.
2. WordPerfect graphic. WordPerfect identifies which graphics it can import, based on the extension.
3. Select the Rotate option from the editing screen and use the + and − keys to change the value of the indicator in the lower right-hand corner. For exact rotation, select option 3 and provide the exact number of degrees you want the image to rotate.
5. d~=~{(C - CL)} over L

Index